LIFE ST[ORY]

GU01019149

BIOLOGY · FOR · SCHOOL

Experiment Guide

—— F M SULLIVAN ——

▷ Contents

▣ Section 1: Cells and mitosis

1.1 Investigating cells   4–5
1.2 Mitosis in a root tip   6–7
1.3 The growing region in a root   8–9

▣ Section 2: Photosynthesis

2.1 Plants, light and starch (1)   11
2.2 Plants, light and starch (2)   12
2.3 Plants, sugar and starch   13
2.4 Plants, carbon dioxide and starch   14
2.5 Plants, chlorophyll and starch   15
2.6 Chloroplasts   16–7
2.7 The waste gas of photosynthesis   18
2.8 Light intensity and photosynthesis   19

▣ Section 3: Enzymes

3.1 Enzymes: biological catalysts   21
3.2 Enzymes and living tissues   22
3.3 Phosphorylase: a 'building-up' enzyme   23–4
3.4 Amylase: a 'breaking-down' enzyme   25
3.5 The effect of pH on the activity of catalase   26
3.6 The effect of temperature on the activity of amylase   27–8

▢ Section 4: Respiration and gas exchange

4.1 Releasing energy from food/Burning foods in oxygen   30
4.2 The signs of respiration   31–2
4.3 Heat production in respiration   33–4
4.4 Alcoholic fermentation   35
4.5 Organisms and the atmosphere   36–7
4.6 Gas analysis: inhaled and exhaled air   38–40
4.7 The effect of exercise on breathing   41
4.8 Breathing models   42
4.9 Vital capacity and tidal volume of the lungs   43
4.10 Examining stomata   44–5

▢ Section 5: Food

5.1 The water content of food   47
5.2 Testing foods for carbohydrates, proteins and fat   48–50
5.3 Measuring vitamin C concentration   51
5.4 The effect of cooking on vitamin C   52
5.5 The energy in a peanut   53
5.6 The energy content of food   54

▢ Section 6: Feeding and digestion

6.1 Feeding adaptations   56–7
6.2 The effect of acid on teeth   58
6.3 Toothpastes   59

6.4 The need for digestion   60–1
6.5 Digestion in a model gut   62–3
6.6 The effect of saliva on starch   64–5
6.7 The effect of pepsin on protein   66–7
6.8 The effect of lipase on fat   68
6.9 Bile salts   69

Section 7: Water and organisms

7.1 Water and organisms   71
7.2 Sweat pores   72
7.3 Diffusion   73
7.4 Osmosis in living tissue   74–5
7.5 Osmosis in a model cell   76
7.6 The effect of heat and chemicals on the cell membrane   77
7.7 Turgor and plasmolysis in plant cells   78–9
7.8 Osmosis and turgor in plant tissue   80
7.9 Osmosis and red blood cells   81
7.10 Water loss from plants   82–3
7.11 Root hairs   84

Section 8: Transport

8.1 Cyclosis/Cytoplasmic streaming   86–7
8.2 Looking at blood   88
8.3 Pulse rates   89
8.4 Water transport in plants   90–1

Section 9: Size, support and movement

9.1 Surface area to weight ratios   93–4
9.2 Surface area to weight ratio and heat loss   95
9.3 Surface area and water loss   96
9.4 Stability and weight   97
9.5 The strength of bones   98
9.6 The components of bone   99
9.7 Muscle force   100

Section 10: Detecting and responding to the environment

10.1 Skin sensitivity   102–3
10.2 Forming an image   104
10.3 How lenses work   105

10.4 Some limits of vision   106–7
10.5 Reaction times   108
10.6 Reflexes   109
10.7 Responding to the environment   110–1
10.8 Positive geotropism in roots   112
10.9 The sensitive part of a root   113
10.10 The effect of one-sided light on stems   114
10.11 The effect of indole acetic acid (IAA) on stems   115

Section 11: Reproduction and heredity

11.1 Reproduction in yeast   117
11.2 Vegetative reproduction in angiosperms   118–9
11.3 Flower structure   120–1
11.4 Growing pollen tubes   122
11.5 The structure of seeds   123–4
11.6 Conditions for seed germination   125
11.7 Drosophila: the monohybrid cross   126–8

Section 12: Soil

12.1 Soil particles   130–1
12.2 Water and humus in soils   132
12.3 The air content of soils   133–4
12.4 The pH of soil   135–6
12.5 Soil properties   137–8
12.6 The effect of lime on soil   139
12.7 Collecting soil animals   140–2
12.8 Micro-organisms in the soil   143–4

Section 13: Micro-organisms

13.1 Food spoilage   146
13.2 Culturing micro-organisms   147–8
13.3 Bacteria and antibiotics   149–50

Section 14: Ecology and pollution

14.1 Investigating an ecosystem: collecting   152–3
14.2 Investigating an ecosystem: plant distribution   154–6
14.3 Monitoring water pollution   157–8
14.4 Air pollution: smoke on leaves   159
14.5 Sulphur dioxide and plants   160

SECTION 1

Cells
and
mitosis

1.1 Investigating cells
   (pupil's book pages 14, 15, 17, 92, 143, 188, 193)
1.2 Mitosis in a root tip
   (pupil's book pages 16, 17, 193)
1.3 The growing region in a root
   (pupil's book pages 17, 48, 193)

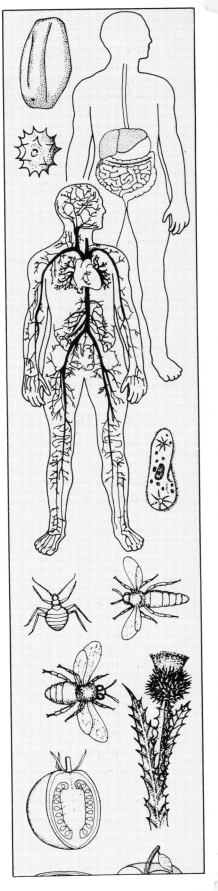

▷ 1.1 Investigating cells

Since cells are so tiny, a microscope must be used to study them. Two types of microscope are shown below.

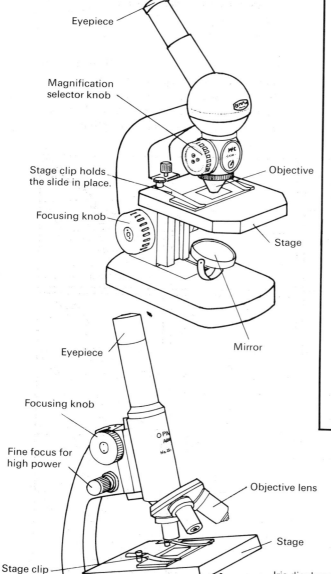

Eyepiece

Magnification selector knob

Stage clip holds the slide in place.

Focusing knob

Objective

Stage

Mirror

Eyepiece

Focusing knob

Fine focus for high power

Objective lens

Stage

Stage clip

Iris diaphragm adjusts light.

Mirror directs light to specimen.

Using the microscope

a Turn to the lowest magnification – the lenses must click *firmly* into place.

b Point a bench lamp at the mirror. By angling the mirror, get as much light as possible up to the eyepiece (or use a built-in light).

c Put a slide on the stage. The part you wish to see must be right in the middle of the hole in the stage.

d Looking from the side, turn the focusing knob until the stage is *almost* touching the objective.

e Look down the eyepiece. Turn the focusing knob *slowly* to separate stage and objective until you have a clear picture.

f Move the slide around until you find the best bits of the specimen. Move these to the centre of your field of view.

g Change to a higher magnification for a closer look.

Note: On the upper model, the magnification is on the selector knob. On the lower, you must multiply the eyepiece (eg × 10) with that on the objective (eg × 30) to find the magnification used (× 300).

SPECIMEN SLIDE
A specimen on a glass slide is placed on the stage.

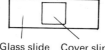

Glass slide   Cover slip

Fields of view

The circular picture you see with a microscope is called the field of view. This, and cells, we measure in tiny units called **micrometres** or **microns** (κm). A micron is one millionth of a metre.

$$1\,000\,000\ \mu m = 1\,m$$

Collect a slide which has a scale stuck on it. Find out the length in microns of the smallest division on the scale. Look at it under the low power of the microscope. Use it, as shown, to measure the field of view.

Note this in your Student Record. Repeat for medium and high powers. You will now be able to estimate the sizes of cells you see with a microscope. For example, if it takes four cells to stretch across a field of view 1600 μm long, each cell must be 400 μm long.

Prepare the specimens below. Observe them under your microscope. In your Student Record, draw three or four cells from each. Draw big (at least 2 cm across). Beside each drawing, mark the estimated length in microns.

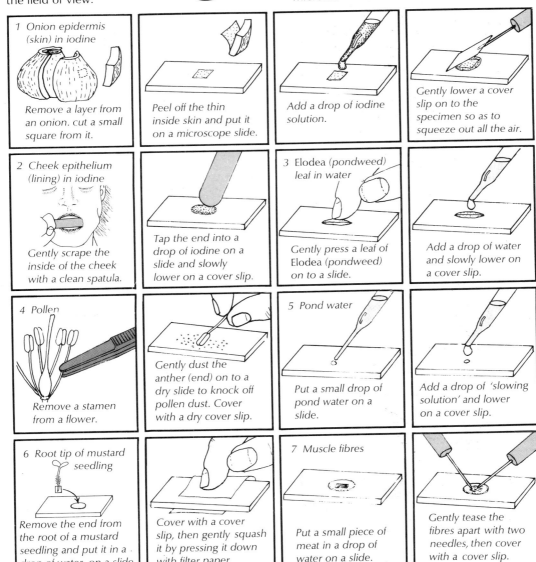

1 Onion epidermis (skin) in iodine

Remove a layer from an onion. cut a small square from it.

Peel off the thin inside skin and put it on a microscope slide.

Add a drop of iodine solution.

Gently lower a cover slip on to the specimen so as to squeeze out all the air.

2 Cheek epithelium (lining) in iodine

Gently scrape the inside of the cheek with a clean spatula.

Tap the end into a drop of iodine on a slide and slowly lower on a cover slip.

3 Elodea (pondweed) leaf in water

Gently press a leaf of Elodea (pondweed) on to a slide.

Add a drop of water and slowly lower on a cover slip.

4 Pollen

Remove a stamen from a flower.

Gently dust the anther (end) on to a dry slide to knock off pollen dust. Cover with a dry cover slip.

5 Pond water

Put a small drop of pond water on a slide.

Add a drop of 'slowing solution' and lower on a cover slip.

6 Root tip of mustard seedling

Remove the end from the root of a mustard seedling and put it in a drop of water, on a slide.

Cover with a cover slip, then gently squash it by pressing it down with filter paper.

7 Muscle fibres

Put a small piece of meat in a drop of water on a slide.

Gently tease the fibres apart with two needles, then cover with a cover slip.

▷ 1.2 Mitosis in a root tip

1 Grow an onion bulb in the dark over water for a few days until young roots grow. (Mustard seedlings or broad bean roots can also be used.)

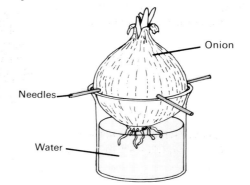

2 Cut off the tip of a young root about 5 mm from the end.

Note: Steps 1 and 2 may have been done for you.

3 Put the tip in a test tube with a little 1 M hydrochloric acid. Sit the tube in a beaker (or water bath) containing water at about 60°C. Leave for 10 minutes. This will soften and loosen the tissues.

4 Carefully pour off the acid. Wash the root tip in water.

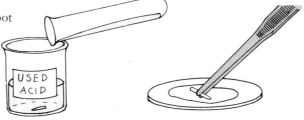

5 Put the root tip on a microscope slide and soak up excess water with filter paper.

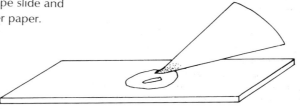

6 Place two small drops of orcein stain on the root tip. Gently tap it with the end of a glass rod until it is completely broken up.

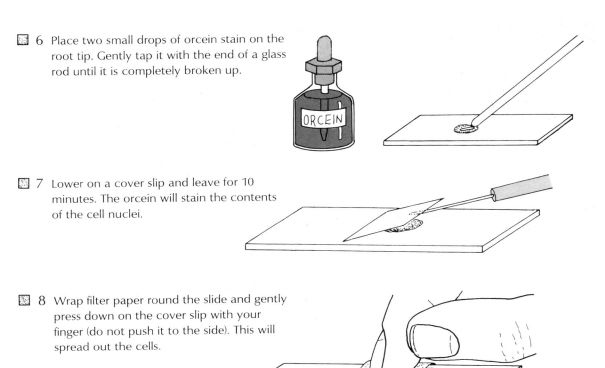

7 Lower on a cover slip and leave for 10 minutes. The orcein will stain the contents of the cell nuclei.

8 Wrap filter paper round the slide and gently press down on the cover slip with your finger (do not push it to the side). This will spread out the cells.

9 Examine the slide under the low power of the microscope. Observe the stained nuclei from all parts of the specimen.

10 Examine the slide under the high power of the microscope. Make careful drawings of as many cells with different-looking nuclei as you can find (especially those just behind the tip). Compare these with photographs and diagrams of plant cells undergoing mitosis.

Think about it!
1 Are all the cells the same size?
2 Where are the smallest cells?
3 Should small cells be younger or older than large cells?
4 In which part of a root are new cells being formed?
5 These cells have little cytoplasm. Why?
6 Are chromosomes visible in any cells?
7 Where are these cells located?
8 How many different-looking kinds of nuclei can you see in them?
9 For each one, at what stage of mitosis is the cell?
10 Where is the region of cell division in a root?

▷ 1.3 The growing region in a root

1 Flatten 6 paper towels one on top of another (or use pieces of newspaper). Wet them under the tap, then allow all excess water to drain off.

2 Space 5 broad bean seeds, which have been soaked overnight, about 40 mm from the top of the paper. Make sure they are all the right way up with their radicles pointing downwards.

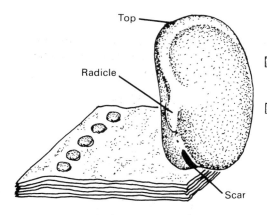

3 Roll up the seeds in the paper, keeping them all in position. Tie thread loosely round the paper to keep it rolled up (or use elastic bands). Do not constrict it in any way.

4 Stand the roll in a beaker of water. Leave it for about a week to allow the beans to germinate.

Water

Note: Steps 1 to 4 may have been done for you.

5 Unroll the beans. Select 2 which have straight radicles, perhaps about 20 mm long.

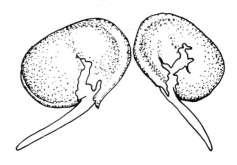

6 Using a soft tissue, gently dry the seedlings. Be careful not to damage them.

7 Take a piece of wire with thread stretched across it. Dip it into Indian ink and blot off any drips.

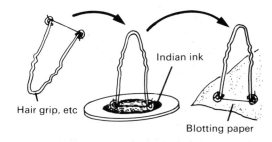

Indian ink

Hair grip, etc

Blotting paper

8 Use the thread to mark the radicles at intervals of 2 mm, starting at the tip. Do not smudge – mark cleanly. Allow to dry.

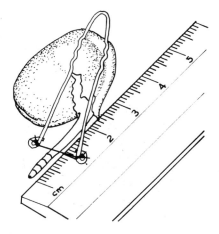

9 Put a layer of cotton-wool (about 3 cm wide) to one side of a large Petri dish. Moisten, but do not soak, it with water.

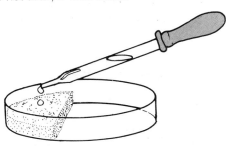

10 Place the two seedlings on the cotton-wool with the radicles sticking out as shown.

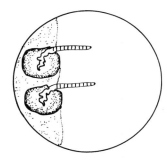

11 Cover the seedlings with another layer of cotton-wool and moisten it. Leave the radicles clear. Be careful not to wash off the ink.

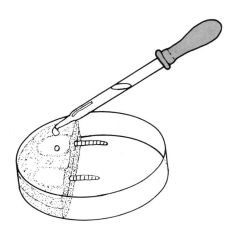

12 Fix a lid on the dish with an elastic band. The seedlings should be held firmly in place. If not, add more moist cotton-wool. Put your name on the dish.

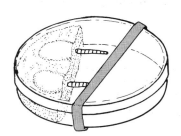

13 Place the Petri dish on its side in the box provided so that the radicles are pointing directly downwards.

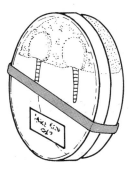

14 In your Student Record, draw the seedlings as they are now. Leave them like this for 2 or 3 days.

15 Examine the seedlings. In your Student Record, draw them as they are now.

Think about it!
1 If the root grows, what should happen to the distances between the ink marks?
2 Did this happen to any marks? Where?
3 Where does growth in length take place in a root?
4 Which structure takes up most of a mature plant cell?
5 Apart from producing more cells, is there any other way root growth could come about?

Photosynthesis

2.1 Plants, light and starch (1)
(pupil's book pages 58, 88, 92, 102)
2.2 Plants, light and starch (2)
(pupil's book pages 58, 88, 92, 102)
2.3 Plants, sugar and starch
(pupil's book pages 88–9)
2.4 Plants, carbon dioxide and starch
(pupil's book pages 88, 90, 95, 112)
2.5 Plants, chlorophyll and starch
(pupil's book pages 14, 88–9)
2.6 Chloroplasts
(pupil's book pages 14, 89, 92, 112)
2.7 The waste gas of photosynthesis
(pupil's book pages 88, 92, 112)
2.8 Light intensity and photosynthesis
(pupil's book pages 90, 102)

▷ 2.1 Plants, light and starch (1)

1 Keep one geranium plant well-lit and one in complete darkness for 2 days.

2 Take a leaf from each plant. Cut a small triangle from the 'light' leaf and a small square from the 'dark' leaf. This step may have been done for you.

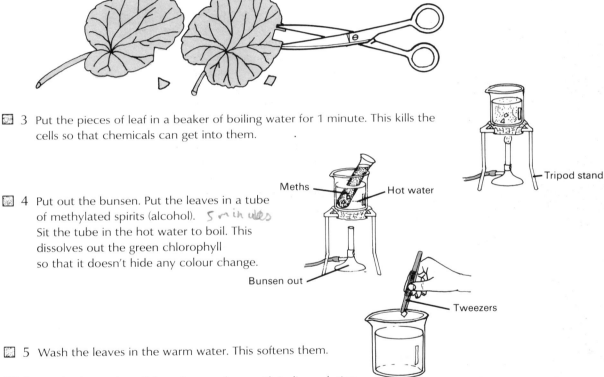

Meths — Hot water

Tripod stand

3 Put the pieces of leaf in a beaker of boiling water for 1 minute. This kills the cells so that chemicals can get into them.

4 Put out the bunsen. Put the leaves in a tube of methylated spirits (alcohol). 5 minutes Sit the tube in the hot water to boil. This dissolves out the green chlorophyll so that it doesn't hide any colour change.

Bunsen out

Tweezers

5 Wash the leaves in the warm water. This softens them.

6 Put the leaves in a dish and cover them with iodine solution.

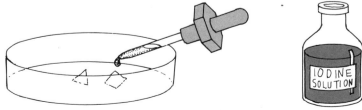

IODINE SOLUTION

7 After a few minutes, wash off excess iodine in clean water. If the leaves contain starch, they will have turned a blue-black colour.

▷ 2.2 Plants, light and starch (2)

▢ 1 A plant is kept in complete darkness for 2 days so that it uses up all its starch. It is now said to be destarched.

▢ 2 Select, *but do not pick*, a leaf near the top of a shoot. Make a sleeve of black paper, as shown, wide enough to just fit over the leaf.

▢ 3 Cut a small pattern on the top paper surface.

▢ 4 Fold the paper over the leaf and secure it with paper clips. Take care not to damage the leaf.

▢ 5 In your Student Record, carefully draw the leaf as it is now. Colour it in.

▢ 6 Leave the plant in bright light for several hours.

▢ 7 Detach the leaf. Test the whole leaf for starch as shown in the previous experiment (2.1). Make sure all the colour is out of the leaf before you add iodine.

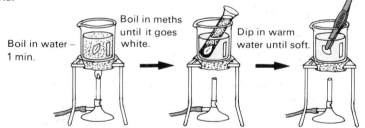

Boil in water – 1 min.

Boil in meths until it goes white.

Dip in warm water until soft.

▢ 8 Carefully flatten out on a dish. Flood with iodine solution. Iodine turns starch blue-black. Wash in clean water.

▢ 9 Beside your first drawing, draw the leaf as it is now. Colour it in.

Iodine KI solution

Think about it!
1 *What does a starch molecule look like?*
2 *Was starch made in this experiment?*
3 *Could it have been made by photosynthesis? Explain.*
4 *How could starch be made in this experiment?*
5 *What does leaf A tell us?*
6 *If a plant made sugar by photosynthesis, but we couldn't find any in the leaves, what could have happened to it?*

▷ 2.3 Plants, sugar and starch

☐ 1 A plant is kept in complete darkness for 2 days so that it uses up all its starch. It is now said to be destarched.

☐ 2 Label 2 test tubes with your initials. On one write 'A water', on the other 'B glucose'.

☐ 3 Cut a small square and a small triangle from the leaf. (This may have been done for you.)

☐ 4 Put the square in test tube A and the triangle in test tube B. Fill test tube A with water. Fill test tube B with 5% glucose solution (sugar). Stopper the tubes.

☐ 5 Keep both test tubes in complete darkness for 48 hours.

☐ 6 Discard the liquids. Test both pieces of leaf for the presence of starch as shown on page 11.

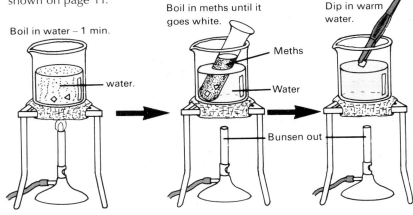

Boil in water – 1 min.

Boil in meths until it goes white.

Meths

Water

Bunsen out

Dip in warm water.

IODINE SOLUTION

☐ 7 Cover with iodine solution. Iodine turns starch blue-black.

Think about it!
1 Which parts of the leaf contained starch?
2 What effect did the black paper have on the leaf's ability to make starch?
3 This effect is because the black paper keeps out the light. Can you think of other reasons and how you could test to see if they had any effect?

▷ 2.4 Plants, carbon dioxide and starch

1 Label two geranium plants A and B and keep them in the dark for 2 days. During this time they use up all their starch. They are now said to be destarched.

2 Beside one plant, put a dish of dampened soda-lime. *This absorbs carbon dioxide.* Beside the other, put a dish of saturated potassium bicarbonate. *This gives off carbon dioxide.* Seal both plants inside polythene bags and keep them well-lit for 48 hours.

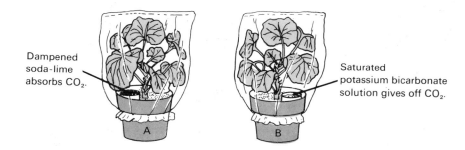

Dampened soda-lime absorbs CO_2.

Saturated potassium bicarbonate solution gives off CO_2.

3 Take a leaf from each plant. Cut a small triangle from the 'high CO_2' plant and a small square from the 'low CO_2' plant. This step may have been done for you.

4 Test both pieces of leaf (see page 11) to see if they contain starch.

Reminder
Boil in water to kill cells.
Boil in alcohol to remove colour.
Wash in warm water to soften leaf.
Cover in iodine.
If the leaf contains starch, it goes blue-black.

▷ 2.5 Plants, chlorophyll and starch

1 Take a whole leaf from a variegated plant which has had plenty of light.

   Note: A variegated plant is one whose leaves are only partly green, for example:

Wandering sailor   Variegated geranium

2 Make a careful drawing of the leaf in your Student Record. Colour it in.

White area
Green area

3 Test the whole leaf for starch as shown on page 11. Make sure all the colour is out of the leaf before you add iodine.

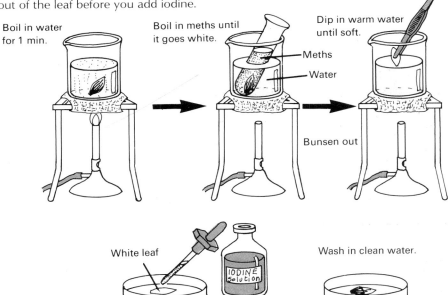

Boil in water for 1 min.

Boil in meths until it goes white.

Dip in warm water until soft.

Meths
Water

Bunsen out

White leaf

IODINE Solution

Wash in clean water.

4 Beside your first drawing, draw the leaf as it is now. Colour in the blue-black areas.

▷ 2.6 Chloroplasts

☐ Method A: Chlorophyll/starch ─────────────

1 Take a whole *Elodea* (pondweed) or moss leaf which has had plenty of light. Place it, top side uppermost, on a microscope slide. Add a drop of water.

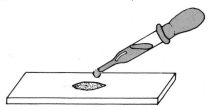

2 Gently lower on a cover slip so as to squeeze out all the air.

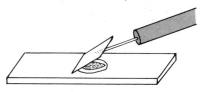

3 Examine the leaf under the low, then the high power of the microscope.

4 Look closely inside the cells to see where the green substance (chlorophyll) is located.

5 In your Student Record, make a large labelled drawing of a few cells. Colour them in. They may look something like this:

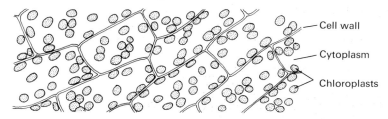

6 Obtain a fresh leaf. Prepare another slide. Mount this leaf in iodine solution instead of water. Leave for 5 minutes. The iodine will turn starch (food) in the leaf blue-black.

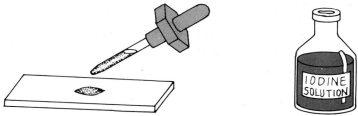

7 Look closely at the cells as before. Find where the starch grains are located.

8 In your Student Record, make a large labelled drawing of a few cells. Colour them in.

☐ Method B: Distribution ───────

☒ 1 Hold a firm dicotyledon leaf (eg privet) between two pieces of carrot or other suitable material. Cut the leaf flush with the carrot.

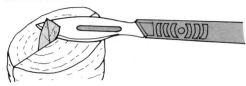

☒ 2 Cut a very thin slice of the leaf – a gentle sawing action will help. Transfer the section to water in a watch glass.

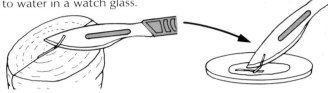

☒ 3 Your section should be almost transparent. Keep trying until you get a really thin section.

☒ 4 Transfer your best section to a drop of water on a slide. Make sure it is flat. Gently lower on a cover slip.

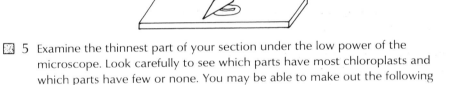

☒ 5 Examine the thinnest part of your section under the low power of the microscope. Look carefully to see which parts have most chloroplasts and which parts have few or none. You may be able to make out the following tissues:

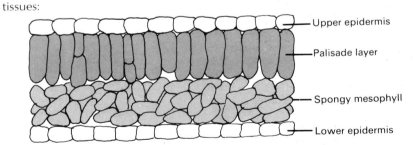

Upper epidermis

Palisade layer

Spongy mesophyll

Lower epidermis

☐ 6 In your Student Record, make a large labelled drawing to show which tissues you can see. Colour it in to show where most chloroplasts are located.

Think about it!
1 In which parts of a plant cell is chlorophyll found?
2 In which parts of a plant cell are starch grains found?
3 Give two pieces of evidence that chloroplasts are the actual sites of photosynthesis.
4 Which tissue in a dicotyledon leaf contains most chloroplasts?
5 Of what advantage is this to the leaf?

▷ 2.7 The waste gas of photosynthesis

1 Take a large healthy sprig of *Elodea* (pondweed). Trap it under a filter funnel in a trough or large beaker of water.

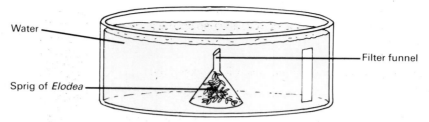

Water

Filter funnel

Sprig of *Elodea*

2 Sink a test tube in the water. Place the test tube full of water on to the funnel. Keep the mouth of the test tube under the water at all times.

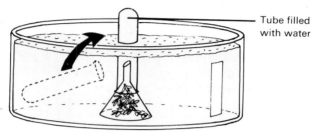

Tube filled with water

3 Keep well-lit for a few days. Bubbles of an invisible gas should rise from the plant and collect in the test tube.

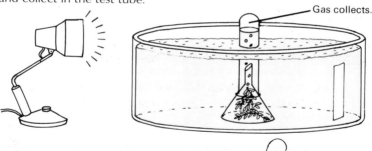

Gas collects.

4 Keeping the mouth of the test tube under the water at all times, put a cork on the tube.

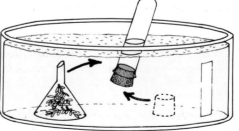

5 When ready, take off the cork and immediately put a glowing wood splint into the gas. If the splint relights, the gas is oxygen.

Remains of water

Gas

Glowing wood splint

▷ 2.8 Light intensity and photosynthesis

▣ 1 Cut a sprig of *Elodea* (pondweed) about 8 cm long.

▣ 2 Attach a paper clip to the top of the sprig to weigh it down. Now sink it in a test tube of weak potassium bicarbonate solution. This supplies the plant with dissolved carbon dioxide.

▣ 3 Stand the test tube in a large beaker of water. This will help keep the temperature steady.

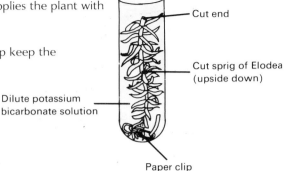

Cut end

Cut sprig of Elodea (upside down)

Dilute potassium bicarbonate solution

Paper clip

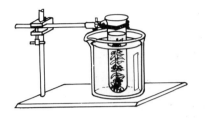

▣ 4 Shine a lamp on the sprig from about 60 cm away. Use a light meter to measure the intensity (strength) of the light falling on the plant.

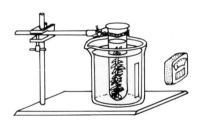

▣ 5 Leave it to settle down for a few minutes. You should see a stream of oxygen bubbles coming from the cut end of the sprig. Count how many bubbles are given off in 1 minute.

▣ 6 Do this twice more. Work out the average of the three counts and note it in the Result table in your Student Record.

▣ 7 Change the light intensity by moving the lamp closer or by adding more lamps. Allow it to settle down, then count the bubbles. Do this for a range of different light intensities.

Bubbles of oxygen

▣ 8 Draw a graph showing the bubble count per minute along the side (vertical axis) with light intensity units along the bottom (horizontal axis). Stick your graph in the space provided in your Student Record.

Think about it!
1 *What effect does light intensity have on the rate of bubbling?*
2 *What effect does light intensity have on the rate of photosynthesis? Explain.*
3 *Why must the plant have carbon dioxide?*
4 *Why must the temperature be kept steady?*

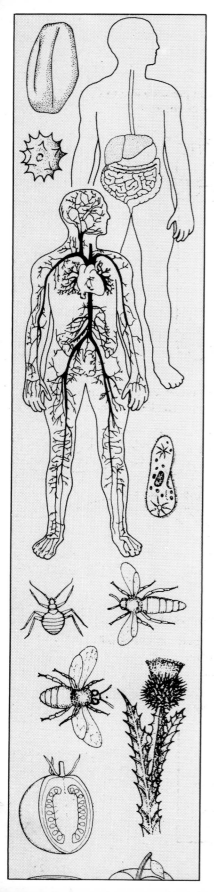

SECTION 3

Enzymes

3.1 Enzymes: biological catalysts
    (pupil's book pages 54–5)
3.2 Enzymes and living tissues
    (pupil's book pages 54–5, 132)
3.3 Phosphorylase: a 'building-up' enzyme
    (pupil's book page 54)
3.4 Amylase: a 'breaking-down' enzyme
    (pupil's book page 54)
3.5 The effect of pH on the activity of catalase
    (pupil's book page 55)
3.6 The effect of temperature on the activity of amylase
    (pupil's book pages 55, 76)

▷ 3.1 Enzymes: biological catalysts

1 Put 10 ml of hydrogen peroxide into a test tube. Add a *tiny* pinch of sand.

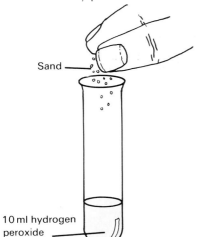

Sand

10 ml hydrogen peroxide

3 Put 10 ml of hydrogen peroxide in a test tube. Add a cylinder of potato.

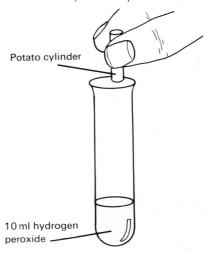

Potato cylinder

10 ml hydrogen peroxide

2 Put 10 ml of hydrogen peroxide into a test tube. Add a *tiny* pinch of manganese dioxide, then wash your hands.

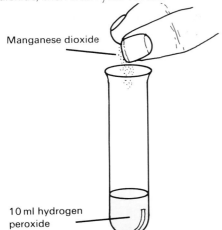

Manganese dioxide

10 ml hydrogen peroxide

4 If any bubbles are given off, wait until some froth collects, then put in a glowing wood splint.

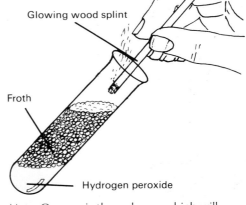

Glowing wood splint

Froth

Hydrogen peroxide

Note: Oxygen is the only gas which will relight a glowing splint.

Think about it!

1 Hydrogen peroxide breaks down by itself into oxygen and water, but very, very slowly. What effect would a catalyst have on it?

2 What effect did manganese dioxide have on it?
Is manganese dioxide a catalyst for this reaction?

3 Did the manganese dioxide seem to be used up? Is this what you would expect in a catalyst? Explain your answer.

4 Manganese dioxide is a powder. Could it be that it is powders which speed up the reaction? Explain your answer.

5 Potato speeds up the reaction because it contains a catalyst, a substance called catalase. So catalase is a biological catalyst. What do we call biological catalysts?

▷ 3.2 Enzymes and living tissues

☐ 1 Select a variety of fresh plant and animal tissues.

☐ 2 Set up a row of test tubes, one for each tissue.

☐ 3 ~~Half-fill~~ 10 ml each test tube with 5% hydrogen peroxide solution.

☐ 4 Cut a cube, about 1 cm³, from each tissue.

☐ 5 Drop the cubes of tissue, one after the other, into the hydrogen peroxide, putting a different tissue into each test tube. A few examples are shown below.

Diagram
Results
Concl.

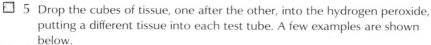

Blood

5% hydrogen peroxide solution

☐ 6 Watch the test tubes to see if they froth. If they do, this shows that the tissue contains the enzyme, catalase. In your Student Record award points for each tissue – 10 for the best, 9 for the next, and so on.

Think about it!
1 The gas given off is oxygen. How could you prove this?
2 How widespread does the enzyme catalase seem to be?
3 Do all tissues contain the same amount of catalase?

---

1 Cut a peeled potato into slices about 1 cm thick.

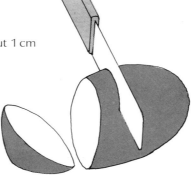

2 Cut out 4 pieces about 1 cm³ in size.

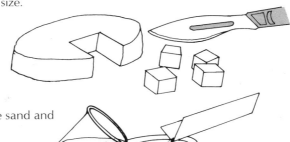

3 Put them in a mortar. Add some sand and just cover with water.

4 Grind up thoroughly with a pestle.

5 Pour the liquid into 2 centrifuge tubes. Leave behind the largest solids. Make sure both tubes contain equal amounts.

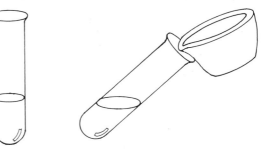

6 Put the tubes *opposite* each other in a centrifuge and spin them for 5 minutes.

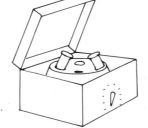

7   Add a drop of the supernatant liquid to a drop of iodine on a tile. If the test is positive (blue-black), centrifuge again until the liquid, the potato extract, is starch-free and gives a negative result.

Note: Steps 1 to 7 may have been done for you.

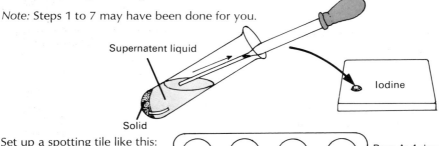

8   Set up a spotting tile like this:

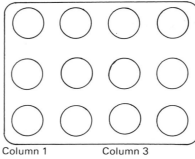

Row A: 4 drops of glucose-1-phosphate solution

Row B: 4 drops of distilled water

Row C: 4 drops of glucose-1-phosphate solution and 4 drops of distilled water

9   When ready, add one drop of the potato extract to all of row A and row B.

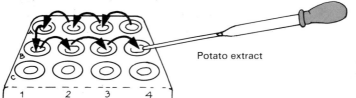

Potato extract

10 Three minutes after adding the potato extract, add a drop of iodine solution to all of column 1. Three minutes later, add iodine to column 2. After another three minutes, add to column 3, then finally to column 4.

Note the time.

Think about it!
1 *What colour does starch turn iodine?*
2 *Does potato tissue contain starch?*
3 *How was the starch removed from the extract?*
4 *What substance was formed in row A?*
5 *What does a starch molecule look like?*
6 *Does glucose-1-phosphate turn into starch by itself? Explain your answer.*
7 *Does potato extract produce starch by itself? Explain your answer.*
8 *What does potato extract contain that can convert glucose-1-phosphate into starch?*

▷ 3.4 Amylase: a 'breaking-down' enzyme

1 In a mortar and pestle grind up 5-day-old barley seedlings with their own volume of water.

2 Squeeze this through muslin to get your extract. This extract of barley seedlings contains the enzyme amylase.

3 Label 3 test tubes A, B and C and fill them as shown below.

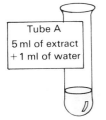 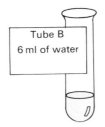 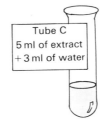

Tube A	Tube B	Tube C
5 ml of extract + 1 ml of water	6 ml of water	5 ml of extract + 3 ml of water

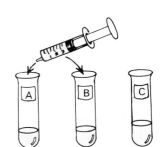

4 When ready, add 2 ml of 1% starch solution to test tube A and test tube B.

5 Immediately (waste no time), take a drop from each test tube and mix it with a drop of iodine on a spotting tile. Use a different dropper for each test tube.

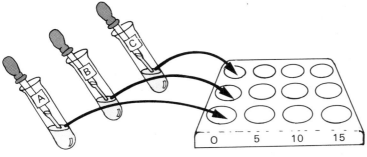

Note the time.

6 Repeat this every 5 minutes for 25 minutes.

7 Add a dropperful of Benedict's solution (or Fehling's solution to each of the test tubes and heat them for 5 minutes (see page 48).

Think about it!

1 Did test tube A contain starch at the start? How do you know?
2 Did test tube A contain starch at the finish? How do you know?
3 Did test tube A contain sugar at the finish? How do you know?
4 What is a starch molecule made of?
5 Where could the sugar in test tube A come from?
6 Did something in the extract cause the starch to disappear? How do you know?
7 Did the extract contain sugar at the start? How do you know?
8 Could the extract have made sugar without starch? How do you know?

▷ 3.5 The effect of pH on the activity of catalase

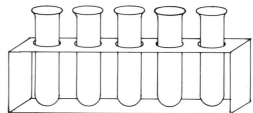

▢ 1 Place 5 test tubes in a rack.

▢ 2 You are provided with 5 solutions of hydrogen peroxide, each at a different pH. Put 10 ml from the lowest pH into the first test tube (take care – acid), 10 ml from the second lowest into test tube 2 and so on. Put a label with the pH number on each tube.

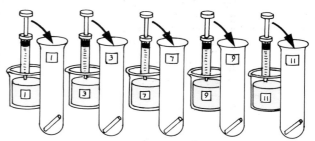

▢ 3 Using a cork borer, cut cylinders from a potato. Cut 5 cylinders to the same length. These are a source of the enzyme catalase. Catalase converts hydrogen peroxide to oxygen and water.

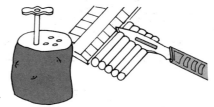

▢ 4 Put a cylinder into each test tube, one after the other.

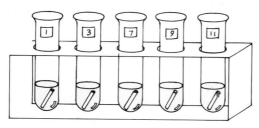

▢ 5 After 5 minutes, measure from the bottom of each test tube to the top of the foam (oxygen) which forms. This will be a rough measure of the volume of oxygen given off. If the froth gets to the top of any test tube before 5 minutes are up, then measure all the test tubes as soon as this happens.

▢ 6 In your Student Record, make a graph showing the height of the oxygen foam against the pH.

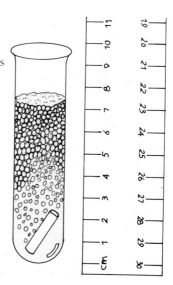

Think about it!
1 Which of your solutions were acid and which were alkali?
2 At which pH did the catalase work best?
3 What is the best pH of an enzyme called?
4 Can catalase work at more than one pH?
5 Over what range of pH does catalase work?
6 Why should all the potato cylinders be the same size?
7 How could you show that the foam contained oxygen?

▷ 3.6 The effect of temperature on the activity of amylase

▦ 1 Set up water baths at four different temperatures, like this:

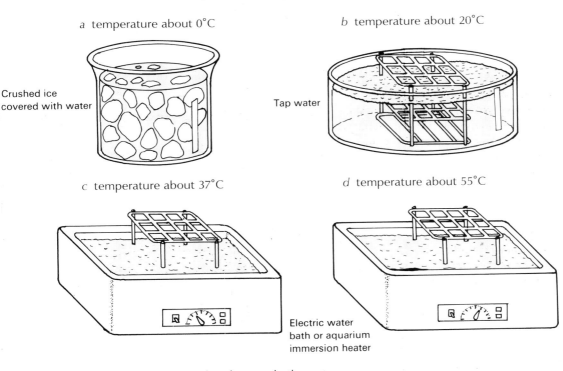

a temperature about 0°C

b temperature about 20°C

Crushed ice covered with water

Tap water

c temperature about 37°C

d temperature about 55°C

Electric water bath or aquarium immersion heater

Note the exact temperature of each water bath.

☐ 2 Into each of 4 test tubes put 2 ml of 1% starch solution and 4 drops of 10% iodine solution.

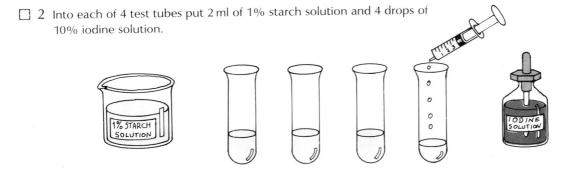

☐ 3 Mix the contents thoroughly. They will turn blue-black. Put one test tube into each water bath.

☐ 4 Rinse out your mouth. Collect some saliva in a beaker (chewing an elastic band will help). Saliva contains the enzyme amylase. Add the same amount of water and mix well.

☐ 5 Take another 4 test tubes. Put 2 ml of the saliva/water mixture into each test tube. Put one test tube into each of the four water baths.

6 Allow about 10 minutes for all the test tubes to get to the same temperature as their water bath. Note the time, then add the saliva to each starch/iodine test tube. Shake the test tube to mix the liquids, then quickly return it to the water bath.

Note the time.

0°C
20°C

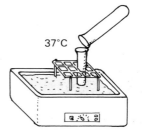
37°C

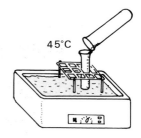
45°C

7 Watch each test tube carefully. As the starch is digested by the amylase, the blue-black colour will fade. Time, to the nearest minute, how long it takes for the colour to disappear completely.

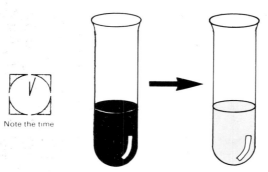
Note the time

8 Each test tube contained about 20 mg of starch. For each test tube, divide the number 20 by the time it took for the colour to disappear. This gives the number of milligrams of starch digested each minute:

Amount of starch digested $= \dfrac{20}{\text{time taken}}$ mg/min

9 In your Student Record, draw a graph of the number of milligrams of starch digested per minute against the temperature.

Think about it!
1 At what temperature did the amylase work best?
2 What is this temperature called?
3 Did the amylase only work at one temperature or over a range of temperatures?
4 What happens to an enzyme if it is heated much above its best temperature?
5 Was there any sign in your results that this might have happened here?
6 In this experiment can you say for sure that it was the amylase which caused the starch to disappear?
7 If not, how could the experiment be changed to get round this?
8 What is the product of amylase?

S E C T I O N 4

Cell

Respiration and gas Exchange

4.1 Releasing energy from food/Burning foods in oxygen
(pupil's book pages 59, 62)

4.2 The signs of respiration
(pupil's book pages 20, 94–5, 106)

4.3 Heat production in respiration
(pupil's book pages 58, 95)

4.4 Alcoholic fermentation
(pupil's book page 97)

4.5 Organisms and the atmosphere
(pupil's book page 95)

4.6 Gas analysis: inhaled and exhaled air
(pupil's book page 109)

4.7 The effect of exercise on breathing
(pupil's book pages 96, 109, 131)

4.8 Breathing models
(pupil's book page 108)

4.9 Vital capacity and tidal volume of the lungs
(pupil's book page 109)

4.10 Examining stomata
(pupil's book pages 90, 92, 112, 122, 123)

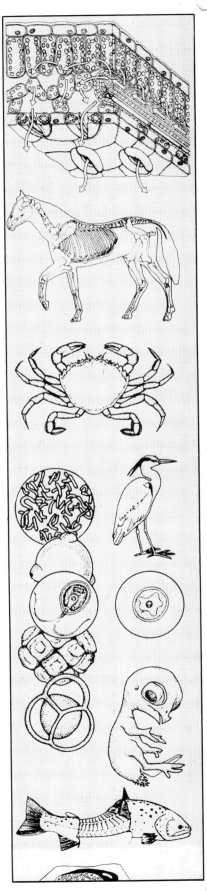

▷ 4.1 Releasing energy from food/Burning foods in oxygen

▣ Method A: Teacher demonstration

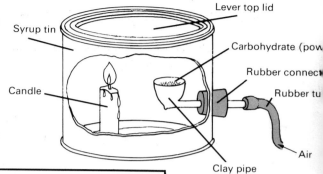

□ 1 Some finely powdered carbohydrate is put in the clay pipe in the apparatus shown opposite.

□ 2 The candle is lit.

□ 3 The lid is put tightly on the tin.

□ 4 Using a bicycle pump, a jet of air is shot into the pipe to fill the tin with fine dust.

Labels on diagram: Syrup tin; Lever top lid; Carbohydrate (pow...; Rubber connect...; Rubber tu...; Candle; Air; Clay pipe

> **Think about it!**
> 1 Did the food contain energy?
> 2 What kind of energy did it have to start with?
> 3 What kinds of energy was this released as?
> 4 Was the carbohydrate rich in energy?
> 5 Why is it a good idea for our cells to release energy from food in a number of small steps?

▣ Method B: Pupil activity

□ 1 Collect a gas jar full of pure dry oxygen.

□ 2 Fill a deflagrating (burning) spoon with dried food and roast it over a blue bunsen flame until it begins to burn (or glow).

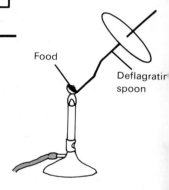

Labels: Food; Deflagratin... spoon

□ 3 Immediately, slide off the gas jar lid and put in the deflagrating spoon. The food should start to burn brightly in the oxygen.

□ 4 Observe closely. Can you see water (condensation) forming on the sides of the gas jar?

□ 5 When the flames go out, remove the spoon and quickly replace the lid.

□ 6 Slide back the lid. Pour in 2 cm of lime water. Replace the lid and shake the gas jar.

Note: Carbon dioxide gas turns lime water milky.

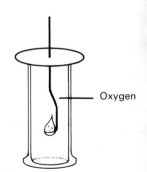

Label: Oxygen

> **Think about it!**
> 1 Was there oxygen in the jar at the end? Explain.
> 2 Was energy released from the food? If so, what kinds?
> 3 What gas was left at the end?
> 4 What else was produced by the reaction?
> 5 What would be a simple word equation to sum up this experimental result?

▷ 4.2 The signs of respiration

These experiments may be done in any order.

☐ Method A: Oxygen content ────────────────

▢ 1 Take a gas jar filled with unbreathed air. Slide back the lid and put in a burning wood splint. Quickly close the lid.

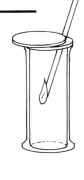

▢ 2 Time exactly how long the flame stays alight.

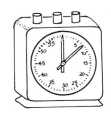

▢ 3 Fill a gas jar with breathed air as outlined on the next page (*) and repeat.

> **Think about it!**
> *1 Which gas allows things to burn in it?*
> *2 How could you tell when all this gas had been used up?*

☐ Method B: Carbon dioxide content ──────────

▢ 1 Collect 2 boiling tubes with stoppers. Fill one with breathed air as outlined on the next page (*).

▢ 2 Lift off each stopper a little and pour in 3 cm of bicarbonate indicator. Replace the stoppers.

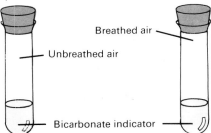

Breathed air

Unbreathed air

Bicarbonate indicator

▢ 3 Shake each tube for 3 minutes. Place them side by side and compare the colours. Note the result.

> **Think about it!**
> *1 What colour does carbon dioxide turn bicarbonate indicator?*
> *2 Which has the greater effect on bicarbonate indicator – unbreathed or breathed air?*
> *3 Which contains most carbon dioxide?*

Method C: Water content

1 Place a dry boiling tube, fitted as shown below, into a beaker of crushed ice and water.

2 Each time you inhale (breathe in), draw (unbreathed) air through the tube. Do not breathe *into* the tube. Do this for 5 minutes.

3 Fit up a second dry boiling tube. This time breathe into the tube each time you exhale (breathe out). Do not blow hard. Continue for 5 minutes.

4 Compare the two boiling tubes. Note any difference in the amount of water *inside* the tubes.

> **Think about it!**
> 1 Is there water in the air around us?
> 2 Is it in liquid or vapour form?
> 3 What effect does cooling have on water vapour?

Method D: Heat production

1 Take a thermometer and read off the temperature of the air in the room. Do not touch the bulb of the thermometer.

2 Breathe on the bulb of the thermometer for 2 minutes and note the reading in your Student Record. Do *not* put it in your mouth.

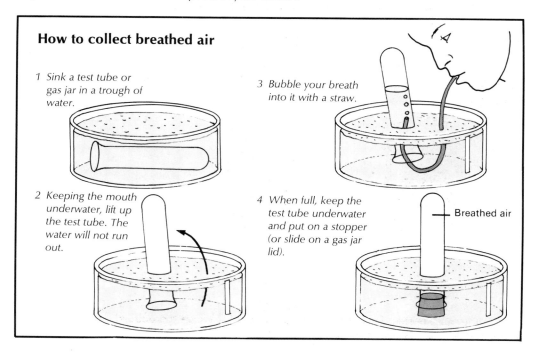

How to collect breathed air

1 Sink a test tube or gas jar in a trough of water.

2 Keeping the mouth underwater, lift up the test tube. The water will not run out.

3 Bubble your breath into it with a straw.

4 When full, keep the test tube underwater and put on a stopper (or slide on a gas jar lid).

Breathed air

▷ 4.3 Heat production in respiration

▭ Method A: Teacher demonstration

▢ 1 Soak a quantity of seeds in water for 24 hours.

▢ 2 Boil a similar amount of soaked seeds in water for 5 minutes to kill them, then leave them to cool.

   Note: Steps 1 and 2 may have been done for you.

▢ 3 Put each portion of seeds into a beaker. Cover them with a mild disinfectant and leave them for 5 minutes. This will prevent them being infected by fungi or bacteria.

▢ 4 Rinse the seeds with water a few times to remove the disinfectant.

▢ 5 Half-fill a small vacuum flask with the live seeds. Label this Flask A.

▢ 6 Half-fill another small flask with the killed seeds. Label this Flask B.

▢ 7 Put a thermometer into each flask and secure it with a cotton-wool plug.

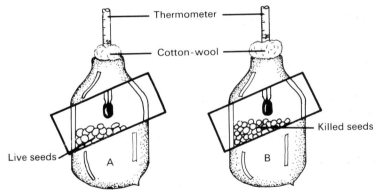

▢ 8 Carefully turn the flasks upside down and clamp them in position. The bulbs of the thermometers must be surrounded by seeds.

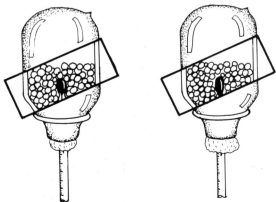

Turning the flasks upside down allows any carbon dioxide which is produced to escape, since it is heavier than air.

9 Leave for 5 minutes then take the temperature. Note it in your Student Record. Take it every day for the next few days.

Method B: Pupil Activity

1 Set up the apparatus shown below. This is known as a **differential air thermometer**.

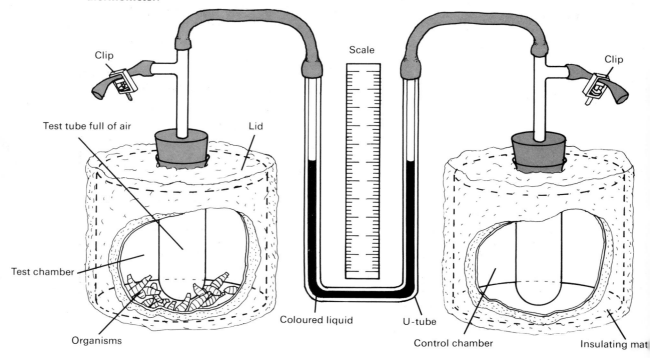

Clip

Scale

Clip

Test tube full of air

Lid

Test chamber

Organisms

Coloured liquid

U-tube

Control chamber

Insulating mat

2 Seal the organism(s) to be tested in one chamber – the other is left empty as a control. Suitable organisms could be woodlice, maggots, mealworms, locust nymphs, earthworms, a small mammal, living plant material, etc.

3 Open both clips to make the liquid levels in both arms of the U-tube the same, then close them.

4 In your Student Record, note the liquid levels in both arms of the U-tube. Leave for 30 minutes, then record again. If heat energy is given off, the air in the test tube will expand and push the liquid in that arm of the U-tube down.

5 Repeat with as many small organisms as possible.

> **Think about it!**
> 1 Which type of energy does food contain?
> 2 To which other forms of energy can organisms convert this? Give examples.
> 3 What name is given to the process by which organisms do these energy changes?
> 4 What kind of respiration is being observed in this experiment?
> 5 What kind of energy is always released in respiration?

▷ 4.4 Alcoholic fermentation

▭ Method A: Brewing and yeast

▭ 1 Put glucose solution into a large test tube to a depth of 2 cm. (The solution has previously been boiled to drive off dissolved oxygen then allowed to cool.)

▭ 2 Add a small amount of dried yeast.

▭ 3 Cover the solution with a thin layer of oil to keep out oxygen.

▭ 4 Set up the test tube as shown below.

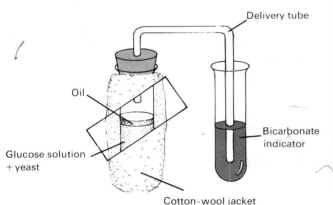

Delivery tube

Oil

Glucose solution + yeast

Bicarbonate indicator

Cotton-wool jacket

▭ 5 Set up a second test tube in the same way, but don't add any yeast. This is the control.

▭ 6 Leave the test tubes in a warm place for about an hour, then:

    a Smell the contents. Can you smell alcohol?
    b Note the temperature of each test tube.
    c Note the colour of the indicator.

> **Think about it!**
> 1 How did you ensure that the yeast was kept in anaerobic conditions?
> 2 If heat energy is released, what process is this a sign of?
> 3 What is the cotton-wool jacket for?
> 4 Where does the energy released in this experiment come from?
> 5 What does the colour change of the indicator show?
> 6 What other chemical could be used to show this?
> 7 What does the control test tube prove?

▭ Method B: Baking and yeast

▭ 1 Collect two 100 ml beakers. Label one A and one B.

▭ 2 Into beaker A put:
    6 level scoops of plain flour;
    2 scoops of water;
    $\frac{1}{4}$ scoop of sugar;
    1 scoop of yeast suspension.

▭ 3 Into beaker B put:
    6 level scoops of plain flour;
    3 scoops of water;
    $\frac{1}{4}$ scoop of sugar.

▭ 4 Using a spatula or stirring rod, thoroughly mix the ingredients to form a smooth dough.

▭ 5 Leave in a warm place for an hour. Note any change in the volume.

▭ 6 Transfer the dough samples to suitable greased baking trays. Bake in a hot oven (230°C) for 30 minutes.

▭ 7 Cut open the bread. Note any difference in texture or appearance between the two samples.

> **Think about it!**
> 1 Which gas could make the dough rise?
> 2 Where does this gas come from?
> 3 What other substance is formed?
> 4 What happens to this when the bread is baked?
> 5 What advantage is there in using yeast for bread-making?

▷ 4.5 Organisms and the atmosphere

These experiments are set up as demonstrations.

▨ Method A: Organisms and carbon dioxide————

▢ 1 Seal as many different kinds of small organisms as possible with (red) bicarbonate indicator. Some examples are shown below.

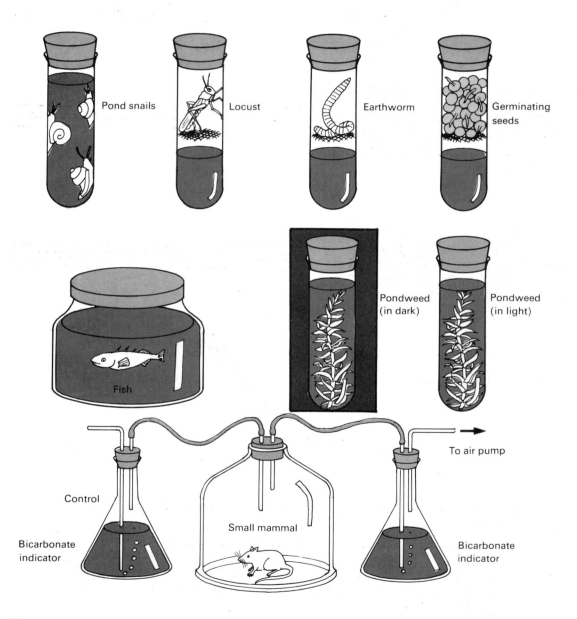

Pond snails

Locust

Earthworm

Germinating seeds

Fish

Pondweed (in dark)

Pondweed (in light)

To air pump

Control

Small mammal

Bicarbonate indicator

Bicarbonate indicator

▨ 2 Observe the set-ups for any change in the colour of the bicarbonate indicator (carbon dioxide turns it yellow). Note any changes in your Student Record.

Method B: Gas absorption by small organisms——

1 Place various small organisms inside large test tubes as shown below.

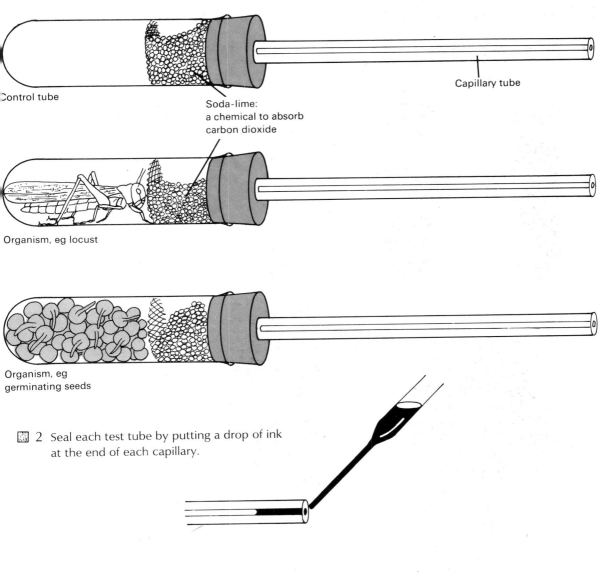

Control tube

Capillary tube

Soda-lime:
a chemical to absorb
carbon dioxide

Organism, eg locust

Organism, eg
germinating seeds

2 Seal each test tube by putting a drop of ink
at the end of each capillary.

3 Observe the test tubes for about 10 minutes. In your Student Record, note
any movements of the ink drops.

Think about it!
1 If the organisms absorb gas, what should happen to the ink drops?
2 The organisms are giving off carbon dioxide gas. What effect should this have
   on the drops?
3 Why does this not happen?
4 If the test tube got cooler, what would happen to the drops? Why?
5 How can we tell if the temperature is, in fact, affecting the experiment?

▷ 4.6 Gas analysis: inhaled and exhaled air

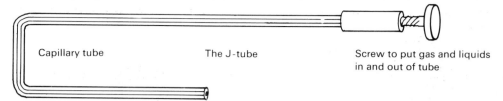

Capillary tube   The J-tube   Screw to put gas and liquids in and out of tube

The J-tube shown above, is used to analyse small samples of gas for the presence of carbon dioxide and oxygen and to calculate the quantity present. When the screw is turned anti-clockwise, gases and liquids are sucked into the tube. When the screw is turned clockwise, they are forced out of the tube. The J-tube is used as explained below.

1 Turn the screw clockwise as far as it will go.

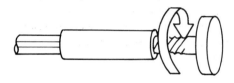

2 Dip the end of the J-tube in water. *Slowly* turn the screw anti-clockwise to draw in about 4 cm of water.

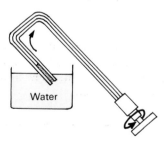

3 Remove the tube from the water. *Slowly* turn the screw anti-clockwise to draw in about 10 cm of air.

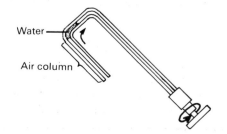

4 Put the end back in the water. *Slowly* turn the screw anti-clockwise to draw in water. Keep turning until the air column is in the position shown below.

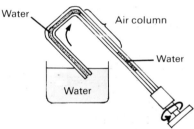

5 Lay the J-tube flat for a few minutes. Do not touch it. Measure the air column carefully and note the length (A) in your Student Record.

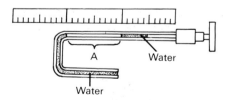

6 *Slowly* turn the screw clockwise to force out all but the last 2–3 mm of water. The air column must remain trapped throughout.

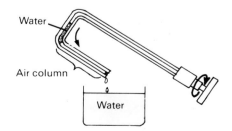

7 Dip the end of the J-tube in potassium hydroxide solution. (Take care – this chemical burns.) *Slowly* turn the screw anti-clockwise, drawing up hydroxide to replace the water.

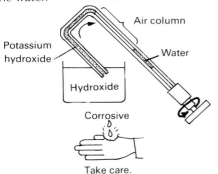

10 Dip the end of the J-tube in potassium pyrogallate solution. (Take care – this chemical burns.) *Slowly* turn the screw anti-clockwise to draw in pyrogallate to replace the hydroxide.

SAFETY

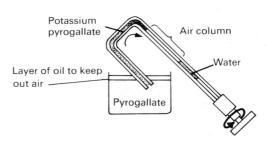

8 Lay the J-tube flat. The hydroxide absorbs carbon dioxide from the air column, causing it to shrink. When it stops shrinking, measure it carefully and note the length (B) in your Student Record.

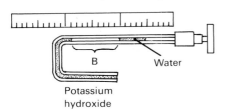

11 Lay the J-tube flat. The pyrogallate absorbs oxygen from the air column, causing it to shrink. When it stops shrinking, measure it carefully and note the length (C) in your Student Record.

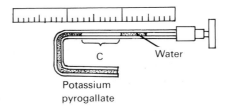

9 *Slowly* turn the screw clockwise to force out all but the last 2–3 mm of hydroxide (into a beaker!!). Keep the air column trapped.

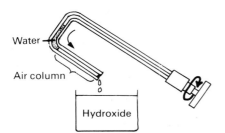

12 Use your results to work out the percentage of carbon dioxide and oxygen in unbreathed (inhaled) air. You are shown how to do this in your Student Record.

Precautions

a Temperature affects the volume of a gas, so, for accuracy, the J-tube should be immersed in a bath of water for a minute before measuring the air column (Steps 5,8,11).

b Potassium pyrogallate absorbs carbon dioxide as well as oxygen, so, if it was used before the hydroxide, the experiment would not work. Thus, the hydroxide must always be used first.

39

13 Fill a clean J-tube with breathed (exhaled) air as shown below and repeat the experiment.

Sink a test tube in a trough of water.

Stand the test tube, still full of water, upright.

Fill it with breathed air.

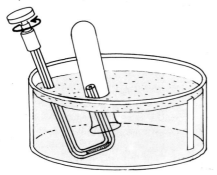

At Step 3 in the experiment, draw a 10 cm sample into the J-tube.

The J-tube and similar devices work as explained below.

1 A column of air is trapped between water and measured carefully – call this length A.

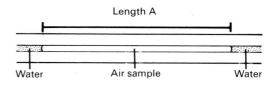

2 Most of the water on one side is replaced with potassium hydroxide solution, a chemical which absorbs carbon dioxide from the air sample. As this happens, the column shrinks. It is then measured again – length B.

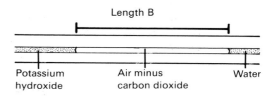

Therefore, the length of column due to carbon dioxide is equal to (A − B).

3 The hydroxide is then replaced with potassium pyrogallate solution, a chemical which absorbs oxygen. The column shrinks and, when it stops, it is measured again – length C.

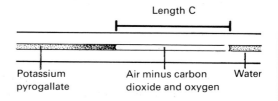

The length of column due to oxygen is therefore equal to (B − C). Using these results, the percentages of carbon dioxide and oxygen can be calculated (see Student Record).

▷ 4.7 The effect of exercise on breathing

☐ 1 Collect 2 boiling tubes and a straw. Put 20 ml of (red) bicarbonate indicator into each tube.

☐ 2 Now sit down and breathe quietly for a few minutes until your breathing rhythm is settled.

☐ 3 Count how many breaths you take in one minute. Try to keep breathing normally as you count. Make a note of the number in your Student Record.

☐ 4 Do this twice more. Note the numbers and work out the average of the three counts.

☐ 5 Using the straw, blow gently through the bicarbonate indicator in one of the tubes. Time how long the indicator takes to turn yellow. Make a note of the time in your Student Record.

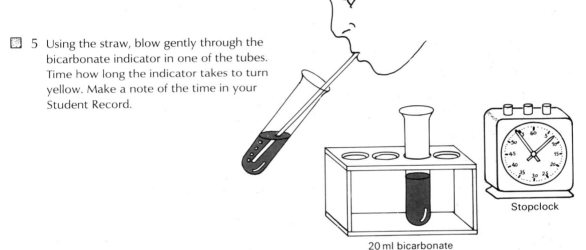

Stopclock

20 ml bicarbonate indicator

☐ 6 Run on the spot for 2 minutes.

☐ 7 Now blow gently through the indicator in the second tube. In your Student Record, note the time it takes to turn yellow.

☐ 8 Count how many breaths you are now taking in 1 minute. Note the number in your Student Record. Repeat twice more and work out your average.

☐ 9 Apart from the number of breaths, has your breathing changed in another way? Are you now breathing more deeply – taking in more air with each breath? Note your observations in Result 2 in your Student Record.

Think about it!
1 When you exercise, which gas must you have more of?
2 Why is more needed?
3 In which ways did you obtain more of this gas?
4 Which gas is produced during tissue respiration?
5 How is this gas disposed of?
6 How does this gas affect the bicarbonate indicator?

41

▷ 4.8 Breathing models

▭ Method A: Diaphragm action ─────────

▦ 1 With the back of your hand, gently push the
rubber sheet a few centimetres upwards. In
your Student Record, draw what happens to
the balloons.

▦ 2 Lower your hand to straighten the rubber
sheet. In your Student Record, draw what
happens to the balloons.

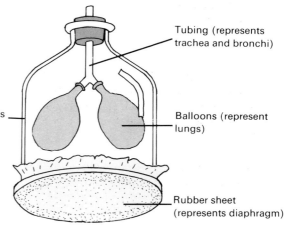

Tubing (represents
trachea and bronchi)

Bell jar (represents
ribcage)

Balloons (represent
lungs)

Rubber sheet
(represents diaphragm)

▭ Method B: Intercostal muscle action ─────────

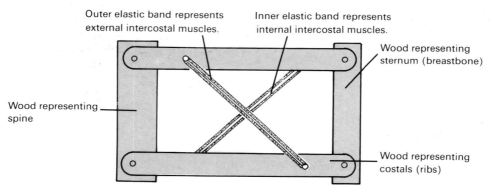

Outer elastic band represents
external intercostal muscles.

Inner elastic band represents
internal intercostal muscles.

Wood representing
sternum (breastbone)

Wood representing
spine

Wood representing
costals (ribs)

▦ 1 Raise the sternum. In your Student Record, note whether the elastic bands
are stretched (muscles relaxed) or loose (muscles contracted).

▦ 2 Lower the sternum. Again note the condition of the elastic bands.

Think about it!
1 Why is the bell jar in model A not a good representation of the rib cage in
 breathing?
2 Are the balloons an accurate representation of lung structure? Explain.
3 What would happen if:
  a the model trachea was blocked?
  b the rubber sheet had a hole in it?
4 What other organ is found inside the thorax?
5 In model B, are the elastic bands a good representation of the way the
 intercostal muscles work? Explain.

▷ 4.9 Vital capacity and tidal volume of the lungs

1 Fill a graduated (volume-marked) container right to the top with water. Put on a stopper or screw-top.

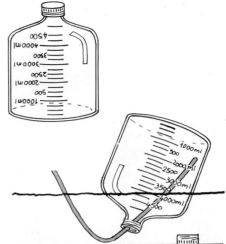

2 With the stopper still on, turn the graduated container upside-down in a basin (or sink) of water. Keeping the mouth of the container under the water, remove the stopper or top. The water will stay inside the container.

3 Pass a length of tubing into the container as shown. Hold the container steady.

Maximum breath in, then maximum breath out

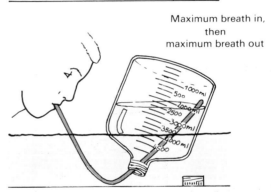

4 Take a long, deep breath until you cannot take any more air into your lungs. Now blow into the container. Keep going until you can do no more.

5 In your Student Record, note the volume of air you have blown into the container. This is the **vital capacity** of your lungs.

6 Refill the container with water and set it up as before.

7 Breathe quietly for a minute or so until your breathing rhythm is steady.

8 When ready, wait until you have taken a breath in, then breathe out through the tube into the container. Try to keep this breath the same as the others. In your Student Record, note how much air you have breathed into the container. This is your **tidal volume**.

9 Do this twice more. Note the results in your Student Record and work out the average.

Think about it!
1 Why does the body need oxygen?
2 When would the body need more oxygen?
3 Why should the vital capacity be so much greater than the tidal volume?

▷ 4.10 Examining stomata

▦ Method A: Structure

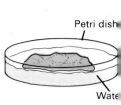

Petri dish

Wate

1. Take a piece of fresh lettuce (or other suitable green leaf). Leave it covered with water in a Petri dish for 5 minutes. This will make the leaf turgid (firm).

2. With the top surface facing up, bend the leaf so that it breaks but leaves the lower epidermis (skin) intact.

Upper leaf surface

Lower epidermis

3. Pull a piece of the lower epidermis from the leaf and place it (torn side down) on a microscope slide.

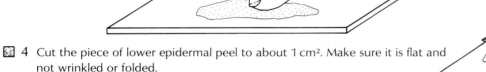

4. Cut the piece of lower epidermal peel to about 1 cm². Make sure it is flat and not wrinkled or folded.

5. Add a drop of water. Gently lower on a cover slip, squeezing out air bubbles as you do so.

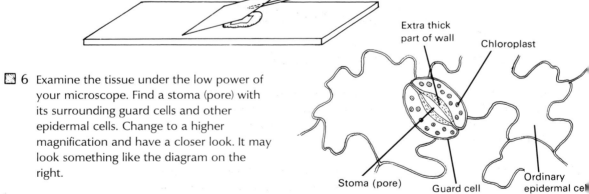

Extra thick part of wall

Chloroplast

6. Examine the tissue under the low power of your microscope. Find a stoma (pore) with its surrounding guard cells and other epidermal cells. Change to a higher magnification and have a closer look. It may look something like the diagram on the right.

Stoma (pore)   Guard cell   Ordinary epidermal cel

7. In your Student Record, draw and label the stoma and its surrounding cells. Draw big – the guard cells should be drawn about 3 cm long. Colour the chloroplasts green.

Think about it!
1 *In what ways do guard cells differ from other epidermal cells?*
2 *What plant process can guard cells carry out which other epidermal cells cannot? Explain.*
3 *Because of their unevenly-thickened walls, guard cells straighten as they lose water. What effect would this have on the stoma?*

1 Paint a small part (about 1 cm²) of the lower surface of a leaf with clear nail varnish. Apply the varnish as thinly as possible.

2 Leave the nail varnish for at least 5 minutes until it is completely dry.

3 Peel off the varnish with a pair of tweezers and place it on a microscope slide.

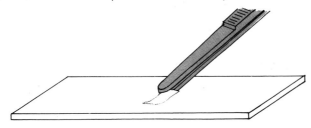

4 Add a drop of water. Gently lower on a cover slip, squeezing out air bubbles as you do so.

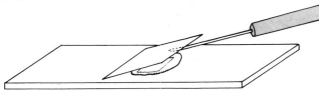

5 Examine the varnish under the low power of the microscope. The varnish will have picked up an exact impression of the lower epidermis. Count how many stomata (pores) you can see in your field of vision and note the figure in your Student Record.

6 Repeat the procedure on the upper surface of the leaf. Count and note down in your Student Record the number of stomata you can see on the upper epidermis of the leaf.

Think about it!
1 Leaves have stomata (pores) to allow oxygen and carbon dioxide in and out. What else could escape through these pores?
2 In what way might this be a problem for a plant?
3 When would this problem be greatest?
4 Which surface of a leaf will be heated most by the sun?
5 Is there any difference between the number of stomata on the upper and lower epidermis? If so, how would this benefit the plant?

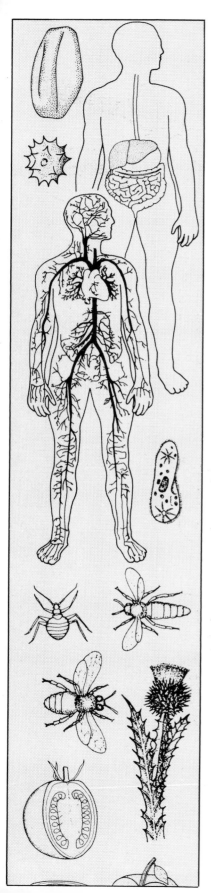

S E C T I O N 5

Food

5.1 The water content of foods
     (pupil's book page 62)
5.2 Testing foods for carbohydrates, proteins and fat
     (pupil's book page 62)
5.3 Measuring vitamin C concentration
     (pupil's book page 63)
5.4 The effect of cooking on vitamin C
     (pupil's book page 63)
5.5 The energy in a peanut
     (pupil's book page 59)
5.6 The energy content of food
     (pupil's book page 59)

▷ 5.1 The water content of foods

☐ 1 Weigh an empty porcelain basin or similar dish. Note the weight in your Student Record.

☐ 2 Chop a foodstuff into small pieces and fill the dish with it.

☐ 3 Weigh the dish with the food in it. Note the weight. Calculate the weight of fresh food in the dish. (Subtract the weight of the empty dish from the weight of the full dish.)

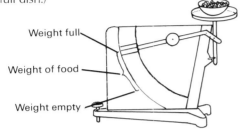

☐ 4 Heat the dish in an oven at 80–90°C for a few hours.

☐ 5 Reweigh the dish. Note the weight. The food is lighter because water has been driven from it.

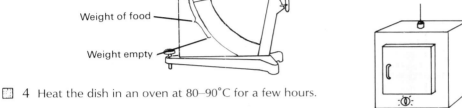

☐ 6 The food may still contain some water. Put it back in the oven for a few more hours, then reweigh it.

☐ 7 Repeat the drying and weighing until you get two weights the same, one after the other. The food is now completely dried.

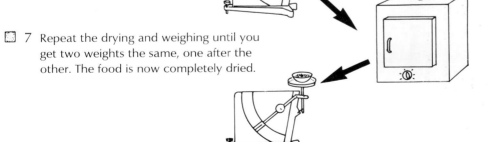

☐ 8 Fill in the results in your Student Record and calculate the percentage of water which the fresh food contained. (You are shown how to do this in your Student Record.)

☐ 9 Try the experiment on as many different foods as you can in order to complete the table in your Student Record.

▷ 5.2 Testing foods for carbohydrates, proteins and fat

▨ Tests for sugar

▨ Method A: Reducing sugars ──────────

The sugars, such as glucose, fructose and maltose, which give a positive result with this test, are known as **reducing sugars**.

▨ 1 Put a small piece of food in a mortar. Add about twice as much water. Grind it up with a pestle.

Note: This step may have been done for you.

▨ 3 Add about the same amount of Benedict's solution, a blue liquid.

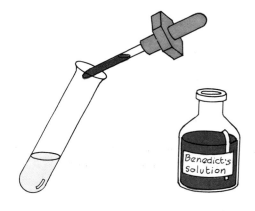

▨ 2 Pour the food suspension into a test tube to a depth of about 1 cm.

▨ 4 Heat for about 5 minutes in a beaker of hot water (or a water bath).

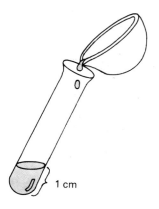

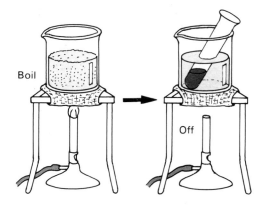

If the food contains sugar, it will go orange (or sometimes green).

Method B: Non-reducing sugars

Some sugars, such as sucrose (common table sugar) cannot be detected directly with Benedict's solution. These **non-reducing sugars** can be detected as follows.

1 Pour the food suspension into a test tube to a depth of about 1 cm.

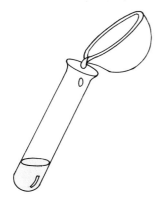

3 Heat for 2 minutes in a beaker of hot water, using a low bunsen flame.

Gentle heat

2 Add 5 drops of dilute hydrochloric acid. (Take care – this causes burns.)

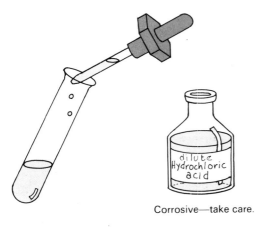

Corrosive—take care.

4 Switch off the bunsen. Add about 1 cm of the blue Benedict's solution. Leave the test tube sitting in the beaker of hot water for 5 minutes.

Off

If the food contains sugar, it will go orange (or sometimes green).

c

▢ Test for protein ─────────────

▢ 1 Pour food suspension into a test tube to a depth of about 1 cm.

▢ 2 Add the same amount of 5% sodium hydroxide solution.

▢ 3 Add 6 drops of 1% copper sulphate solution.

▢ 4 Gently shake the tube to mix the contents.

If the food contains protein, it will turn purple or lilac. This is called the **Biuret test** for protein.

▢ Test for starch ─────────────

▢ 1 Put a small piece of food on a spotting tile.

▢ 2 Add a few drops of brown iodine solution. If the food contains starch, it will go a blue-black colour.

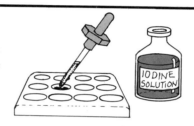

▢ Tests for fat ─────────────

▢ Method A: The simple test

▢ 1 Rub a piece of the food on to dry filter paper. Discard excess.

▢ 2 Write your name and the name of the food on the paper, then heat it in an oven for an hour at 40°C.

▢ 3 Hold the filter paper up to the light.

A translucent (greasy-looking) stain on the paper is a sign that the food contains fat.

▢ Method B: The emulsion test

▢ 1 Put a small piece of food (a 5 mm cube will do) into a mortar.

▢ 2 Add 10 ml of alcohol and grind with a pestle.

▢ 3 Filter into a dry test tube.

▢ 4 Add an equal volume of water to the filtered liquid. If the food contains fat, a white suspension (called an **emulsion**) will form.

▷ 5.3 Measuring vitamin C concentration

▢ The test

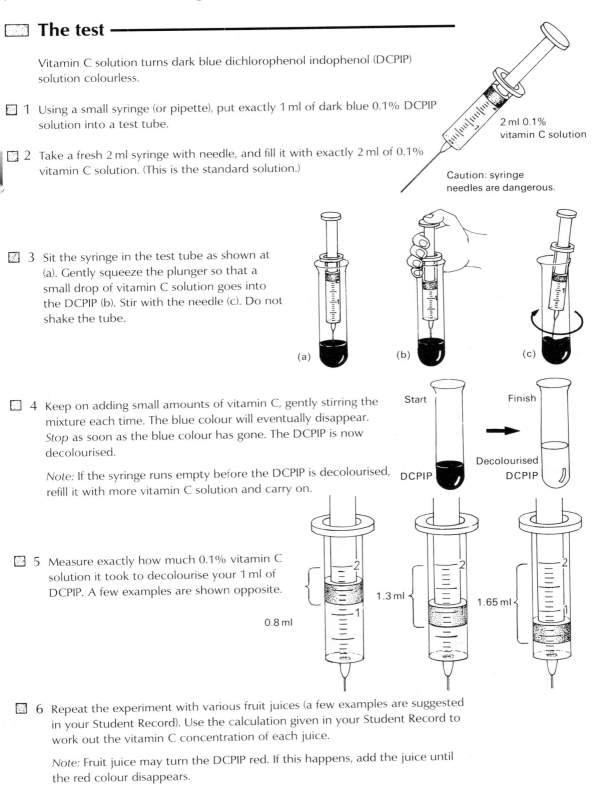

Vitamin C solution turns dark blue dichlorophenol indophenol (DCPIP) solution colourless.

☑ 1 Using a small syringe (or pipette), put exactly 1 ml of dark blue 0.1% DCPIP solution into a test tube.

☑ 2 Take a fresh 2 ml syringe with needle, and fill it with exactly 2 ml of 0.1% vitamin C solution. (This is the standard solution.)

2 ml 0.1% vitamin C solution

Caution: syringe needles are dangerous.

☑ 3 Sit the syringe in the test tube as shown at (a). Gently squeeze the plunger so that a small drop of vitamin C solution goes into the DCPIP (b). Stir with the needle (c). Do not shake the tube.

(a)   (b)   (c)

☑ 4 Keep on adding small amounts of vitamin C, gently stirring the mixture each time. The blue colour will eventually disappear. *Stop* as soon as the blue colour has gone. The DCPIP is now decolourised.

Note: If the syringe runs empty before the DCPIP is decolourised, refill it with more vitamin C solution and carry on.

Start   Finish

DCPIP   Decolourised DCPIP

☑ 5 Measure exactly how much 0.1% vitamin C solution it took to decolourise your 1 ml of DCPIP. A few examples are shown opposite.

0.8 ml   1.3 ml   1.65 ml

☑ 6 Repeat the experiment with various fruit juices (a few examples are suggested in your Student Record). Use the calculation given in your Student Record to work out the vitamin C concentration of each juice.

Note: Fruit juice may turn the DCPIP red. If this happens, add the juice until the red colour disappears.

▷ 5.4 The effect of cooking on vitamin C

1 Squeeze the juice from a fresh orange. Filter the juice through glass wool to remove debris.

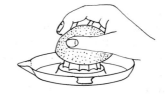 

Glass wo

2 Gently simmer a known volume of fresh orange juice until half has boiled off. Make up the original volume with fresh water.

3 Peel a fresh orange carefully, then boil it in plenty of water for 20 minutes. Keep the water and allow it to cool. Use in Step 5.

4 Squeeze the boiled orange to remove the juice. Filter the juice through glass wool to remove debris.

Note: Steps 1 to 4 may have been done for you.

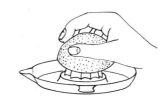 

Glass woo

5 Using the DCPIP test (Experiment 5.3), measure the vitamin C concentration of the juices prepared in Steps 1 to 4. If you are unsure of the method, revise Experiment 5.3 before you start.

Think about it!
1 *Does heating destroy vitamin C?*
2 *Does heating affect vitamin C?*
3 *Would boiling a food (potato or cabbage say) in water reduce its vitamin C content?*
4 *If so, is the heat to blame or what?*
5 *How could we stop waste of vitamin C when boiling vegetables?*

▷ 5.5 The energy in a peanut

To find out how much energy a peanut contains, we burn it and use the heat to warm up a known weight of water. The temperature of the water is taken immediately before and after the peanut is burned. If we know the weight of the peanut, we can work out how much energy it contains in kilocalories per gram, where one kilocalorie is the amount of heat needed to raise the temperature of one kilogram of water by one Centigrade degree.

Nowadays, another unit, the kilojoule, is also used. To convert kilocalories to kilojoules we simply multiply by 4.2.

1 Measure out 20 ml (0.02 kg) of water into a test tube.

2 Clamp the test tube in a stand as shown. Take the temperature of the water and note it in your Student Record. Remove the thermometer.

3 Weigh a peanut accurately and note the weight in your Student Record.

4 Stick the peanut on a mounted needle and roast it in a bunsen flame until it starts to burn.

5 Hold the peanut beneath the test tube until it stops burning.

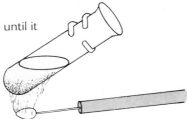

6 Stir the water with the thermometer and note the final temperature in your Student Record.

7 Work out the calorific value of the peanut in kilocalories per gram and kilojoules per gram. Write your answer in your Student Record.

Think about it!
1 What kind of energy does a peanut contain?
2 To what kinds of energy is it converted in this experiment?
3 Which kind of energy is actually measured?
4 Does all the energy of the peanut go into the water? Explain.
5 Why should the water be stirred before taking the temperature?
6 Would you expect the result from this experiment to be too high or too low?

▷ 5.6 The energy content of food

To measure how much energy a food contains in kilocalories (calories) or kilojoules, we use a food calorimeter. A food calorimeter is a device which burns a known weight of food very rapidly in pure oxygen. The heat given off is used to heat a known weight of water. The temperature of the water is taken immediately before and immediately after the food is burned. The more energy the food contains, the greater is the rise in temperature. The result is calculated in kilocalories per gram, where one kilocalorie is the amount of heat needed to raise the temperature of one kilogram of water by one Centigrade degree. Nowadays, the calorie has been replaced by the kilojoule. To convert calories to kilojoules we simply multiply by 4.2.

A simple type of food calorimeter is shown opposite.

1 Fill the calorimeter with cold water, carefully measuring the volume it takes.

2 Weigh a small amount of food (see Student Record for suggestions) and put it in the crucible.

3 Gently lower the igniter coil into the food and put the water container on top.

4 Switch on the oxygen and let it flow for a minute or so.

5 Take the temperature of the water.

6 Switch on the igniter. The food should burn strongly.

7 As burning stops, stir the water vigorously and note the highest temperature it reaches.

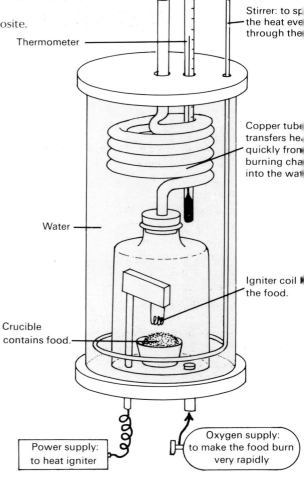

Stirrer: to sp the heat eve through the

Thermometer

Copper tube transfers he quickly from burning cha into the wa

Water

Igniter coil the food.

Crucible contains food.

Power supply: to heat igniter

Oxygen supply: to make the food burn very rapidly

Think about it!
1 Why is the oxygen allowed to flow for a while before ignition?
2 Why do we need oxygen?
3 Why must the stirrer be used before taking the temperature?
4 What is the copper tube for?
5 Name two sources of error in this experiment.
6 Why is the igniter coil essential?
7 Why must the final temperature be taken as quickly as possible?

SECTION 6

Feeding and digestion

6.1 Feeding adaptations
(pupil's book pages 24, 36, 39, 68, 83, 84)

6.2 The effect of acid on teeth
(pupil's book page 71)

6.3 Toothpastes
(pupil's book page 71)

6.4 The need for digestion
(pupil's book page 75)

6.5 Digestion in a model gut
(pupil's book pages 75, 76)

6.6 The effect of saliva on starch
(pupil's book page 76)

6.7 The effect of pepsin on protein
(pupil's book pages 62, 76)

6.8 The effect of lipase on fat
(pupil's book pages 62, 76)

6.9 Bile salts
(pupil's book pages 76, 89)

▷ 6.1 Feeding adaptations

🔲 Method A: *Amoeba*

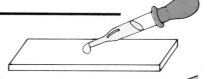

🔲 1 Put a drop of water containing *Amoeba* on to a clean microscope slide.

🔲 2 Leave for 2 minutes to allow the *Amoeba* to stick to the slide.

🔲 3 Gently lower on a cover slip so as to squeeze out any air bubbles.

🔲 4 Find an *Amoeba* using the lower power of the microscope, then use the high power for a closer look.

🔲 5 In your Student Record, draw the shape of the *Amoeba* every minute to show how it changes as it moves. Your drawings may look something like this:

🔲 6 Look closely at the cytoplasm. Try to locate food vacuoles. In your Student Record, draw or describe any you see.

🔲 Method B: Mussel

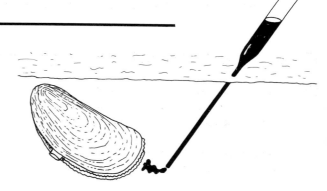

🔲 1 Lay a common mussel (*Mytilus*) in a dish of sea water for a few minutes until the valves (shells) open a little.

🔲 2 Place a drop of ink in the water near the inhalent siphon as shown. In your Student Record, draw what happens.

🔲 3 Insert a coin or blunt scalpel in the straight edge of the mussel as shown and prise the valves apart. This tears the muscles holding the shell together so that you can now open out the mussel. Replace the mussel in salt water and allow it to recover.

4 In your Student Record, draw the opened mussel. Identify and label the foot, gill plates and palps.

5 Place a drop of ink on the gills. Put arrows on your drawing to show where it goes.

6 Cut a small piece of gill and put it on a microscope slide. Add a drop of sea water and lower on a cover slip.

7 Examine the piece of gill under the lower power of the microscope. In your Student Record, write about what you see.

Method C: Housefly

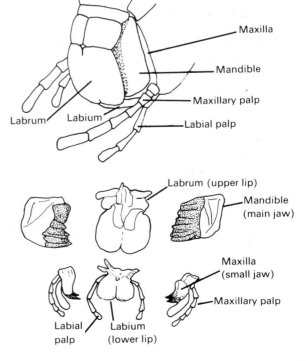

1 Collect a fly which has a piece of thread attached to it with wax.

2 Put the fly near a drop of sugar solution on a microscope slide.

3 Using a lens or a binocular microscope, observe the fly feeding.

4 In your Student Record, write a few lines about your observations.

5 Obtain a prepared slide of a housefly's mouthparts. Examine it under the microscope. In your Student Record, draw the channels which suck up the food.

Method D: Locust

1 You are supplied with a dead locust. Lift it up and examine its mouthparts with a lens. Identify the parts shown opposite.

2 Use tweezers to pull off the labrum (upper lip). Put it at the top of a piece of moist filter paper.

3 You can now see the main jaws called mandibles. Carefully pull them off and put them on the paper. Remove, in turn, the labium (lower lip) and the two smaller jaws or maxillae. Arrange them as shown on the right.

4 Use a lens or binocular microscope to examine the parts. In your Student Record, draw and label each part.

5 Find the cutting and grinding surfaces of the mandibles and label them.

Maxilla

Mandible

Maxillary palp

Labial palp

Labrum   Labium

Labrum (upper lip)

Mandible (main jaw)

Maxilla (small jaw)

Maxillary palp

Labial palp   Labium (lower lip)

▷ 6.2 The effect of acid on teeth

🔲 1 You are supplied with 3 similar teeth from a human or other mammal. Wash them, then use a paper towel to clean and polish them thoroughly. Remove all traces of flesh or soft tissue.

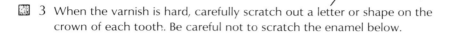

🔲 2 Paint each tooth all over with a thin coat of coloured nail varnish. Allow 5 minutes to dry, then apply a second coat.

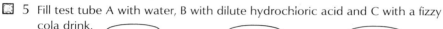

🔲 3 When the varnish is hard, carefully scratch out a letter or shape on the crown of each tooth. Be careful not to scratch the enamel below.

🔲 4 Set up 3 test tubes. Label them with your initials and A, B and C. In your Student Record, draw and colour the teeth as they appear now and put them into the appropriate test tubes.

🔲 5 Fill test tube A with water, B with dilute hydrochloric acid and C with a fizzy cola drink.

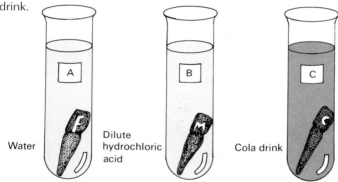

Water   Dilute hydrochloric acid   Cola drink

🔲 6 Dip a piece of pH paper into each liquid (take care with the acid) and compare the papers with a pH colour chart. Note each pH in your Student Record.

🔲 7 Leave the test tubes for 3 or 4 days. Remove the teeth with tweezers. Rinse them in water and dry them.

🔲 8 Peel off the varnish (use nail varnish remover if necessary) and examine the teeth.

🔲 9 In your Student Record, draw each tooth. Write a short description of each tooth.

Think about it!
1 What effect does acid have on teeth?
2 What was the purpose of test tube A?
3 What is the usual source of acid in the mouth?
4 Are there other sources? Could these have harmful effects? Explain.
5 Should toothpastes have a high or low pH? Explain.

▷ 6.3 Toothpastes

▨ 1 You are supplied with a number of popular toothpastes. Collect a piece of pH paper for each one. Moisten each piece with a drop of water.

▨ 2 Rub a small drop of a toothpaste on one piece of pH paper. Compare the colour with a pH colour chart.

Note the pH number in your Student Record. Repeat for the other toothpastes.

▨ 3 Each toothpaste has also been diluted with water. Collect a bottle of this, shake it up and put one drop on a microscope slide.

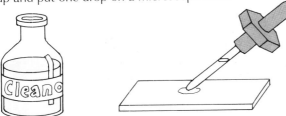

▨ 4 Gently lower on a cover slip so as to squeeze out all air bubbles.

▨ 5 Examine it under the low power of the microscope first. Toothpastes contain a gritty substance. Find this, then look at it under the high power. It may look like the example on the right.

▨ 6 In your Student Record, make a drawing of this. Note especially how much there is and how big the grit particles are. Repeat for the other toothpastes.

▨ 7 Look at your Result table. Decide which toothpaste you think seems best. (Assume that fine grit is better than coarse grit.)

Think about it!
1 If fluoride is so good for teeth, why don't all toothpastes contain it?
2 Which pH values are acid and which alkali?
3 What causes tooth decay?
4 Which pH values in toothpaste would help resist tooth decay? Why?
5 How would grit in toothpaste be of help?

▷ 6.4 The need for digestion

Note: **Visking tubing** is made from a cellulose material which behaves very like the wall of the gut (alimentary canal).

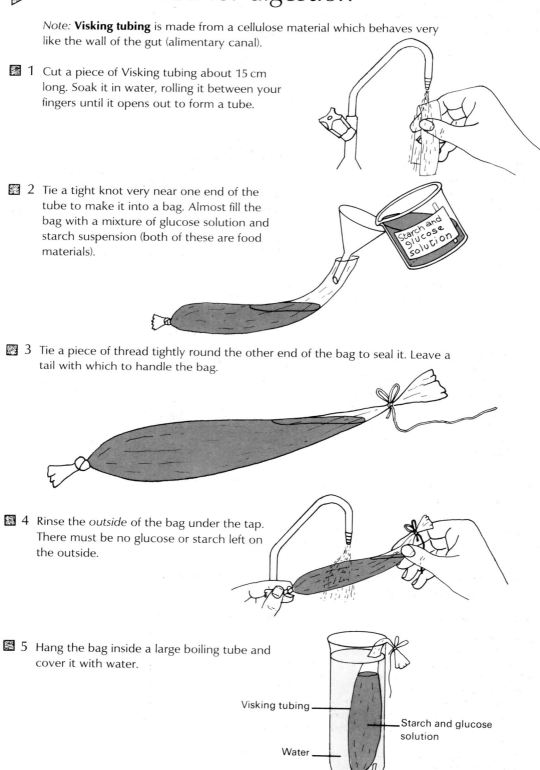

1 Cut a piece of Visking tubing about 15 cm long. Soak it in water, rolling it between your fingers until it opens out to form a tube.

2 Tie a tight knot very near one end of the tube to make it into a bag. Almost fill the bag with a mixture of glucose solution and starch suspension (both of these are food materials).

Starch and glucose solution

3 Tie a piece of thread tightly round the other end of the bag to seal it. Leave a tail with which to handle the bag.

4 Rinse the *outside* of the bag under the tap. There must be no glucose or starch left on the outside.

5 Hang the bag inside a large boiling tube and cover it with water.

Visking tubing

Starch and glucose solution

Water

6 Immediately, use a dropper to take a sample of the water from the *outside* of the Visking tubing bag.

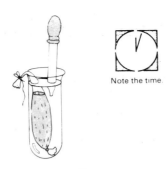

Note the time.

7 Add a drop of this water to a drop of (brown) iodine solution on a spotting tile. If the mixture goes blue-black, starch is present in the water.

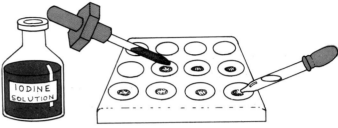

IODINE SOLUTION

8 Put the rest in a test tube. Add a dropperful of (blue) Benedict's solution (or Fehling's solution) and heat for 5 minutes in a water bath. If the mixture goes orange (or green), glucose is present in the water.

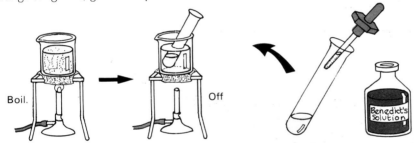

Boil.   Off

Benedict's Solution

9 These first two tests *must* be negative. If not, there is something wrong. Set up the apparatus again and restart.

10 Take samples of the water every 10 minutes for the next 40 or 50 minutes, and test each sample with iodine and Benedict's solution.

11 Note each result in the table in your Student Record. Write the quantity of glucose or starch detected as 0/ + / + +/ + + +/ + + + +/ + + + + +

Think about it!
1 Did glucose or starch leak from the bag?
2 What must the Visking tubing have to allow things to get through it?
3 Which must be bigger – glucose or starch molecules? Explain.
4 What are starch molecules made of?
5 If Visking acts like the gut wall, could intact glucose or starch molecules get from inside the gut to the rest of the body?
6 What could be done to starch molecules to allow the body to get the benefit from them?
7 What other large food molecules might need similar treatment before the body could use them?

▷ 6.5 Digestion in a model gut

Note: **Visking tubing** is made from a cellulose material which behaves very like the wall of the gut (alimentary canal).

1 Rinse your mouth thoroughly with water. This should get rid of sugar, etc, in the mouth. Collect about 10 ml of saliva in a small beaker. Add about the same amount of water and mix well.

Note: Saliva contains an enzyme called salivary amylase (or ptyalin) which converts starch to maltose (a kind of sugar).

2 Cut a piece of Visking tubing about 15 cm long. Soak it in water, rolling it between your fingers until it opens out to form a tube.

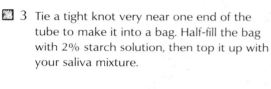

3 Tie a tight knot very near one end of the tube to make it into a bag. Half-fill the bag with 2% starch solution, then top it up with your saliva mixture.

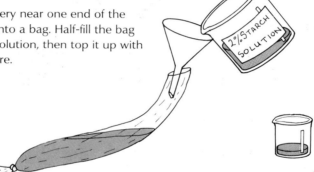

4 Tie a piece of thread tightly round the other end of the bag to seal it. Leave a tail with which to handle the bag.

5 Rinse the *outside* of the bag under the tap.

6 Hang the bag inside a large boiling tube and cover it with water.

7 Immediately, use a dropper to take a sample of the water from the *outside* of the Visking tubing bag.

Note the time.

8 Add a drop of this water to a drop of (brown) iodine solution on a spotting tile.

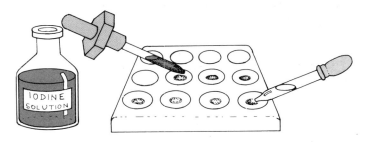

If the mixture goes blue-black, starch is present in the water.

9 Put the rest in a test tube. Add a dropperful of (blue) Benedict's solution (or Fehling's solution) and heat for 5 minutes in a water bath.

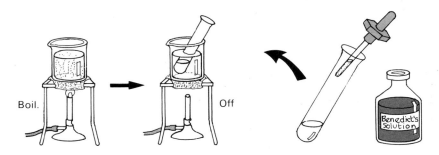

Boil.   Off

If the mixture goes orange (or green), sugar is present in the water.

10 These first two tests *must* be negative. If not, there is something wrong. Set up the apparatus again and restart.

11 Take samples of the water every 10 minutes for the next 40 or 50 minutes, and test each sample with iodine and Benedict's solution.

12 Note each result in the table in your Student Record. Write the quantity of sugar or starch detected as 0/+/++/+++/+++++/+++++

Think about it!
1 What must Visking tubing be like if things are able to pass through it?
2 Did any starch molecules escape from the bag? How do you know?
3 What could be the reason for starch molecules being unable to escape from the bag?
4 What is the structure of a starch molecule?
5 Did sugar leak out of the bag during the experiment? How do you know?
6 Was there sugar in the bag at the start?
7 Where could sugar have come from?
8 What could cause sugar to be produced?
9 What important job do digestive enzymes (like amylase) do for us?

▷ 6.6 The effect of saliva on starch

🔲 1 Take a clean spotting tile. Put 1 *drop* of iodine solution into each dimple.

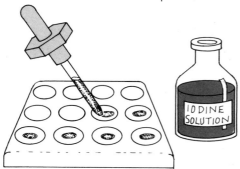

🔲 2 Rinse your mouth thoroughly with water. This should get rid of sugar, etc, in the mouth. Collect about 5 ml of saliva in a small beaker (chewing an elastic band will help). Add about the same amount of water and mix well.

Note: Saliva contains an enzyme called salivary amylase. This is also known as ptyalin.

🔲 3 Take up 2 ml of 1% starch solution into a clean 5 ml syringe.

🔲 4 Wash the outside of the syringe.

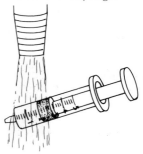

🔲 5 Keep your eye on the time. This experiment starts as soon as you do Step 6.

Note the time.

🔲 6 Take up 2 ml of your saliva into the syringe. Then draw in a little air and mix the contents very quickly.

Work fast!
Waste no time!

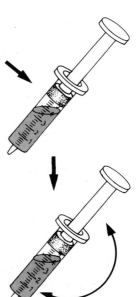

7 Immediately, add one drop of the starch/saliva mixture to the first drop of iodine on your tile. Note the time.

Note the time.

A blue-black colour shows that starch is present.

8 Keep testing single drops of your starch/saliva mixture with iodine every 30 seconds until no more colour changes occur. (Prepare a second tile if necessary.)

9 Put what's left of your mixture into a clean test tube. Add a dropperful of (blue) Benedict's solution (or Fehling's solution) and heat for 5 minutes in a water bath.

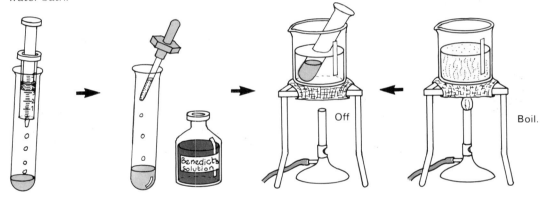

Off

Boil.

If it turns orange, sugar is present. Note the result in your Student Record.

10 Colour in the table in your Student Record to show the result of each iodine test.

Think about it!
1 Was starch present:
   a at the start?
   b at the end of the experiment?
2 How could you have checked that no sugar was present at the start of the experiment?
3 Was sugar present at the end of the experiment?
4 Of what smaller molecules are starch molecules made?
5 What has happened to the starch molecules in this experiment?
6 Of what use might this be to the body?
7 In this experiment, can you say for sure that the saliva caused the change? How could you show that it did?
8 If you had boiled and cooled the saliva before starting, what would have happened? Explain.

▷ 6.7 The effect of pepsin on protein

You only need to try one of these methods.

▨ Method A: Egg albumen

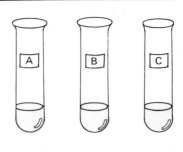

▨ 1 Label 4 test tubes A, B, C and D.

▨ 2 Put 9 ml of egg albumen (egg white) suspension into each test tube. This is a suspension in water of the protein (called albumen) found in egg white. As long as the protein is intact and undamaged, this suspension is white and cloudy.

▨ 3 Add 1 ml of 1% pepsin solution to test tubes A, C and D. Add 1 ml of water to test tube B. Pepsin is an enzyme found in the stomach.

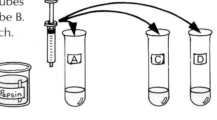

▨ 4 Add 5 drops of dilute hydrochloric acid to test tubes A and B. Add 5 drops of water to test tube C. Add 5 drops of dilute alkali to test tube D.

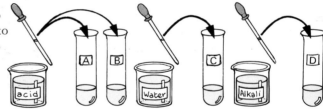

▨ 5 Incubate the 4 test tubes in a water bath at 37°C for 20–5 minutes.

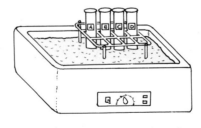

Or mix hot and cold tap water in a large beaker to get a temperature of around 40°C.

▨ 6 Examine each test tube. In your Student Record, note whether the contents are clear or cloudy. If the protein has been broken into smaller, soluble molecules (digested), it will have gone clear.

Method B: Hard-boiled egg

1 Label 4 test tubes A, B, C and D.

2 Collect some hard-boiled egg white (egg albumen). Cut 4 cubes of the same size (about 1 cm³) from the egg white. (This may have been done for you.)
Put one cube into each test tube.

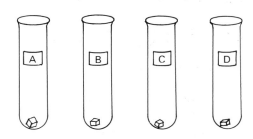

3 Add 10 ml of 1% pepsin solution to test tubes A, C and D. Add 10 ml of water to test tube B. Pepsin is an enzyme found in the stomach.

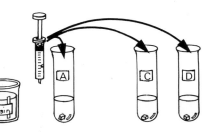

4 Add 5 drops of dilute hydrochloric acid to test tubes A and B. Add 5 drops of water to test tube C. Add 5 drops of dilute alkali to test tube D.

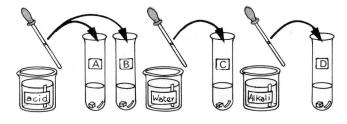

5 Incubate the 4 test tubes in a water bath at 37°C for 48 hours (or keep in a warm place).

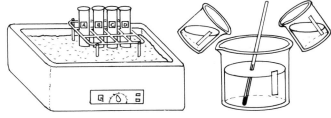

6 Examine each cube. In your Student Record, note down the size of the cube – is it smaller or unchanged?

Think about it!

1 In which test tube(s) has the protein been digested? How do you know?
2 Has pepsin digested the protein? If so, how can you be sure?
3 What kind of conditions does pepsin need in which to work? Why should this be so?
4 Does hydrochloric acid digest protein? How do you know?
5 Of which smaller molecules are proteins made?
6 Why does the body digest proteins?

▷ 6.8 The effect of lipase on fat

1 Label 3 test tubes A, B and C.

2 Add 5 ml of milk to each tube. The milk is being used as a convenient source of fat.

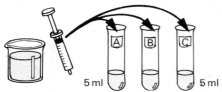

3 Add 1 ml of 1% bile salts solution to test tube B and test tube C.

4 Add 1 ml of water to test tube A and 5 ml to test tube C.

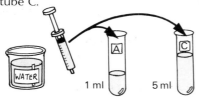

5 Add 5 ml of 5% lipase solution to test tube A and B.

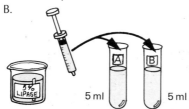

6 Add 5 drops of 0.01% phenol red solution to each test tube. Gently shake each test tube to mix the contents.

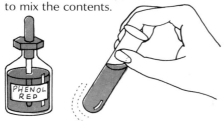

Phenol red is an indicator which is red in alkali and yellow in acid solution.

7 Add dilute sodium hydroxide, one drop at a time, until the contents go pink. Shake the test tube after each drop.

8 Incubate the test tubes in a water bath at 37°C for 30 minutes.

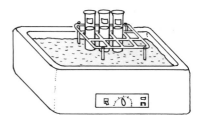

Or mix hot and cold tap water in a large beaker to get a temperature of about 40°C.

9 Observe the test tubes every 5 minutes for 30 minutes and record the colour in your Student Record. Use coloured pencils to colour in each box in the Result table.

Think about it!

1 What is the structure of a fat molecule?
2 If the contents of a test tube go yellow, acid has been formed. Where could this acid come from?
3 What could happen to a fat molecule to produce acid in the solution?
4 Did lipase cause this to happen? How do you know lipase was needed?
5 Could the bile salts cause this to happen? Explain.
6 What effect did bile salts have on the lipase?
7 Why were the test tubes incubated at 37°C?
8 Why was water added?

▷ 6.9 Bile salts

1 Label 2 test tubes with your initials and A or B.

2 Put a small knob of butter (a 5 mm cube will
   do) into each test tube. Put it to the bottom
   of the tube.

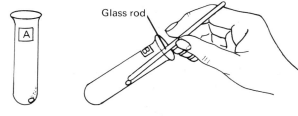

Glass rod

3 Add 10 ml of water to test tube A.

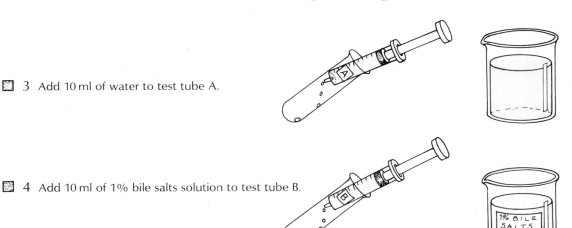

4 Add 10 ml of 1% bile salts solution to test tube B.

1% BILE
SALTS

5 Stopper the test tubes and put them in a water bath at 37°C until the butter
   melts.

6 Shake both test tubes thoroughly. Observe their appearance and return them
   to the water bath. Note the time.

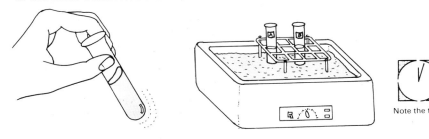

Note the time.

7 Examine the test tubes every 5 minutes. In your Student Record, draw and
   colour each tube as you go along.

Think about it!
1 *What is the temperature of the human body?*
2 *What will happen to butter inside the body?*
3 *What happens when fats like butter are mixed with water?*
4 *What effect do bile salts have?*
5 *How could this help the digestion of fats?*

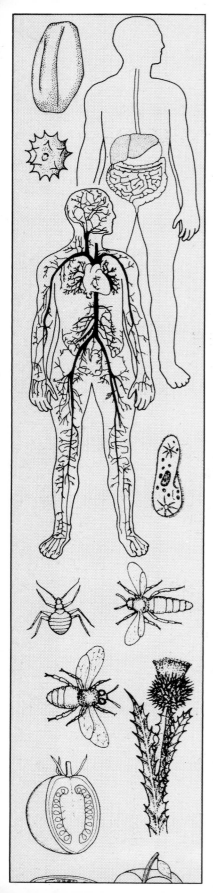

Water
and
organisms

7.1 Water and organisms
     (pupil's book page 114)
7.2 Sweat pores
     (pupil's book page 115)
7.3 Diffusion
     (pupil's book pages 116, 126)
7.4 Osmosis in living tissue
     (pupil's book pages 116–7, 120–2, 126)
7.5 Osmosis in a model cell
  · (pupil's book page 116)
7.6 The effect of heat and chemicals on the cell membrane
     (pupil's book pages 115, 116–7)
7.7 Turgor and plasmolysis in plant cells
     (pupil's book pages 115, 117, 122, 148)
7.8 Osmosis and turgor in plant tissue
     (pupil's book pages 115–7, 122, 148)
7.9 Osmosis and red blood cells
     (pupil's book page 117)
7.10 Water loss from plants
     (pupil's book pages 122–3, 147)
7.11 Root hairs
     (pupil's book page 134)

▷ 7.1 Water and organisms

☐ 1 Weigh an empty porcelain basin or similar dish. Note the weight in your Student Record.

☐ 2 Chop some fresh plant or animal tissue into small pieces and fill the dish with them.

☐ 3 Weigh the dish with the tissue in it. Note the weight. Calculate the weight of tissue in the empty dish. (Subtract the weight of the empty dish from the weight of the full dish.)

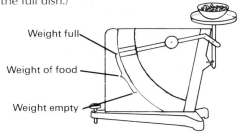

Weight full

Weight of food

Weight empty

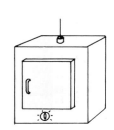

☐ 4 Heat the dish in an oven at 80°–90°C for a few hours.

☐ 5 Reweigh the dish. Note the weight. The tissue is lighter because water has been driven off.

☐ 6 The tissue may still contain some water. Put it back in the oven for a few more hours, then reweigh it.

☐ 7 Repeat the drying and weighings until you get two weights the same, one after the other. The tissue is now completely dried.

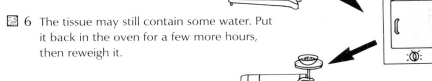

☐ 8 Fill in the Result table in your Student Record and calculate the percentage of water which the fresh tissue contained. You will find the calculation in your Student Record.

☐ 9 Obtain results for other tissues and complete the table in your Student Record.

7.2 Sweat pores

1 Rub a few drops of iodine solution on the palm of your hand. Allow to dry completely.

2 Put a drop of iodine solution on to a piece of starch paper. Observe the result.

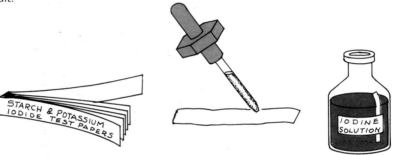

3 Put a fresh piece of starch paper over the iodine stain on your palm. Hold firmly in place for 5 minutes.

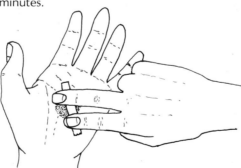

4 Examine the paper. Use clear tape to stick it in your Student Record.

5 Repeat the experiment on other parts of the skin, for example the forearm, back of the hand, the armpit, a leg, a foot.

> **Think about it!**
> 1 *Dry iodine will not turn starch paper blue-black, only iodine solution. Where did water come from?*
> 2 *Where is sweat made?*
> 3 *How does sweat get on to the skin?*
> 4 *What is sweat for?*

▷ 7.3 Diffusion

🔳 Method A: Diffusion of gas ───────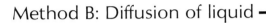

🔳 1 You are supplied with a gas jar filled with a brown gas.

🔳 2 Take another jar of the same size. Place it, upside down, on top of the first jar.

🔳 3 Carefully slide away the gas jar cover.

🔳 4 Leave the jars for 5 minutes, then examine them. In your Student Record, draw what they look like.

Method B: Diffusion of liquid ──────

🔳 1 Fill 2 test tubes three-quarters full with water. Place them in a stand.

🔳 2 Fill a long dropper with concentrated potassium permanganate solution (a purple liquid). Wipe the outside of the dropper with a tissue. (Take care – this liquid will stain your skin and clothes.)

🔳 3 Place the dropper in one of the test tubes as shown.

🔳 4 Slowly squeeze liquid out of the dropper to form a layer about 2 cm deep at the bottom of the test tube. Carefully withdraw the dropper.

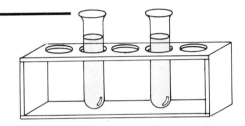

🔳 5 There should be a sharp boundary between the permanganate and the water. If there isn't, have another try.

🔳 6 Fill the dropper with a more dilute permanganate solution and put a layer of this at the bottom of the second test tube.

🔳 7 Leave the test tubes to stand for a few hours. Do not shake or disturb them! Examine the two test tubes closely. In your Student Record, draw what they look like.

Think about it!
1 Were the gas and permanganate particles moving? How can you tell?
2 Which particles moved faster?
3 Which permanganate tube had the higher concentration gradient?
4 Did this affect the rate of diffusion? If so, in what way?

D

▷ 7.4 Osmosis in living tissue

▦ Method A: Potato

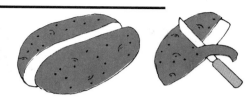

1 Obtain 3 potato halves. Peel round each half about 1 cm back from the cut.

2 Make a neat cavity in the top of each potato, like this:

3 Boil one potato half in water for 10 minutes. This disrupts the cell membranes.

4 Label 3 Petri dish bases with your initials and A, B and C. Put the boiled potato into dish A and the others into dishes B and C.

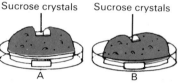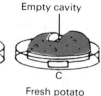

Sucrose crystals   Sucrose crystals   Empty cavity

A   B   C
Boiled potato   Fresh potato   Fresh potato

5 Put some sucrose (sugar) crystals into the cavities of potato halves A and B. Leave C empty.

6 Pour water into the Petri dishes. Put aside for 24 hours.

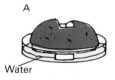

A   B   C

Water

7 Examine the cavities. In your Student Record, draw what has happened.

Think about it!
1 What effect does the sucrose have on the water concentration in the cavity?
2 Where is water concentration highest in each dish?
3 Define osmosis.
4 Into which cavity did water move? Why?
5 Are semi-permeable membranes needed for this to happen? Explain.
6 Explain the result in C in terms of water concentration.

▦ Method B: Grapes

1 Use scissors to cut 2 undamaged grapes from a bunch. Make sure the stalks are left intact.

2 Label 2 boiling tubes with your initials. On one, write 'A–water'. On the other write 'B–salt'.

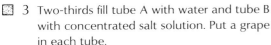 3 Two-thirds fill tube A with water and tube B with concentrated salt solution. Put a grape in each tube.

4 Leave aside for 48 hours.

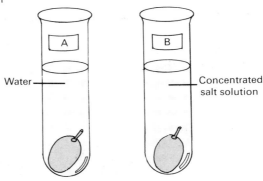

Water

Concentrated salt solution

5 In your Student Record, draw what has happened. Examine each grape. Note its condition – normal, swollen, shrunken.

> **Think about it!**
> 1 In A, where is water concentration higher – inside or outside the grape?
> 2 In B, where is water concentration higher – inside or outside the grape?
> 3 Define osmosis.
> 4 Which grape got lighter? How do you know it did? Why would you expect it to get lighter?
> 5 Which grape got heavier? How do you know it did? Why would you expect it to get heavier?

Method C: Shelled eggs

1 The shells are removed from 2 fresh eggs by leaving them in dilute acid for a few hours.

2 Put one egg in a beaker of water and the other in a beaker of concentrated salt solution. Label each beaker.

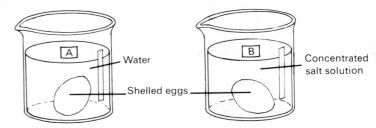

Water

Concentrated salt solution

Shelled eggs

3 Leave aside for 48 hours.

4 In your Student Record, draw what has happened. Note the condition of the eggs – normal, swollen, shrunken.

> **Think about it!**
> 1 In A, where is water concentration higher – inside or outside the egg?
> 2 In B, where is water concentration higher – inside or outside the egg?
> 3 Define osmosis.
> 4 Which egg got lighter? How do you know it did? Why would you expect it to get lighter?
> 5 Which egg got heavier? How do you know it did? Why would you expect it to get heavier?

▷ 7.5 Osmosis in a model cell

Note: **Visking tubing** is made from a type of semi-permeable membrane. It will let water molecules diffuse through it easily, but will hold back larger particles such as sucrose and starch molecules.

1 Cut a piece of Visking tubing about 15 cm long. Soak it in water, rolling it between your fingers until it opens out to form a tube.

2 Tie a tight knot at one end of the tube to make it into a bag. Half-fill the bag with 20% sucrose solution.

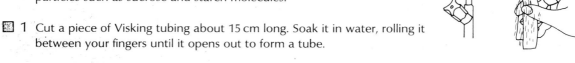

3 Carefully squeeze out any air and tie a knot at the other end to seal the bag.

4 Dry the outside of the bag with a tissue. Weigh the bag. Note the weight in the table in your Student Record.

5 Immerse the bag completely in a large beaker of water. Label it A.

6 Prepare a second Visking tubing bag. Half-fill this one with water, seal it, dry the outside and weigh it. Again note the weight in your Student Record.

7 Immerse this bag in 20% sucrose solution. Label it B.

8 Your experiment now looks like the diagram on the right.

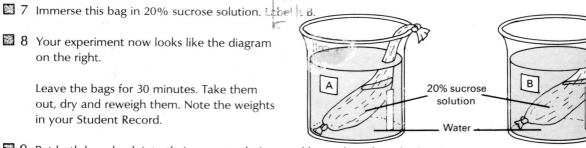

Leave the bags for 30 minutes. Take them out, dry and reweigh them. Note the weights in your Student Record.

9 Put both bags back into their *correct* solutions and leave them for a further 30 minutes. If this is inconvenient, they can be left for a few days. Remove the bags, dry them and weigh them. Note the weights in your Student Record.

Think about it!
1 In A, where is the higher water concentration – inside or outside the bag?
2 Which way should water move? Will the bag become heavier or lighter?
3 In B, where is the higher water concentration – inside or outside the bag?
4 Which way should water move? Will the bag become heavier or lighter?
5 If the bag of 20% sucrose solution had been immersed in 15% sucrose solution, what would have happened?

▷ 7.6 The effect of heat and chemicals on the cell membrane

1 Using a cork borer, cut cylinders from a fresh beetroot. Cut 6 cylinders to the same length. Wash the cylinders in water until no more colour leaks from them.

Note: This step may have been done for you.

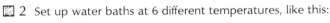

2 Set up water baths at 6 different temperatures, like this:

a Temperature about 0°C

Crushed ice covered with water

b Temperature about 20°C

Tap water

c Temperature about 40°C

Electric water bath or aquarium immersion heater

d Temperature about 60°C

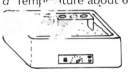

e Temperature about 80°C

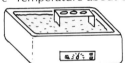

f Temperature about 100°C

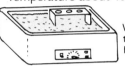

Water brought to boil then heat turned off

Electric water bath or aquarium immersion heater

3 Label 6 test tubes with your initials and one of each of the 6 temperatures. One-third fill each test tube with water.

4 Put one test tube into each water bath. Leave for 5 minutes to let them reach the temperature of their bath.

5 Put a beetroot cylinder into each tube. Check the colour of the water after 2 minutes, 5 minutes and 15 minutes.

Note: The red beetroot juice is actually cell sap which is found inside the vacuole.

Note the time

6 Colour in the appropriate boxes in your Student Record to show the colour of the water in each test tube.

Note: This step may have been done for you. Two more beetroot cylinders are put into tubes of different chemicals as shown, and the colour checked at the same times as the others.

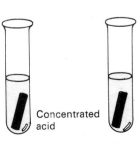

Concentrated acid

Ether

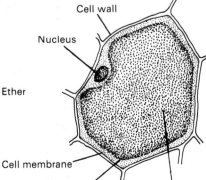

Beetroot cell
Cell wall
Nucleus
Cell membrane
Cytoplasm
Red cell sap

Think about it!
1 Is the membrane permeable to the red substance? Explain.
2 Why should the red substance escape at high temperatures?
3 Could heat have any other effects?
4 Is the membrane damaged by chemicals? Explain.
5 Give another explanation for your observations?

▷ 7.7 Turgor and plasmolysis in plant cells

▣ Method A: Onion epidermis ─────────────

▣ 1 Remove a layer from an onion. Cut it into small (1 cm³) pieces.

Note: This step may have been done for you.

▣ 2 Peel off the thin inside epidermis (skin) and place it (torn side down) on to a microscope slide.

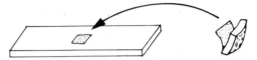

▣ 3 Add a drop of water to the skin.

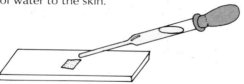

▣ 4 Slowly lower a cover slip over the specimen, squeezing out air bubbles as you do so.

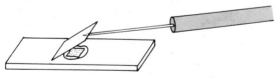

▣ 5 Examine the epidermis under the microscope for a few minutes. In your Student Record carefully draw a few of the cells. Draw the cells big – 2–3 cm long!

▣ 6 Place a drop of 20% sucrose solution at one side of the cover slip and a piece of filter paper at the other.

The paper will suck up the water, drawing the sugar solution across. Keep adding sugar solution until the water has been replaced. This is known as **irrigating** the slide.

7 Observe the tissue again. Try to find the same cells as before. Watch them for several minutes. Look out for cells which look like this:

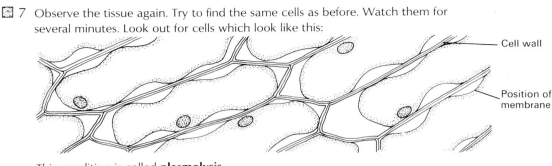

Cell wall

Position of membrane

This condition is called **plasmolysis**.

8 In your Student Record, make careful labelled (wall, position of membrane, protoplasm) drawings of a few plasmolysed cells.

9 Irrigate the slide again – this time with water. Observe for 5 minutes or so.

Method B: Rhubarb epidermis

1 Make a light cut across a piece of red rhubarb stalk.

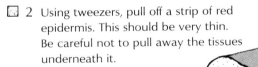

2 Using tweezers, pull off a strip of red epidermis. This should be very thin. Be careful not to pull away the tissues underneath it.

3 Place the epidermis, torn side down, on a microscope slide. Cut it to about 1 cm².

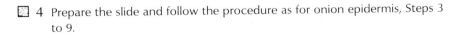

4 Prepare the slide and follow the procedure as for onion epidermis, Steps 3 to 9.

Think about it!
1 Which bathing liquid caused water to enter the plant cells? Explain why.
2 Which bathing liquid caused water to leave the plant cells? Explain why.
3 If its cells were plasmolysed, in what condition would the plant be?
4 Is plasmolysis a permanent state? If not, how is it reversed?
5 When you water a wilted plant, its drooping leaves begin to straighten out. Why?
6 Does the cell wall keep out sucrose? Explain your answer.

▷ 7.8 Osmosis and turgor in plant tissue

1 Cut off the ends of a large potato.

2 Use a cork borer to cut out cylinders of potato tissue.

   Note: Steps 1 and 2 may have been done for you.

3 Take 3 potato cylinders and cut them squarely to exactly the same length. Note the length in the Result table in your Student Record.

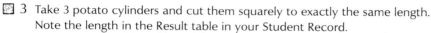

4 Label 3 test tubes A, B and C. Put a potato cylinder into each test tube.

5 Three-quarters fill test tube A with water, test tube B with 5% sucrose solution and test tube C with 20% sucrose solution.

6 Leave the test tubes for 1 or 2 days (if longer, put them in a fridge).

7 Pour off the liquid and dry the cylinders with a tissue. Feel each cylinder – is it particularly firm or flabby or much as it was? Note their condition in the Result table in your Student Record.

8 Measure the cylinders and note the lengths in the table.

Think about it!

1 Which has the higher water concentration – 5% sucrose or 20% sucrose solution?
2 If a potato cell took in water, would it be likely to get longer or shorter?
3 Which potato cylinder absorbed water?
4 Which potato cylinder lost water?
5 If a cylinder stayed more or less the same, what could you say about the water concentration of the cell contents compared to the bathing solution?
6 In what condition would the cells of cylinder C be?

Drawing blood: Warning
* Do not attempt to draw blood without supervision.
* Wash and dry hands thoroughly before starting.
* Use disposable lancets *once* only. Do not re-use or exchange lancets.
* Return lancets immediately after use for safe disposal.

1 Label 3 microscope slides: 'distilled water', '0.85% salt solution' and '2% salt solution'.

2 Put a drop of the appropriate liquid on each slide.

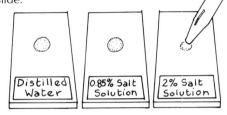

3 Tie an elastic band round one finger.

4 Wipe the finger with cotton-wool dipped in alcohol (ethanol). This will help kill germs and prevent infection.

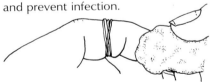

5 Prick the finger with a sharp jab with an unused sterile lancet.

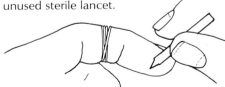

Note: Steps 3–5 may have been done for you.

6 Add a *very small* drop of blood to the liquid on each slide. Wipe again with cotton-wool and alcohol.

7 Gently lower a cover slip on to each slide so as to squeeze out all air bubbles.

8 Observe each slide under the high power of the microscope. You should be able to see red blood cells which look like this:

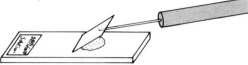

9 Keep looking at the 3 slides, especially the distilled water slide, for the next 10–15 minutes. Watch what happens to the red blood cells.

10 In your Student Record, make large drawings of the red blood cells to show how they appear. Describe what effect the bathing solutions had on them.

Think about it!
1 In the distilled water slide, where is the higher water concentration – inside or outside the blood cells?
2 Define osmosis.
3 Which way would water move by osmosis in the distilled water slide?
4 Eventually, what effect does this have on the cells?
5 This would not happen to plant cells. Why not?
6 What happens to the cells in the 2% salt solution?
7 In this case, where is the higher water concentration – inside or outside the cells?
8 What can you say about the water concentration of 0.85% salt solution compared to red blood cells? Explain.
9 Why does the body not allow the water concentration of the blood to vary much?

▷ 7.10 Water loss from plants

Method A: Source of loss

1 Take 2 well-watered pot plants. Remove all the leaves from one. Put each pot into a polythene bag and tie the bag round the stem.

Plant A   Plant B

2 Put each plant inside a bell jar. Leave them for 24 hours or so.

Bell jar

3 Look closely for moisture on the insides of the jars. Draw the appearance of the jars in your Student Record.

> **Think about it!**
> 1 How could you prove that the moisture was water?
> 2 From where do plants lose water?

Method B: Rate of loss

1 Take 2 large test tubes. Put a fresh-cut leafy shoot into one of them.

2 Three-quarters fill each test tube with water. Carefully mark the water level on each tube.

3 Place a thin layer of oil over the water in each test tube. This will prevent water evaporating from the surface.

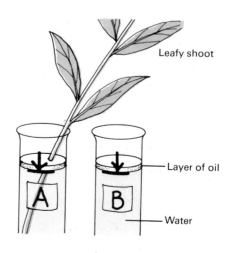

Leafy shoot

Layer of oil

Water

4 Note the time (to the nearest hour) in your Student Record. Leave the test tubes for about 24 hours.

5 After about 24 hours, fill a 2 ml syringe with water. Add water, drop by drop, to test tube A until the water level is back to where it was. Note the volume of water needed. Repeat with test tube B if necessary.

6 Note the finishing hour in your Student Record. Work out how many hours the experiment took. Calculate the volume of water being lost from the shoot per hour.

Think about it!
1 If water evaporates from the leaves of a plant, what effect could this have on the leaf temperature?
2 When would this be:
  a an advantage?
  b a disadvantage?
3 What do leaves have which allows water molecules to escape from them?

Method C: Loss from upper and lower epidermis

1 Take 2 leaves of about the same size. Smear the upper surface of one leaf (leaf A) and the lower surface of the other leaf (leaf B) with a layer of Vaseline.

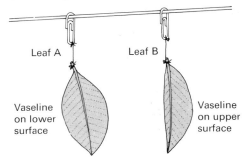

2 Carefully weigh both leaves. (Don't get any Vaseline on the balance.) Note the weights in your Student Record. Hang the leaves up for 24–48 hours.

3 Reweigh the leaves. Calculate the percentage weight loss of each.

Think about it!
1 What would cause the leaves to lose weight?
2 How could Vaseline prevent this?
3 Which leaf surface allowed more water to escape through it?
4 Why should this surface allow this?
5 What does the upper epidermis of a leaf have to reduce water loss?
6 Is this completely efficient? Explain your answer.
7 Why is the percentage weight loss more useful than the actual weight loss?

▷ 7.11 Root hairs

1 You are provided with a cress seedling, 3 or 4 days old, growing on black paper. Examine the seedling with a hand lens or binocular microscope. Draw it in your Student Record. Note especially the size and position of the root hairs (i).

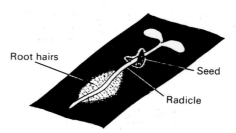

Root hairs
Seed
Radicle

2 Gently remove the seedling from the paper. Try not to damage the root hairs. Put the seedling on a microscope slide.

3 Cut off the bottom 1 cm of the radicle. Discard the rest of the seedling.

4 Add a drop of iodine solution and gently lower on a cover slip.

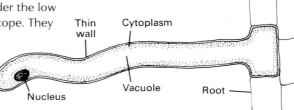

5 Examine the root hair cells under the low and high power of the microscope. They have this sort of structure:

Thin wall   Cytoplasm

Nucleus   Vacuole   Root

6 Make a large labelled drawing of a root hair cell in your Student Record (ii).

7 Collect another seedling and cut it as before. Add a drop of dye to the radicle before putting on the coverslip.

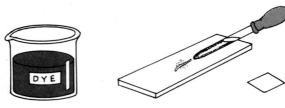

DYE

8 Observe the root hairs under the microscope. Watch how the dye is absorbed. Make coloured drawings in your Student Record to show how the dye moves into the root (iii).

Think about it!
1 Where are the youngest (smallest) root hairs?
2 Are root hairs found all over a root?
3 Where is the nucleus of a root hair cell?
4 How does water enter a root?
5 Root hairs increase a root's surface area many times over. How is this of advantage?

SECTION 8

Transport

8.1 Cyclosis/Cytoplasmic streaming
(pupil's book pages 25, 126)

8.2 Looking at blood
(pupil's book pages 132–3)

8.3 Pulse rates
(pupil's book pages 129–31)

8.4 Water transport in plants
(pupil's book pages 92, 96, 134–5)

▷ 8.1 Cyclosis/Cytoplasmic streaming

▭ Method A: *Paramecium* ———————————

Note: Paramecium is a single-celled animal – a protozoan. Its membrane is covered with tiny hairs called cilia. The cilia beat to move the animal around and to draw in food particles.

1 Place a drop of water containing *Paramecium* on to a microscope slide. (It could be pond water or a specially-prepared culture.)

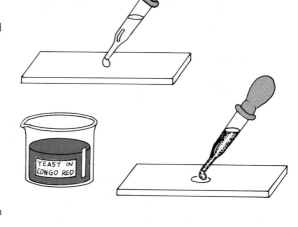

2 Add a drop of yeast suspension which has been stained with Congo red. Leave for 2 minutes.

The yeast cells will act as food for the *Paramecium*, while the congo red stain will allow you to follow its movements. Also, if the yeast is digested, the Congo red will turn blue.

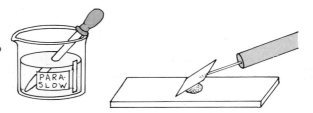

3 Add a drop of 'slowing solution' (Polycell) to the slide. This will stop the *Paramecium* moving about and enable you to see them properly. Gently lower on a cover slip.

4 Examine the slide under the microscope. Find a stationary animal surrounded by red yeast cells. Observe it closely under high power for 10–15 minutes. It should look something like this:

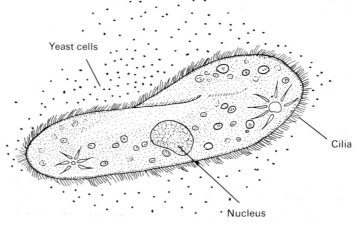

Yeast cells

Cilia

Nucleus

5 In your Student Record, make a series of drawings (colour if possible) to show what happens to the yeast cells as the animal feeds on them.

> **Think about it!**
> 1 Can you see the cilia? What do they look like?
> 2 What effect are the cilia having on the yeast cells?
> 3 Is the Paramecium digesting the yeast? How can you tell?
> 4 What path does the yeast take inside the cell?
> 5 How could moving its food around be of use to the cell?

Method B: *Elodea*

1 Take a whole *Elodea* (pondweed) leaf. Place it, top side uppermost, on a microscope slide. Add a drop of water.

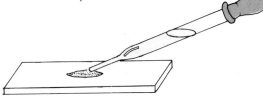

2 Gently lower on a cover slip so as to squeeze out all the air.

3 Examine the slide under the microscope. Look at the cells near the mid-line of the leaf under the high power. They should look something like this:

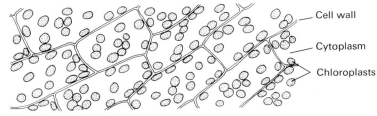

4 Focus carefully on 2 or 3 cells and watch them closely for a few minutes. Try to see the cytoplasm as well as the chloroplasts.

5 In your Student Record, make a large drawing of 2 or 3 cells. (Colour the chloroplasts green.) Add arrows to show clearly the directions in which the chloroplasts were moving.

> **Think about it!**
> 1 If the chloroplasts aren't moving around by themselves, what could cause them to move?
> 2 Could you see any signs of the cytoplasm moving (streaming)?
> 3 How could such movement be useful to the cell?

▷ 8.2 Looking at blood

SAFETY

Drawing blood: Warning
* Do not attempt to draw blood without supervision.
* Wash and dry hands thoroughly before starting.
* Use disposable lancets *once* only. Do not re-use or exchange lancets.
* Return lancets immediately after use for safe disposal.

1 Tie an elastic band round one finger.

2 Wipe the finger with cotton-wool dipped in alcohol (ethanol). This will help kill germs and prevent infection.

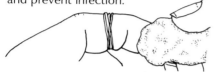

3 Prick the finger with a sharp jab with an unused sterile lancet.

Note: Steps 1–3 may have been done for you.

4 Place a drop of blood about 1 cm from the end of a *very* clean slide.

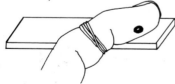

5 Take another very clean slide. Place it at an angle of about 45° to the first slide. Bring it along until it just touches the blood, then push it away along the slide to smear out the blood.

6 Wave the slide in the air to dry it quickly.

7 Add 8 drops of Leishman's stain. Leave for 45 seconds.

8 Add 8 drops of phosphate buffer (or distilled water). Gently rock the slide to mix the liquids.

9 Leave the slide for 10 minutes.

10 Carefully wash off the liquids with distilled water. Dry the *back* of the slide, then stand it on one end and allow it to dry completely.

11 Look at the slide under the low power of the microscope. Find the blood cells, then look at them under the high power. They may look something like this:

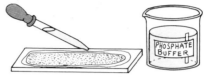

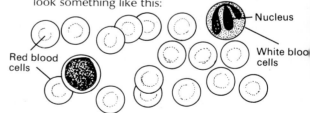

Red blood cells

Nucleus

White blood cells

12 In your Student Record, draw and colour all the different kinds of blood cell you can see. Draw large – about 3 cm across.

Think about it!
1 *Which cells are most abundant?*
2 *What is unusual about these cells?*
3 *How many different kinds of white blood cell did you find? What is the most outstanding part of these cells?*

8.3 Pulse rates

1 Sit down comfortably for a few minutes and relax.

2 Hold your hand out, bent back, palm upwards as shown.

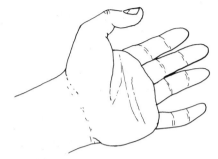

3 Gently place the tips of the 3 middle fingers of your other hand on the thumb side of your wrist. Feel for your pulse.

4 When you can feel a regular pulse, count the number of beats you can feel in exactly one minute. This is your resting pulse. Note it down in your Student Record (1).

5 Do this 3 more times. Note the figures.

6 Run on the spot (or do some equivalent exercise) for 3 minutes.

7 Immediately sit down and take your pulse. Note the figure in your Student Record.

8 Wait for one minute and take it again. Keep doing this, writing down each figure as you get it, until you get back down to your resting pulse.

9 Plot the results on the graph in your Student Record.

Think about it!
1 What is the pulse rate a measure of?
2 What effect does exercise have on this?
3 Why does it have this effect?
4 When you stop exercising, it takes some time to recover. Why?
5 Do fit people recover faster?

▷ 8.4 Water transport in plants

▣ Method A: Pathways

1 A leafy shoot is cut and left standing in coloured water for about 1 hour.
Note: This step may have been done for you.

Water containing dye

2 Wipe the dye off the end of the stem. Cut off and discard the part of the stem that was under the water. (Don't get the dye on your clothes!)

3 Start from the bottom and cut the stem in pieces about 2 cm long.

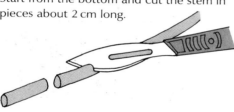

4 Using a hand lens, examine the top end of each piece. Look carefully for any signs of the dye.

5 In your Student Record, draw what each cut end looks like. Add colour to show where the dye is located in each section. Arrange your drawings like this:

Bottom ◯ ◯ ◯ ◯ ◯

These slices are called **transverse sections**.

6 Cut each section in half lengthways. These are called **longitudinal sections**.

7 Once again examine each section with a lens and make drawings in your Student Record, showing the location of the dye. Arrange your drawings like this:

Bottom ▯ ▯ ▯ ▯ ▯

> **Think about it!**
> 1 Why did we use coloured water?
> 2 Do plants draw up water through their whole stem or only certain parts of it?
> 3 Plants have a system of veins or pipes to carry water. Do you agree with this?
> If so, why?
> 4 How could you calculate how fast the water is moving up the stem?

▣ Method B: Veins

1 Stand a variegated plant in the coloured water for 24 hours.

2 Examine the leaves carefully, especially the white parts, for signs of the dye.

3 In your Student Record, make a large coloured drawing of one leaf to show where the dye is located.

> **Think about it!**
> 1 Did the plant manage to raise water up to its leaves? How could you tell?
> 2 Does water travel evenly through a leaf or only through certain parts of it?
> 3 How would you describe the leaf's water supply system?

Method C: Transport tissues

1 Take a small whole plant and carefully wash the soil from its roots.

2 Stand the plant in coloured water for 1 hour.

Note: Steps 1 and 2 may have been done for you.

3 Remove a thick root from the plant. Place it on a microscope slide and carefully cut very thin slices (transverse sections) from it.

4 Select your thinnest section and transfer it to a drop of water on another slide.

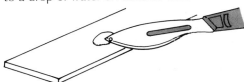

5 Hold the stem between two pieces of carrot or other suitable material. Cut the stem flush with the carrot.

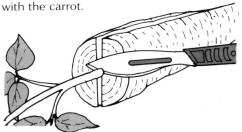

6 Cut a very thin slice from the stem – a gentle sawing action will help. This section should be almost transparent. If it is too thick, keep trying until you get a good specimen.

7 Transfer your best section on to the slide alongside your root section.

8 Gently lower on a cover slip.

9 Examine both sections under the low power of a microscope. In your Student Record, draw an outline of each section to show the location of the dye.

10 Under the high power, look more closely at the coloured areas. In your Student Record, draw a few of the cells, from both root and stem, which contain the dye. Draw them large.

> **Think about it!**
> 1 Does water take the same path through a root as through a stem? If not, what is the difference?
> 2 What do water-carrying cells look like in transverse section?
> 3 Are water-carrying cells in roots similar to those in stems?
> 4 Apart from coloured water, could you see any other contents in these cells?

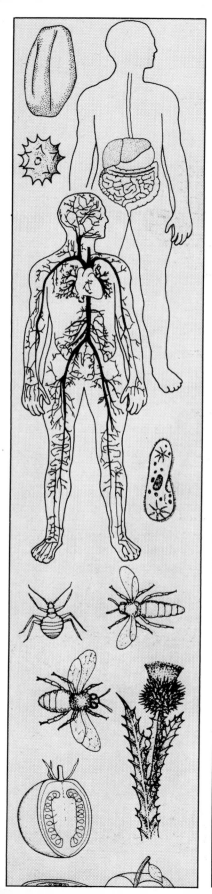

Detecting and responding to the environment

9.1   Surface area to weight ratios
      (pupil's book page 147)
9.2   Surface area to weight ratio and heat loss
      (pupil's book page 147)
9.3   Surface area and water loss
      (pupil's book pages 122, 147)
9.4   Stability and weight
      (pupil's book pages 138, 144)
9.5   The strength of bones
      (pupil's book pages 140, 145)
9.6   The components of bone
      (pupil's book page 140)
9.7   Muscle force
      (pupil's book pages 142, 143)

▷ 9.1 Surface area to weight ratios

▭ Method A: Models ━━━━━━━━━━━━━━━

The shapes below represent organisms of various sizes and shapes.

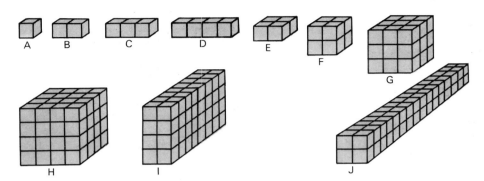

1   Assume that the sides of each small cube have an area of 1 cm². Work out the area of *external* surface of each model. Note them in your Student Record.

2   Assume each small cube has a weight (or mass) of 1 g. Work out the total weight of each model. Note them in your Student Record.

3   For each model divide its surface area by its weight ($\frac{\text{surface area}}{\text{weight}}$). This is the **surface area to weight ratio**. Note these in your Student Record.

▭ Method B: Animals ━━━━━━━━━━━━━━

Note: It is difficult to measure the surface area of an animal exactly. This method gives an estimate only.

1   Imagine your animals to be made up (approximately) of one or more cylinders, for example, the mouse below.

The surface area of the cylinder is circumference × length = c × L cm²

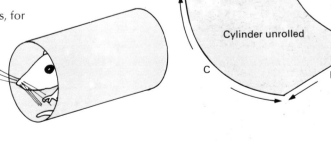

Cylinder unrolled

2   Use a tape measure (or a piece of string and a ruler) and measure the length and circumference of the (imaginary) cylinder round the mouse. Calculate the surface area of the mouse (C × L) and note it in your Student Record.

3 Weigh the mouse. Note the weight in grams.

4 Calculate the surface area to weight ratio of the mouse and enter it in your Student Record.

5 Use the same procedure for other small animals such as gerbils, hamsters and guinea pigs.

6 With larger animals, we must take the surface area of the limbs into account. Imagine them to be made up of a number of cylinders like this:

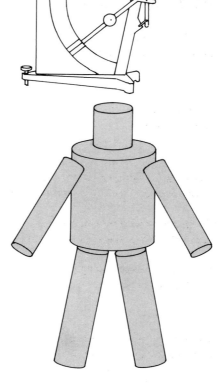

7 Calculate the surface area of each cylinder separately. Note them on a scrap of paper. Don't miss any. Add them up and enter the total surface area (cm²) in your Student Record.

8 Use bathroom scales to find the weight of your animal. Convert it to grams! Enter it in your Student Record.

9 Calculate the surface area to weight ratio of the animal and enter it in your Student Record.

Note: Great care must be taken when using animals in experiments. The animals must be caused no discomfort or distress. Handle them as gently as possible.

Think about it!
1 *Which has more surface area — a large or a small organism?*
2 *Which has more weight — a large or a small organism?*
3 *Which has the higher surface area to weight ratio — a large or a small organism?*
4 *Which will have more cells — a large or a small organism?*
5 *Which will have more surface for each cell — a large or a small organism?*
6 *Which will have more skin in proportion to its weight — a large or a small organism?*
7 *Will the shape of an organism affect its surface area to weight ratio? Explain your answer.*

9.2 Surface area to weight ratio and heat loss

1 Collect a 100 ml and a 500 ml round-bottomed flask and stoppers and thermometers to fit them.

2 Fit each flask to a stand, using a clamp. Do not overtighten the clamps.

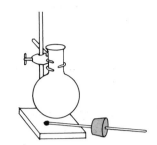

3 The 100 ml flask has a surface area of about 115 cm². The 500 ml flask has a surface area of about 330 cm². Note these figures in your Student Record.

4 When the bulbs are filled with water, the small flask holds about 100 g and the large flask 500 g. Note these figures in your Student Record.

5 Calculate the surface area to weight ratios of the two flasks. Note these in your Student Record.

6 Fill the bulbs of both flasks with boiling water. (Use an electric kettle if possible.) Take care. Fit the stoppers and thermometers to the flasks.

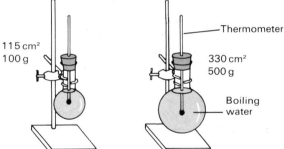

115 cm²
100 g

Thermometer

330 cm²
500 g

Boiling water

7 Wait 1 minute, then take the temperature of both flasks. Note them in the table in your Student Record. Note the time also.

8 Take the temperatures every 5 minutes for as long as possible.

9 In your Student Record complete the graph of Temperature against Time for each flask. These are known as **cooling curves**. Label one curve 'large flask' and the other 'small flask'.

Think about it!

1 Which cools down more quickly – a flask with a large surface area to weight ratio or a flask with a smaller one?

2 Why are birds and mammals from very cold regions larger than those from warm climates?

3 Why are the smallest birds and mammals found in hot regions?

4 Why, when indoors, do very large dogs pant more than small dogs?

5 Which flask contained more heat energy at the start?

6 Which flask had most surface in contact with the air?

7 Which flask would lose more heat energy?

8 If a large animal gives out more heat energy than a small one, why does it cool down more slowly?

▷ 9.3 Surface area and water loss

1 Collect a small (100 ml) beaker and 2 large (250 ml) beakers (or other suitable containers).

2 Label them with your name and A, B and C as shown.

3 Measure the diameter *in centimetres* of the small beaker and one large beaker.

d = diameter

Liquid surface area = 0.8×d²

4 Calculate the liquid surface area of each beaker by multiplying the diameter (in centimetres) squared by 0.8 ($0.8 \times d^2$). Note them in your Student Record.

Note: Steps 3 and 4 may have been done for you.

5 Fill a 200 ml measuring cylinder with water.

Note: 1 ml of water weighs about 1 g.

6 Pour water from the cylinder into beaker A to a depth of about 1 cm. In your Student Record, note the weight (volume) of water needed. An example is shown below.

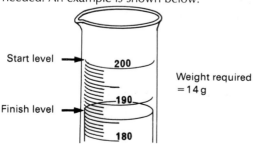

Start level → 200

Weight required = 14 g

Finish level → 190

180

7 Refill the cylinder and pour the same weight of water into beaker B. In your Student Record, note the weight used.

8 Refill the cylinder and half-fill beaker C from it. Note the weight of water used.

9 Your beakers will now look something like this:

For each beaker, work out the surface area to weight ratio. Note them in your Student Record.

10 Put the beakers to one side for 3 or 4 days.

11 Use a measuring cylinder to find out how much water now remains in each beaker.

Note each volume in your Student Record.

12 For each beaker calculate the percentage of water lost, like this:

weight of water lost = weight at start − weight at

$$\text{percentage water lost} = \frac{\text{weight of water lost}}{\text{weight at start}} \times 100$$

Think about it!

1 What effect does surface area have on the weight of water lost? Explain.
2 Which has more surface area – a large or a small body?
3 Would a large organism lose more water through its skin than a small organism?
4 Which could tolerate water loss more – a large or a small organism? Explain.
5 Which has the higher surface area to weight ratio – a large or a small organism?
6 Would the shape of an organism affect the water it loses through its skin? Explain.

▷ 9.4 Stability and weight

▣ 1 Collect a lump of Plasticine (about 100 g) and some milk straws or wooden dowelling.

▣ 2 You are going to use these to make and test, one after the other, the model 'animals' shown below. The top of each model should be flat.

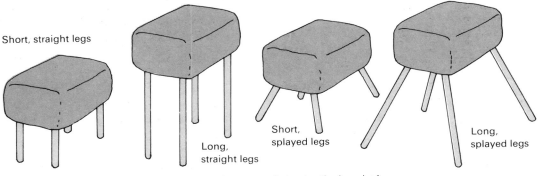

Short, straight legs

Long, straight legs

Short, splayed legs

Long, splayed legs

▣ 3 Put the first animal on the platform, as shown, and slowly tilt the platform until the animal topples over.

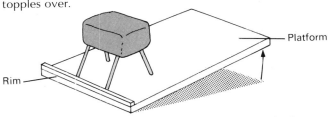

Platform

Rim

▣ 4 Use a protractor to measure the angle at which the platform was tilted. Note this in your Student Record.

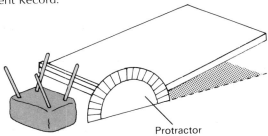

Protractor

▢ 5 Stand the animal up again. Add weights to the back of the animal, 10 g at a time, until the animal collapses. In your Student Record, note the weight required to do this.

▢ 6 Repeat the tests for the other animals.

Think about it!
1 Which animal has the lowest centre of gravity?
2 Which animals have the biggest base?
3 Which animal is most stable?
4 Which can support most weight – splayed legs or legs pointing straight down?

E

▷ 9.5 The strength of bones

This experiment will be done for you behind a perspex safety screen.

1 Fix a length of glass rod between two clamps, 32 cm apart. This will represent a length of bone.

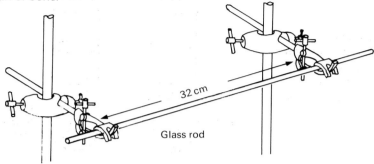

32 cm

Glass rod

2 Hang a scale pan from the centre of the glass rod. Add weights to the pan, 100 g at a time, until the glass breaks. Note this 'breaking strength' in your Student Record.

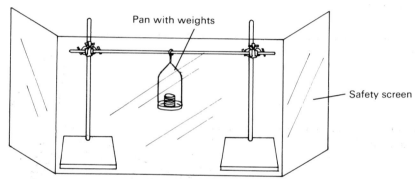

Pan with weights

Safety screen

3 Repeat the experiment with a 16 cm exposed length of glass. Then repeat with an 8 cm and finally a 4 cm length. Note each breaking strength in your Student Record.

4 Find the breaking strength of a 32 cm length of glass tubing of the same weight per centimetre as the glass rod.

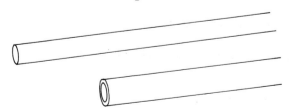

Think about it!
1 Why are you more likely to break a leg than a finger?
2 Why do heavy animals have shorter leg bones than light animals?
3 Why are long bones hollow?

9.6 The components of bone

1 Obtain and clean 3 small chicken bones of about the same size.

2 Label 2 boiling tubes with your initials and A or B. Put a bone into each tube.

3 Cover bone A with water and bone B with dilute hydrochloric acid. Leave for a few days. The hydrochloric acid will dissolve out the mineral component of the bone (mainly calcium phosphate), leaving behind the organic part.

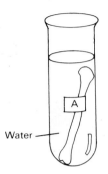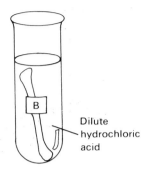

Water

Dilute hydrochloric acid

4 Take out bone A and dry it. Use tweezers to take bone B out of the acid. Rinse it under the tap and dry it.

5 Compare the two bones. In your Student Record, note how they appear and whether they are soft or hard, flexible or brittle.

6 Place the third bone (bone C) on a pipe clay triangle or wire gauze on a tripod stand. Roast the bone strongly for 10 minutes. Roasting will burn off the organic component of the bone (mainly protein fibres), leaving behind the mineral part.

Bone C

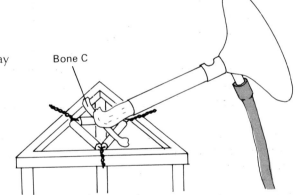

7 Allow the bone to cool down completely before you touch it.

8 In your Student Record, note the appearance of bone C and whether it is soft or hard, flexible or brittle.

> **Think about it!**
> 1 A bone should be slightly flexible. Why?
> 2 Which component of bone gives it this flexibility?
> 3 Why is this component not good enough on its own?
> 4 Which component of bone gives it its hardness?
> 5 Why is this component not good enough on its own?

▷ 9.7 Muscle force

▣ 1 Grip a set of bathroom scales (marked in Newtons) in your hands.

Squeeze.

▣ 2 Squeeze as hard as you can. Read from the scales the maximum force you could apply. Note this in your Student record.

▣ 3 Squeeze again as hard as you can, then release. As soon as the scale stops moving, squeeze again. Do this 30 times.

Release. ◀━━━━━▶ Squeeze.

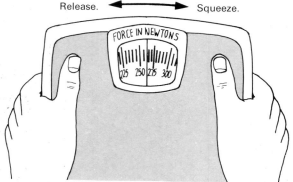

▣ 4 After 30 squeezes, again measure the maximum force you can apply and note it in your Student Record.

▣ 5 Rest for 10 minutes, then squeeze again. Note the force you applied.

▣ 6 For the next 4 lessons, repeat Steps 1 to 4 and note the results in your Student Record.

Think about it!

1 *The muscles being used here are not in your hands but in your arms. How can you tell?*
2 *How are the muscles connected to the fingers?*
3 *What does a muscle do to move a joint?*
4 *What must it use up to do this?*
5 *What is the effect of repeated contraction on a muscle? What causes this?*
6 *What effect does rest have? What might cause this?*
7 *What is the effect of training on muscles?*

SECTION 10

Size, support and movement

10.1 Skin sensitivity
 (pupil's book page 163)

10.2 Forming an image
 (pupil's book pages 39, 159, 160)

10.3 How lenses work
 (pupil's book pages 159, 160)

10.4 Some limits of vision
 (pupil's book page 158)

10.5 Reaction times
 (pupil's book page 156)

10.6 Reflexes
 (pupil's book pages 156, 157)

10.7 Responding to the environment
 (pupil's book pages 149, 152)

10.8 Positive geotropism in roots
 (pupil's book pages 149, 150)

10.9 The sensitive part of a root
 (pupil's book page 150)

10.10 The effect of one-sided light on stems
 (pupil's book pages 149, 150)

10.11 The effect of indole acetic acid (IAA) on stems
 (pupil's book page 150)

▷ 10.1 Skin sensitivity

▭ Method A: Two-point thresholds ──────

1 Work in pairs. Have your partner sit at a table with his/her arm resting upwards on it.

2 Set a pair of dividers about 2 mm apart. Touch the tip of your partner's forefinger with the dividers. Ask him/her how many points he/she feels.

3 If he/she says 'two', reduce the gap and try again. Repeat until your partner can feel only one point.

4 Now start to increase the gap until your partner can just feel two points again. This is the 'two-point threshold'. Measure the gap in millimetres and note it in your Student Record.

5 Find the two-point thresholds for the palm, the back of the hand, the forearm the back of the neck, the cheek and the sole of the foot. Note them in your Student Record.

> **Think about it!**
> 1 Why, if the skin is being touched by two points, can we sometimes feel only one?
> 2 Are touch receptors in the skin the same distance apart? If not, how do they vary?
> 3 Which parts of the skin have most touch receptors? Is there any advantage in this?

▭ Method B: Temperature receptors ──────

1 Put 3 same-size beakers in a row. Fill one with hot water (about 50°C), one with lukewarm water (about 25°C) and one with iced water (about 0°C).

2 Put one forefinger into the hot water and the other into the cold water. Keep them there for about 1 minute.

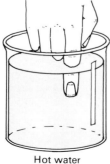
Hot water

Lukewarm water

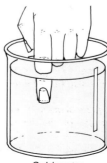
Cold water

3 Transfer them both to the lukewarm water. How do they feel? Repeat a few times and note the sensation in your Student Record.

4 Put 6 thin nails in a beaker of very hot water (90–100°C) and 6 in iced water (about 0°C). Leave them for 5 minutes.

5 Collect a rubber stamp and ink it with 36 dots. Use it to mark your partner's palm and the back of his/her hand. Your Student Record has grids to represent these points.

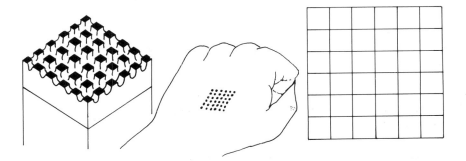

6 Get your partner to look away. Take a nail, dry it *quickly* with a tissue and touch one of the ink dots. Your partner must say immediately 'hot', 'cold' or 'don't know'. If the answer is correct, put a tick (√) in the appropriate box in your grid. If wrong, put a cross (×).

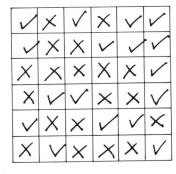

7 Put the nail back in its beaker. Take a fresh nail and repeat. Continue until the grids are filled.

Think about it!
1 Did the lukewarm water feel the same to both fingers? If not, how did they differ?
2 Were both fingers actually at different temperatures when in the lukewarm water?
3 Which finger was losing heat? How did it feel in the lukewarm water?
4 Which finger was gaining heat? How did it feel in the lukewarm water?
5 Does the skin measure temperature or does it measure heat loss and heat gain?
6 Do all parts of the skin respond to heat loss or gain?
7 Does a spot on the skin which responds to heat loss also respond to heat gain?
8 What is thought to be underneath the skin at 'hot spots' and 'cold spots'?

▷ 10.2 Forming an image

▢ 1 Collect a thin convex lens, a thick convex lens, a lens holder, a screen, a metre stick and a candle (or other light source).

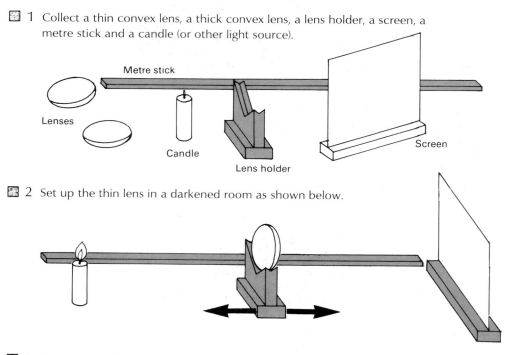

▢ 2 Set up the thin lens in a darkened room as shown below.

▢ 3 Move the lens back and forth until you find a position which gives a clear image (picture) of the candle on the screen.

▢ 4 Measure the distance from the candle to the lens and note it in your Student Record. Write a description of the image.

▢ 5 Keeping the lens holder the same distance from the screen, change the thin lens for the thicker one. What happens to the image.

▢ 6 Now move the candle until you get a sharp image again. Measure the distance from the candle to the lens and note it in your Student Record.

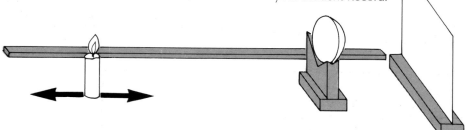

Think about it!
1 Which way up is the image – is it right way up or inverted?
2 Is it in colour?
3 Does a thin lens give a clear image of a near or a distant object?
4 Does a thick lens give a clear image of a near or a distant object?
5 Does the image change in size as the object gets nearer or further away? How?

▷ 10.3 How lenses work

☑ 1 You are supplied with a ray box such as this one:

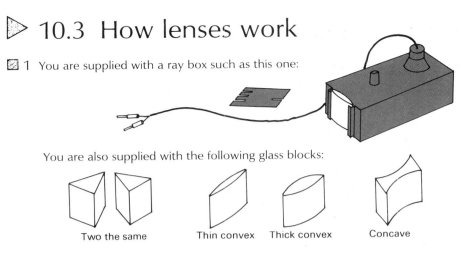

You are also supplied with the following glass blocks:

Two the same   Thin convex   Thick convex   Concave

☑ 2 Set up the ray box to give a single ray of light. Put one prism in its path like this:

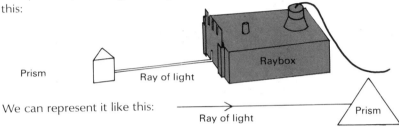

Prism   Ray of light   Raybox   Prism

We can represent it like this: Ray of light   Prism

In your Student Record, draw what happens to the ray of light.

☑ 3 Set up the ray box to give parallel rays of light. Try each of the situations below, recording each result in your Student Record.

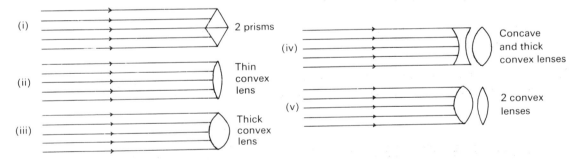

(i) 2 prisms

(ii) Thin convex lens

(iii) Thick convex lens

(iv) Concave and thick convex lenses

(v) 2 convex lenses

Think about it!

1 What effect does a prism have on light rays?
2 What do two prisms do to a row of parallel light rays?
3 What type of lens do the two prisms resemble?
4 How do lenses work?
5 What kind of lens does the eye have?
6 Which way does this lens bend light rays? Do they meet?
7 Which bends light rays more – a thick or a thin lens?
8 If the lens in an eye was bending light too much, which kind of spectacle lens would correct this?
9 If the lens in an eye was not bending light rays enough, which kind of spectacle lens would correct this?

▷ 10.4 Some limits of vision

▨ Method A: Blind spot ──────────

●   **A**   **B**   **C**   **D**   **E**   **F**   **G**

1 Hold this page at arm's length with your left eye directly in line with the black spot.

2 Close your right eye. Now look at each letter in turn with your left. At one letter, the spot will disappear. Circle this letter in your Student Record.

3 Repeat with the page at $\frac{3}{4}$, $\frac{1}{2}$ and $\frac{1}{4}$ arm's lengths. Note the results in your Student Record.

> **Think about it!**
> 1 Why does the spot disappear?
> 2 When it does disappear, what do you see in its place?
> 3 Is the blind spot big? Explain your answer.
> 4 What causes the blind spot?

▨ Method B: Colour sensitivity ──────────

Work in pairs

1 On the wall is a chart like this:

Sit down in front of it with your right eye directly in line with the cross and 30 cm (one ruler length) away from it.

2 Cover your left eye with your hand. Stare at the cross with your right eye. Do not let your eye wander.

3 Your partner slowly moves a felt pen along the chart from the right, wagging it a little as it goes.

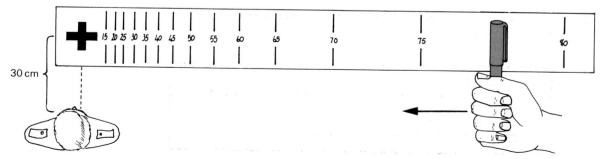

4 Tell your partner when you can just see the pen. He/she reads the angle from the chart and ticks the appropriate box in your Student Record.

5 The pen is then moved slowly further in until you can name the colour correctly. The angle is read and the box ticked.

6 Repeat the experiment for a range of colours. Use the pens to colour in your Student Record.

Think about it!
1 Which cells in the retina detect colours?
2 Which cells in the retina detect dim light, but not colour?
3 Are there colour receptors all over the retina? Explain your answer.
4 Is there more than one kind of colour receptor? Explain your answer.
5 To which colour is the retina:
    a most sensitive?
    b least sensitive?
6 Which colour might be best for an emergency vehicle?

Method C: Binocular vision

Note: Binocular means 'with two eyes'.

1 Stand with your arms by your sides.

2 Raise your hands and touch your forefingers together.

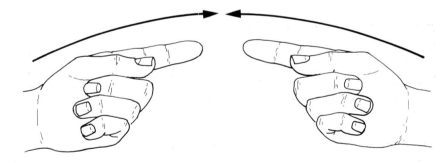

3 Do this 10 times altogether, but change the distance of your fingers from your face each time. Record the number of misses in your Student Record.

4 Repeat with one eye closed. In your Student Record, note the number of misses out of 10.

Think about it!
1 Both eyes do not send exactly the same picture of an object to the brain. Why not?
2 Why are we not usually aware of this?
3 How can this be useful in, for example, sport?

▷ 10.5 Reaction times

Work in pairs for these experiments.

1 Collect a reaction timing card like the one opposite. This has distances in centimetres and reaction times in seconds written on it. You could also use a ruler or a metre stick.

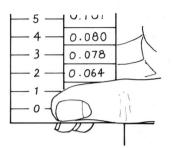

2 With your hand resting on the bench as shown, your partner holds the card vertically between your thumb and forefinger. The centre of your thumb should be exactly in line with the 'O' mark on the card.

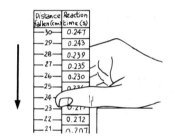

3 Without warning, your partner drops the card. As soon as you see it move, catch it between your thumb and forefinger.

4 Read the time at which your thumb stops, and note it in your Student Record.

5 Do this 5 times in all and work out the average. This is your **visual reaction time**. Work out the average for the class.

6 Repeat the experiment with your eyes closed. This time, your partner says 'Go' as the card is released. Note your reaction times and the average in your Student Record. This is your **auditory reaction time** ('auditory' means by hearing). Work out the average for the class.

7 There may be special reaction timing apparatus available. If there is, follow the instructions carefully and put the results and averages in your Student Record.

Distance fallen (cm)	Reaction time (s)
30	0.247
29	0.243
28	0.239
27	0.235
26	0.230
25	0.226
24	0.221
23	0.217
22	0.212
21	0.207
20	0.202
19	0.197
18	0.192
17	0.186
16	0.181
15	0.175
14	0.168–0.1
13	0.163
12	0.156
11	0.150
10	0.143
9	0.136
8	0.128
7	0.120
6	0.111
5	0.101
4	0.080–0.
3	0.078
2	0.064
1	0.045
0	

Think about it!
1 Did practice improve your performance?
2 What causes the delay in response?
3 What are synapses?
4 There are more synapses in the auditory pathways than in the visual. What effect would this have on the auditory reaction time?
5 How did your auditory reaction time compare with your visual reaction time?
6 How did your times compare with the class average?

▷ 10.6 Reflexes

Work in pairs for these experiments.

Method A: The knee-jerk reflex

1 Your partner sits on the edge of a table with one leg dangling freely.

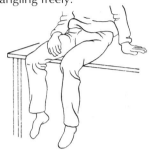

2 Locate his/her knee cap and feel the tendon just beneath it.

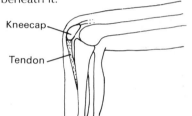

Kneecap

Tendon

3 With a metal rod, *gently* tap the tendon. Note what happens in your Student Record. If nothing happens, keep trying until you do get a response.

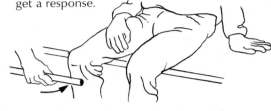

4 Repeat the experiment a few times with your partner trying to prevent the response. Note what happens in your Student Record.

5 In your Student Record, sketch a diagram of the reflex arc involved in the knee-jerk reflex. Label the diagram with these terms: receptors; sensory neurone; ganglion; white matter; grey matter; synapse; motor neurone; effector.

Method B: The pupillar reflex

1 Your partner closes his/her eyes for 2 minutes.

2 As soon as they are opened, look at them closely. In your Student Record, note the size of the pupils and irises.

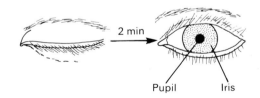

2 min

Pupil   Iris

3 Draw their appearance in your Student Record.

4 Shine a bright light into your partner's eyes for a few seconds while watching the pupils. (Take care – don't dazzle!)

5 Draw their appearance in your Student Record.

6 Your partner closes his/her eyes for 2 minutes, also holding one hand over the left eye.

7 Keeping the left eye closed and shaded, they now open the right eye. Immediately, shine a bright light into it.

8 Watch the response of the right eye. Then look at the left eye and observe its condition.

9 In your Student Record, describe what you saw happening.

> **Think about it!**
> 1 *Was the knee-jerk reflex a voluntary response?*
> 2 *Could you stop it?*
> 3 *What exactly is the pupil of the eye?*
> 4 *Describe the pupillar reflex.*
> 5 *Of what use is the pupillar reflex?*
> 6 *Does this reflex work independently in each eye?*

▷ 10.7 Responding to the environment

▭ Method A: Woodlice and light ─────────────

The apparatus used is called a **choice chamber**. Here is one design:

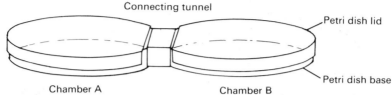

1 Cut 2 pieces of blotting paper so that they fit neatly inside the bases. Put one in each.

2 Moisten, but do not soak, the paper with a few drops of water.

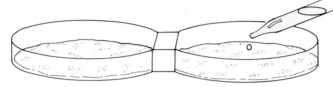

3 Put 6 woodlice of the same species (or other suitable animal) into each dish. Put on the lids.

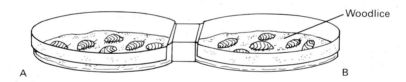

4 Every minute for the next 10 minutes, count the number of woodlice in each chamber. Note the numbers in Table 1 in your Student Record.

5 Start again. Put 6 woodlice in each chamber.

6 Place the black paper hood over chamber A. Switch on a lamp over chamber B. Don't put the lamp too close.

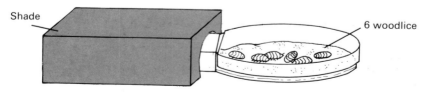

7 Every minute for the next 10 minutes, record the number of woodlice in each chamber in Table 2 (don't lift the shade – use subtraction) of your Student Record.

8 Complete the graphs in your Student Record.

110

Method B: *Paramecium* and chemicals

Note: Paramecium is a single-celled animal – a protozoan – which lives in water. Its membrane is covered with tiny hairs called cilia which it uses like oars to swim around. *Paramecium* looks like this:

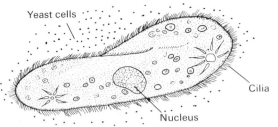

Yeast cells

Cilia

Nucleus

1 Place a drop of water containing *Paramecium* on to a microscope slide. (It could be pond water or a specially-prepared culture.)

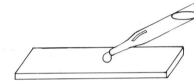

2 Gently lower on a cover slip so as to squeeze out all air bubbles.

3 Observe the animals under the low power of the microscope. In your Student Record, describe how they are distributed about the slide.

4 Using a fine dropper, put a small amount of dilute sodium bicarbonate solution at the edge of the cover slip. This produces weak acid conditions similar to those found around *Paramecium's* food supply.

5 Observe how *Paramecium* responds to this. Note it in your Student Record.

6 Add a small amount of acetic acid – a much stronger acid – to the same region. Observe what happens and in your Student Record, record the reaction of the animals.

Think about it!
1 How do woodlice respond to light?
2 When light causes a whole organism to move, what is this response called?
3 Is the response positive or negative in this case?
4 What, then, do we call woodlice's response to light?
5 When a chemical causes a whole organism to move, the response is called **chemotaxis**. What kind of chemotaxis does sodium bicarbonate solution induce in Paramecium?
6 What kind of chemotaxis does acetic acid induce in Paramecium?
7 Of what advantage could these responses be to Paramecium?

▷ 10.8 Positive geotropism in roots

■ 1 Collect 2 broad bean (or pea) seedlings which have straight radicles about 2 cm long.

■ 2 Put a layer of cotton-wool to one side of 2 large Petri dishes. Moisten, but do not soak, it with water.

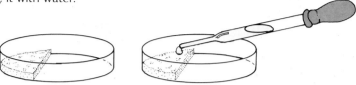

■ 3 Place one seedling in each dish, with the radicle sticking out as shown. Cover with another layer of cotton-wool and moisten it.

■ 4 Fix a lid on each dish with an elastic band. The seedlings should be firmly held in place. If not, add more moist cotton-wool.

■ 5 Fix each Petri dish to the platform of a clinostat. The radicles must stick out horizontally as shown.

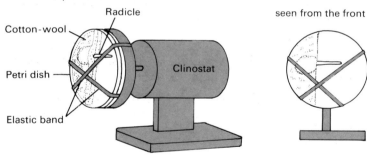

A clinostat is a device with a platform that revolves very slowly.

■ 6 In your Student Record, draw the seedlings as they are set up now.

■ 7 Switch on clinostat B but not clinostat A. Leave for 2 days.

■ 8 Examine the seedlings now. In your Student Record, draw them as they are now.

Think about it!
1 In which direction did radicle A grow?
2 Which stimulus seems to cause this type of growth?
3 Will a root bend if gravity affects it equally from all directions?
4 What will cause a root to bend?
5 What is this response called?
6 Of what use is this response to a plant?

▷ 10.9 The sensitive part of a root

☒ 1 Collect 2 broad bean (or pea) seedlings which have straight radicles about 2 cm long.

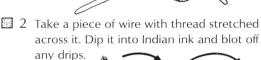

☒ 2 Take a piece of wire with thread stretched across it. Dip it into Indian ink and blot off any drips.

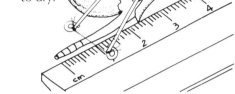

Hair grip, etc   Indian ink   Blotting paper

☒ 3 Use the thread to mark the radicles at intervals of 2 mm, starting at the tip. Allow to dry.

☒ 4 Cut off the last 2 mm from one of your radicles.

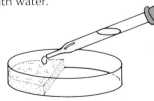

☒ 5 Put a layer of cotton-wool to one side of a large Petri dish. Moisten, but do not soak, it with water.

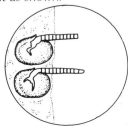

☒ 6 Place the 2 seedlings on the cotton-wool, then cut one at the top, with the radicles sticking out as shown.

☒ 7 Cover the seedlings with another layer of cotton-wool and moisten it. Leave the radicles clear.

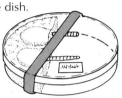

☒ 8 Fix a lid on the dish with an elastic band. The seedlings should be firmly held in place. If not, add more moist cotton-wool. Put your name on the dish.

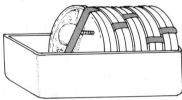

☒ 9 Place the Petri dish on its side in the box provided, so that the radicles are horizontal.

☒10 In your Student Record, draw the seedlings as they are set up now. Leave them for 2 days.

☒11 Examine the seedlings. In your Student Record, draw them as they are now.

Think about it!
1 Were the radicles both exposed to gravity from the same direction?
2 Did they both respond in the same way? How exactly did they respond?
3 What do we call the response shown by the intact radicles?
4 What stimulus caused this response?
5 Which part of the radicle seems to be responsible for detecting and responding to this stimulus?
6 Are all the ink marks the same distance apart as they were at the start?
7 If not, how do they differ?
8 Which part of a root grows most? How do you know?
9 Is there any evidence that the response is connected with root growth?

▷ 10.10 The effect of one-sided light on stems

1 Oat (or other cereal) seeds are germinated on moist cotton-wool in small Petri dishes until their coleoptiles are about 20 mm long. Take 3 dishes, each containing 6 to 12 seedlings. Label the dishes with your name and A, B or C.

2 Moisten, but do not soak, the cotton-wool with water.

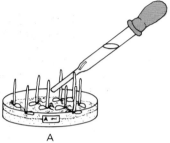

A

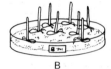 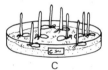

B   C

Note: The coleoptile is the sheath which covers the plumule inside the seed. The coleoptile is the first part of the shoot to appear when the seed germinates.

3 Take dish A and place it directly under a lamp so that the seedlings are evenly lit all round.

A

4 Take dish B and put it in a box which has a slit cut in it so that the seedlings receive light from one side only.

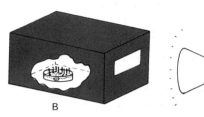

B

5 Cut enough 1 cm squares of cooking foil for each of your seedlings in dish C. Use a matchstick, or something similar, to shape the foil into little caps. Gently cover the tip of each coleoptile in dish C with a foil cap.

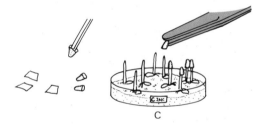

C

6 Once ready, put dish C into the same sort of box as dish B, so that these seedlings, too, receive light only from one side.

7 Leave the seedlings for a few days. Moisten the cotton-wool each day if possible.

8 Examine the seedlings carefully. In your Student Record, make drawings to show how they appear now.

Think about it!

1 Comparing A and B, what effect does one-sided light have on plants?

3 What is the response of B called?

3 What stimulus is causing this response?

4 What effect do the foil caps of C have on this response?

5 Which part of a plant stem seems to detect and respond to one-sided light?

▷ 10.11 The effect of indole acetic acid (IAA) on stems

1 Oat (or other cereal) seeds are germinated on moist cotton-wool in small Petri dishes until their coleoptiles are about 20 mm long. Take 4 dishes, each containing 6–12 seedlings. Label the dishes with your name and A, B, C or D.

Note: The coleoptile is the sheath which covers the plumule inside the seed. The coleoptile is the first part of the shoot to appear when the seed germinates.

2 Take dish A and measure the lengths of the coleoptiles. A pair of dividers would be handiest for this.
Jot down the lengths, add them up and calculate the average length of the coleoptiles. Note this in your Student Record.

A

3 Take dish B, measure the lengths of the coleoptiles and work out the average length. Note this in your Student Record.

4 Pick up a little lanolin containing 0.1% indole acetic acid (IAA), using a matchstick or splint. Put a little blob of lanolin + IAA on the tip of each coleoptile in dish B. Discard the matchstick.

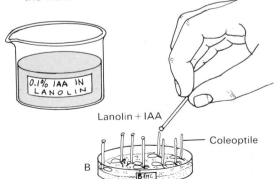

Lanolin + IAA

Coleoptile

B

Note: Lanolin is a fatty substance which helps keep the IAA moist and in contact with the plant.

5 Take dish C. Using a matchstick or splint, smear a small drop (about 5 mm long) of lanolin + IAA on one side of each coleoptile, about 5 mm from the tip. Discard the matchstick.

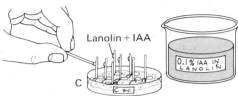

Lanolin + IAA

0.1% IAA IN LANOLIN

C

6 Take dish D. Smear a small drop of pure lanolin (about 5 mm long) on one side of each coleoptile, about 5 mm from the tip.

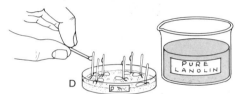

PURE LANOLIN

D

7 Moisten, but do not soak, the cotton-wool in each dish. Put the dishes in darkness for about 2 days.

8 Measure the coleoptiles in dish A and dish B as before. Work out their average lengths and note them in your Student Record. Use these to calculate their average change in length and percentage change in length.

9 Examine the coleoptiles in dishes C and D. In your Student Record, draw them (along with A and B) as they appear now.

Think about it!
1 What effect does IAA have if put on the tip of a shoot?
2 What effect does IAA have if put on one side of a shoot?
3 Why should it have this effect?
4 The IAA was mixed with lanolin. Could it have been the lanolin which caused the effect? Explain your answer.
5 What effect might a blob of lanolin have on the tips of dish A coleoptiles?
6 Why were the coleoptiles kept in the dark?

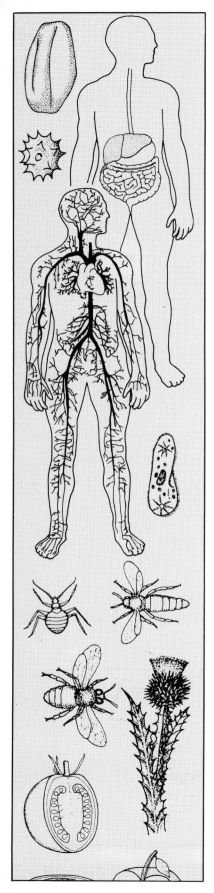

Reproduction and heredity

11.1 Reproduction in yeast
(pupil's book pages 168, 169)

11.2 Vegetative reproduction in angiosperms
(pupil's book pages 170–1)

11.3 Flower structure
(pupil's book pages 186–9)

11.4 Growing pollen tubes
(pupil's book page 189)

11.5 The structure of seeds
(pupil's book pages 190–1)

11.6 Conditions for seed germination
(pupil's book page 192)

11.7 *Drosophila:* The monohybrid cross
(pupil's book pages 206–7)

▷ 11.1 Reproduction in yeast

1 Put your initials on a test tube. Add 5 ml of 5% glucose solution.

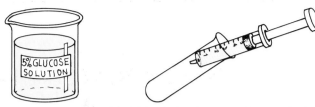

2 Add 1 ml of yeast suspension. Gently shake the test tube to mix the contents.

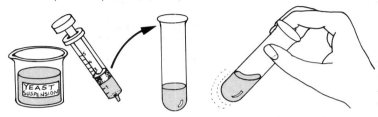

3 Take a drop of the mixture on a glass rod and transfer it to a microscope slide.

4 Gently lower on a cover slip so as to squeeze out all the air.

5 Examine the slide under the high power of the microscope. Find the yeast cells.

6 Made a rough count of the number of yeast cells in your field of view. Note this in your Student Record.

7 Draw a few yeast cells in your Student Record. Draw them big – about 15 mm across.

8 Leave the test tube in a warm place for a few days.

9 Shake the test tube, then make up a slide as before.

10 Using the same microscope as before, count how many cells now appear under the high power. Note this in your Student Record.

11 Look for yeast cells which appear different from before and draw them in your Student Record. They may look like these:

Parent cells

Buds

> **Think about it!**
> 1 What kind of organism is yeast?
> 2 Did the yeast culture look 'alive'? If so, in what way?
> 3 What does the yeast feed on in this experiment?
> 4 Is the yeast reproducing in this experiment? How do you know?
> 5 What method of reproduction is it using?

▷ 11.2 Vegetative reproduction in angiosperms

▭ Method A: Tubers ─────────────────────

▭ 1 Use a hand lens to examine a clean potato
tuber. In your Student Record make a
labelled drawing of the tuber. Your tuber
may look something like the one on the
right.

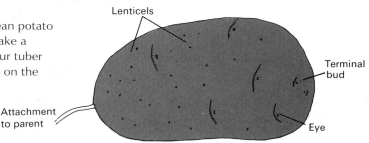

Lenticels

Terminal
bud

Attachment
to parent

Eye

▭ 2 Cut the tuber in half. Put a few drops of
iodine solution on a cut surface. Iodine turns
starch blue-black. Note the result in your
Student Record.

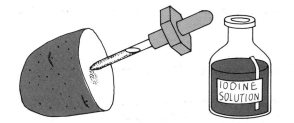

IODINE
SOLUTION

▭ 3 Scrape some potato tissue into a test tube. Add one dropperful of blue
Benedict's solution and heat for 5 minutes in a water bath. Sugar will turn
Benedict's solution orange. Note the result in your Student Record.

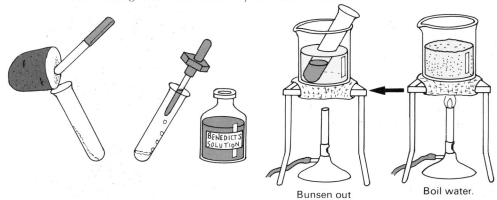

BENEDICT'S
SOLUTION

Bunsen out

Boil water.

▭ Method B: Corms ─────────────────────

▭ 1 Examine a corm of, for example, crocus. In
your Student Record, make a labelled
drawing of the corm. Your corm may look
something like the one on the right.

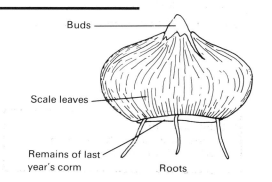

Buds

Scale leaves

Remains of last
year's corm

Roots

2 Cut the corm in half longitudinally (lengthwise). In your Student Record, make a labelled drawing of one section. It may look something like the one on the right.

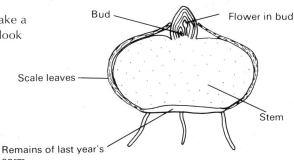

3 Test the cut surface with a few drops of iodine. Note the result in your Student Record.

4 Scrape some stem tissue into a test tube. Add a dropperful of Benedict's solution and heat for 5 minutes. Note the result in your Student Record.

Method C: Bulbs

1 Examine a bulb of, for example, tulip. In your Student Record, make a labelled drawing of the bulb. Your bulb may look something like the one on the right.

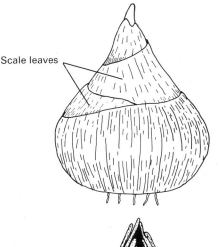

2 Cut the bulb in half longitudinally (lengthwise). In your Student Record, make a labelled drawing of one section.

3 Test the cut surface with a few drops of iodine. Note the result in your Student Record.

4 Scrape some tissue from the fleshy leaves into a test tube. Add a dropperful of Benedict's solution and heat for 5 minutes. Note the result in your Student Record.

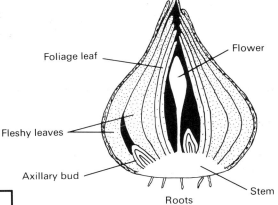

Think about it!
1 These organs are swollen. With what?
2 Why do they need a food store?

11.3 Flower structure

▦ Method A: Insect-pollinated ─────────

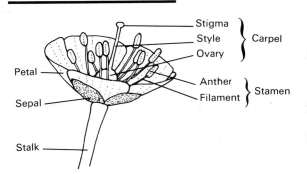

▦ 1 You are supplied with an insect-pollinated flower. In your Student Record draw the flower. Label, if possible, stalk, sepals, petals, carpels, stigma, style, ovary, stamens, filament, anther.

▦ 2 Remove the sepals and petals, lay them out as below, and draw them in your Student Record. Draw and label the inside parts of the flower also, for example:

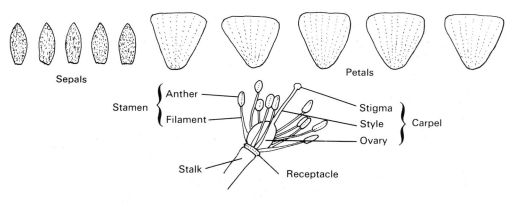

▦ 3 Use a lens or binocular microscope to examine the carpels. Cut the ovary in half.

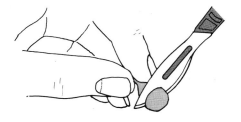

▦ 4 Examine the cut ovary. Make a large labelled diagram in your Student Record, for example:

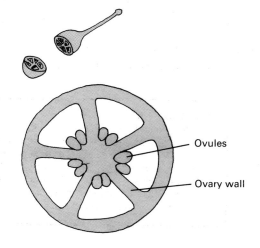

TRANSVERSE SECTION
OF OVARY

5 Dust some pollen from an anther on to a dry microscope slide.

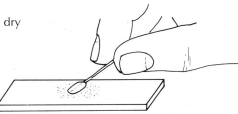

6 Examine this under the high power of the microscope. In your Student Record, draw several pollen grains. Draw large – about 2 cm in diameter.

Method B: Wind-pollinated

1 You are supplied with a wind-pollinated flower. Use a lens or a binocular microscope to examine it. In your Student Record, make a large diagram of the flower. Label, if possible, bracts, stigmas, stamens, anther, filament, for example:

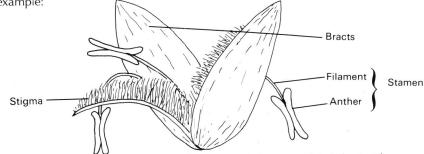

2 Remove the bracts and in your Student Record, draw and label the inside parts of the flower, for example:

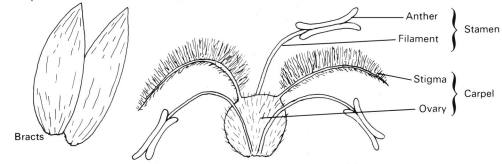

3 Dust some pollen from an anther on to a dry microscope slide.

4 Examine this under the high power of the microscope. In your Student Record, draw several pollen grains.

Think about it!
1 Why do wind-pollinated flowers not have petals?
2 Does the carpel stick up in the insect-pollinated flower? If so, why?
3 Does the carpel stick up in the wind-pollinated flower? Explain.
4 Do the stamens stand up in the insect-pollinated flower? If so, why?
5 Do the stamens stand up in the wind-pollinated flower? Explain.
6 Which flower had more pollen? Why?
7 Which pollen grains were smaller? Why?

F

▷ 11.4 Growing pollen tubes

1 Cut a piece of Visking (cellulose) sheet about 4 cm × 2 cm and place it on a microscope slide.

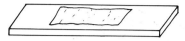

2 Add 4 drops of 10% sucrose (sugar) solution. Leave for a few minutes.

3 Remove a ripe stamen from a flower. Hold it above the sucrose and tap the anther so that pollen falls on to the slide.

4 Examine the slide under the microscope. (Make sure the lens does not touch the slide.) Find the pollen. In your Student Record, draw a few pollen grains. (Draw them big – about 15 mm across.)

5 Put the slide over moist filter paper in a closed Petri dish as shown. Leave in a warm place for 24 hours.

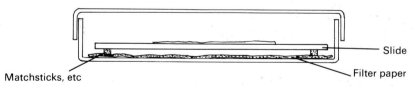

Matchsticks, etc   Slide   Filter paper

6 Use a tissue to dry the underside of the slide. Lower on a cover slip, then look at your pollen under the microscope.

7 Look for pollen grains which have grown pollen tubes. Carefully draw a few of these in your Student Record.

Think about it!

1 Where does pollen usually sprout a tube?
2 What causes it to do this?
3 Where does the pollen tube grow to? Why?
4 Pollen of different species often requires different conditions before it will grow. Why would this be an advantage?

▷ 11.5 The structure of seeds

🔳 Method A: A dicotyledon-broad bean ─────

🔲 1 Collect a broad bean seed which has been soaked in water to soften it. Compare it with the diagram opposite.

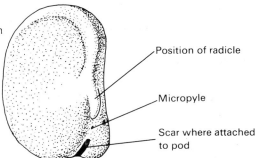

Position of radicle

Micropyle

Scar where attached to pod

🔲 2 Remove the outer coat – the testa.

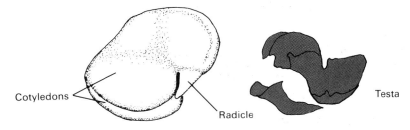

Cotyledons

Radicle

Testa

🔲 3 Gently prise apart the two cotyledons and lay the seed out like this:

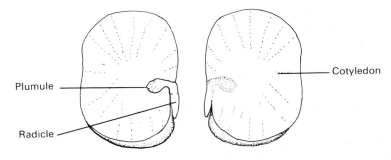

Cotyledon

Plumule

Radicle

🔲 4 Use a hand lens to examine the seed carefully. In your Student Record, draw and label the opened seed.

🔲 5 Flood both inner surfaces with iodine solution. The seed's food store is starch. The iodine turns this blue-black so we can locate it. Leave for 5 minutes.

IODINE SOLUTION

🔲 6 Draw the seed again, this time colouring in the blue-black areas.

123

 Method B: A monocotyledon-maize ——————————

Note: The maize 'seed' is actually a fruit since its 'skin' consists of both the testa and the pericarp fused together.

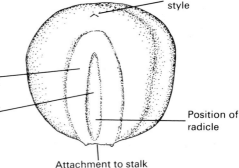

1 Collect a maize 'seed' which has been soaked in water to soften it. Compare it with the diagram opposite.

Remains of style

Position of cotyledon

Position of plumule

Position of radicle

Attachment to stalk

2 Carefully cut the fruit in half along the line shown.

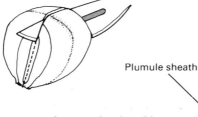

Endosperm

Plumule sheath

3 Examine the inner surfaces with a hand lens. Locate and identify the parts labelled opposite.

Plumule

4 In your Student Record, make a large labelled drawing of the inside of the maize fruit.

Radicle

Radicle sheath

Cotyledon

5 Flood the inner surfaces with iodine solution. The fruit's food store is starch. The iodine turns this blue-black. Leave for a few minutes.

IODINE SOLUTION

6 Draw the insides of the fruit again, this time colouring in the blue-black areas.

Think about it!
1 Why is the broad bean seed said to be a dicotyledon?
2 Which part of a broad bean seed stores its food?
3 Which foodstuff does it store?
4 Why is the broad bean's plumule tucked between the cotyledons?
5 Why is the broad bean radicle near the outside?
6 Why is the maize said to be a monocotyledon?
7 Which tissue stores the food in maize?
8 Which foodstuff does it store?
9 What is the pericarp?

11.6 Conditions for seed germination

1 Label 5 test tubes with your initials and A, B, C, D or E. Push a piece of cotton-wool to the bottom of test tubes A, B, D and E.

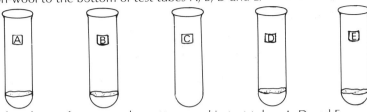

2 Put a few drops of water on the cotton-wool in test tubes A, D and E.

3 Put 6 cress seeds into all 5 test tubes.

4 Cover the seeds in test tube C with 1 cm of water which has been boiled to drive off oxygen (then allowed to cool). Cover the water with a thin layer of oil to keep out oxygen.

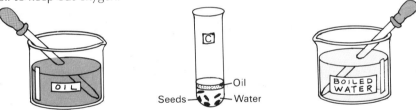

5 Stopper the test tubes and leave them for a few days like this:

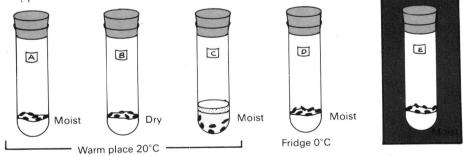

6 Check each test tube and note in your Student Record whether the seeds have germinated.

Think about it!
1 What did test tube B show?
2 What did test tube C show?
3 What did test tube D show?
4 What did test tube E show?
5 What conditions do seeds need before they will germinate?

F *

▷ 11.7 *Drosophila*: the monohybrid cross

Drosophila melanogaster is a tiny fruit fly about 2 mm long, often used in breeding experiments. The flies are kept in culture bottles or tubes like this one:

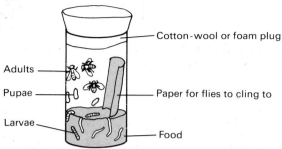

Cotton-wool or foam plug

Adults

Pupae

Paper for flies to cling to

Larvae

Food

The original strain of flies used in these experiments are known as wild type (symbol +) flies. They look like this:

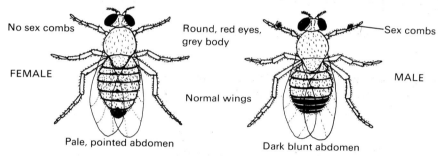

No sex combs

Round, red eyes, grey body

Sex combs

FEMALE

MALE

Normal wings

Pale, pointed abdomen

Dark blunt abdomen

A number of mutant strains are now available. These include:

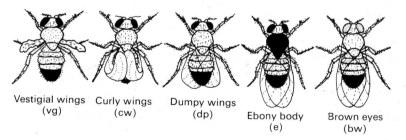

Vestigial wings (vg) Curly wings (cw) Dumpy wings (dp) Ebony body (e) Brown eyes (bw)

Method A: The F₁ generation

1 Collect a culture tube (tube A) containing 6 wild type male flies and a tube (tube B) containing 6 mutant virgin females,
   or
   tube C containing 6 wild type virgin females and tube D containing 6 mutant males.

2 Collect a fresh culture tube and an etheriser.

3 Take off the etheriser lid. Put 2 or 3 drops of ether on the cotton-wool and replace the lid.

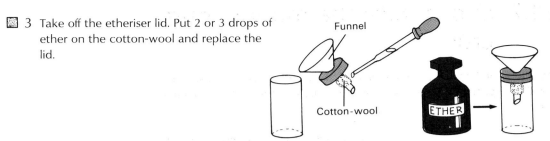

4 Tap the first culture tube to knock down the flies. Remove the plug and quickly invert it over the funnel. Tap again to knock the flies into the etheriser. Don't let them escape.

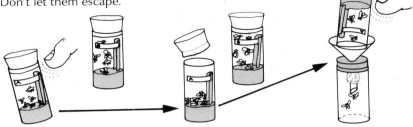

5 Repeat with the second culture tube. Leave the flies in the etheriser until they have all stopped moving.

6 Empty the flies on to a white tile. With a soft paintbrush, gently brush the flies one by one, into the fresh culture tube lying on its side.

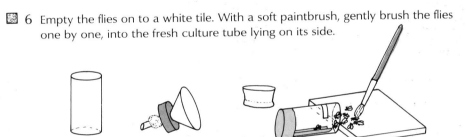

7 The flies should be unconscious for about 10 minutes. If they begin to revive, use an emergency etheriser like this:

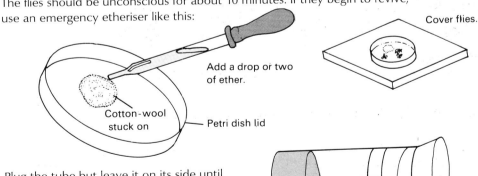

8 Plug the tube but leave it on its side until the flies revive, otherwise they might drown in the food.

9 Label the tube with your initials, the date and the cross, for example:

male wild type ♂ (+) × female dumpy wing ♀ (dp)

Incubate at 25°C for one week.

10 When the eggs have hatched, remove the adults by transferring to the etheriser as before. Put them in 70% alcohol to kill them. Put the tube back in the incubator.

11 A few days later the adults will start to emerge. Wait until they have all emerged (10–14 days after the start of the cross). Transfer them to the etheriser then on to a white tile.

12 Using a lens or binocular microscope, examine the flies. With a paintbrush sort out and count the phenotypes which are present (in this example, either wild type or dumpy wing). Note the number in your Student Record. Add the results from other groups.

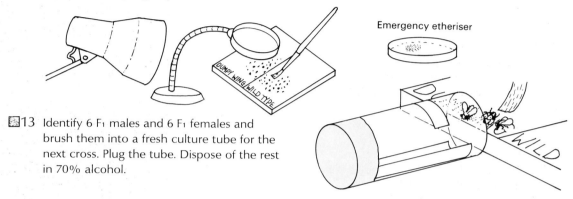

Emergency etheriser

13 Identify 6 F$_1$ males and 6 F$_1$ females and brush them into a fresh culture tube for the next cross. Plug the tube. Dispose of the rest in 70% alcohol.

Method B: The F$_2$ generation

1 Keep the fresh tube on its side until the flies have revived, then label it with your initials, the date and the cross, for example:

    F$_1$ females × F$_1$ males
(phenotype)   (phenotype)

2 Proceed as before with incubation, disposal of F$_1$ parents, then finally etherising and sorting of the F$_2$ flies.

3 In your Student Record, note the number of each phenotype in the F$_2$ generation. Add the results from other groups.

> **Think about it!**
> 1 Which was the dominant characteristic?
> 2 How do you know?
> 3 The parent females must be virgins. Why?
> 4 The F$_1$ females did not have to be virgins. Why?
> 5 In your cross what was the ratio of dominant to recessive flies in the F$_2$ generation?
> 6 What was the dominant to recessive ratio in the F$_2$ generation over all the crosses?
> 7 What was the predicted ratio? If it differs from the other two, explain why.
> 8 Did those groups who started with wild type males report different results from those who had wild type females?

S E C T I O N 12

Soil

12.1 Soil particles
(pupil's book page 218)
12.2 Water and humus in soils
(pupil's book pages 218, 219, 221)
12.3 The air content of soils
(pupil's book page 219)
12.4 The pH of soil
(pupil's book pages 53, 102–3)
12.5 Soil properties
(pupil's book page 219)
12.6 The effect of lime on soil
(pupil's book pages 218, 219)
12.7 Collecting soil animals
(pupil's book page 220)
12.8 Micro-organisms in the soil
(pupil's book pages 220, 229)

▷ 12.1 Soil particles

▨ Method A: Simple method ——————————

▨ 1 Collect a tall narrow container with a lid or stopper. A coffee jar, gas jar or large boiling tube will do.

▨ 2 Quarter-fill the container with soil, then fill it to the top with water. Close it tightly. Label it with your name and the source of the soil sample you used.

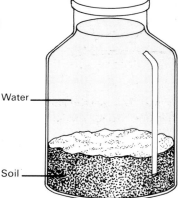

Water

Soil

▨ 3 Shake the container vigorously for a few minutes, then put it aside and leave it completely undisturbed for a few days.

▨ 4 The soil particles will settle to the bottom in order of size – largest first, smallest last. First to settle are gravel particles (diameter over 2 mm), followed by coarse sand (0.02 mm) and fine sand (0.2–0.2 mm), silt (0.002–0.02 mm) and clay (less than 0.002 mm). Very fine clay particles will stay in suspension, making the water cloudy. Organic material, such as humus will float on top.

▨ 5 Examine the container closely, noting the thickness of each layer. In your Student Record, draw how they appear. An example might look like the diagram on the right.

(Record)

Humus

Fine clay

(Result)

Clay
Silt
Fine sand
Coarse sand
Gravel

▨ 6 Compare and record the results for soils from other sources.

▨ Method B: Accurate method ——————————

▨ 1 Heat a sample of soil in a porcelain basin at 90°C for 24 hours. This will dry the soil. Allow it to cool.

Note: This step may have been done for you.

▨ 2 Weigh a sheet of paper and write down its weight on it. Subtract this weight from each other weight as you get it.

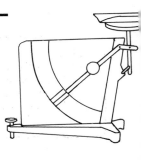

3 Weigh the sample of dried soil. Note the weight in your Student Record. (Remember to subtract the paper.)

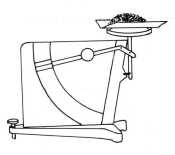

4 Collect a set of soil sieves. Remove the lid, pour in the soil sample and replace the lid.

5 Hold the sieves tightly together and shake them vigorously for 5 minutes.

6 Remove the top sieve (A). Take off the lid, pour the soil on to the paper and weigh it. Note the weight in your Student Record. Discard the soil and brush off the paper.

7 Repeat the weighing for each of the sieves in turn and enter the weights in the table in your Student Record.

8 Find out the type and size of soil particle which each sieve contained and work out the percentage of each in your soil sample, like this:

$$\text{percentage of particle type} = \frac{\text{weight of particle type}}{\text{weight of soil sample}} \times 100$$

Think about it!
1 Which of the soils were loams? Explain.
2 Which is the most common type of particle in each soil?
3 How would you define each soil – clay, sandy, clay loam, etc?
4 Which soil contains most humus?
5 Which soil might be most fertile? Why?

▷ 12.2 Water and humus in soils

▦ Method A: Water content of soils

1 Write your initials on a crucible with a marker. Weigh the crucible. Note the weight in your Student Record.

2 Fill the crucible almost to the top with fresh soil. Reweigh it and calculate the weight of fresh soil like this:
weight of fresh soil = (weight of soil and crucible) − (weight of crucible empty)

3 Heat the crucible in an oven at 105°C for 24 hours. This will evaporate the water without burning off anything else.

4 Using tongs, take the crucible from the oven and allow it to cool.

5 Reweigh the crucible. Note the weight (1) in your Student Record.

6 Put the crucible back in the oven for a further 24 hours, then reweigh it (2).

7 Keep heating and weighing until you get two weights the same. The soil is now dry.

8 Calculate the percentage water in the soil like this:
weight of water in soil = weight of fresh soil − weight of dried soil

$$\text{percentage water in soil} = \frac{\text{weight of water in soil}}{\text{weight of fresh soil}} \times 100$$

Keep the dried soil for the next experiment.

9 Obtain and record in your Student Record results for other types of soil.

▦ Method B: Humus content of soils

1 Take the crucible of dried soil from the previous experiment and roast it strongly over a bunsen burner for 15 minutes. Roasting the soil causes all the organic substances in it to burn and be driven off, mainly as carbon dioxide and water.

Pipe clay triangle — Crucible

Tripod stand

2 Remove the bunsen and allow the crucible to cool. Weigh it (1) and note the weight in your Student Record.

3 Roast for another 15 minutes, cool and reweigh. Note the weight (2).

4 Keep heating and weighing until you get two weights the same. All the humus has now been driven off.

5 Calculate the percentage humus in the soil like this:
weight of humus in soil = weight of dried soil − weight of soil after roasting

$$\text{percentage of humus in soil} = \frac{\text{weight of humus in soil}}{\text{weight of fresh soil}} \times 100$$

6 Obtain and record in your Student Record results for other types of soil.

Think about it!
1 Why it is necessary to reheat and reweigh in these experiments?
2 How would it affect the results if we didn't?
3 Which should hold most water — clay, loam or sand? Explain.
4 Did your results agree? If not, why not?
5 How would a lot of humus affect water content in a soil? Did it?
6 Which of the soils tested should be most fertile? Explain.

12.3 The air content of soils

Note: Steps 1 to 3 may have been done for you.

1 Collect a tin can with its lid removed and several holes punched in its base.

2 Work the tin, open and downwards, into soil until it is completely filled. Do not compress the soil. Avoid stony areas.

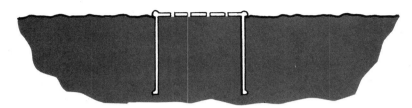

3 Dig out the can with a spade or trowel. Wipe excess soil from the sides of the can and scrape the soil flush with the top.

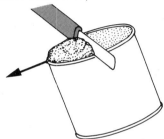

4 Collect another can of the same volume as the soil can. Sink it in a large beaker of water like this:

Mark the level of the water with a line.

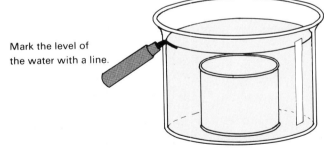

5 Remove the can, now filled with water. Empty it into a measuring cylinder and note the volume in your Student Record. Discard the water. This is the same as the volume of soil in the other can.

6 Place the can filled with soil into the beaker of water. The water should rise up to the line again.

7 Bubbles of air will start to escape from the soil. Stir it with a glass rod to help it. As air escapes, the water level falls.

8 When no more bubbles are coming off, fill a measuring cylinder with water to its top mark. Pour water into the beaker until it reaches the line again.

9 Work out how much water you used. This is equal to the volume of air in the soil. Note this in your Student Record.

10 Work out the percentage of air in the soil like this:

$$\text{percentage air in soil} = \frac{\text{volume of air in soil}}{\text{volume of soil}} \times 100$$

11 Obtain and record in your Student Record results for other types of soil.

Think about it!
1 Why must the can be filled with soil?
2 Why must the soil not be compressed?
3 Why avoid stones?
4 Why not just fill the can with a trowel?
5 Which types of soil should have:
   a most air in them?
   b least air in them?
   Explain.
6 Did your results agree with this? If not, can you suggest why?

12.4 The pH of soil

Note: The pH scale is used to measure how acid or alkaline a solution is. It ranges from pH1 (very acidic) to pH14 (very alkaline). pH7 is neutral (distilled water). Everything below pH7 is acid, while everything above pH7 is alkaline.

Method A: Simple method

1 Put about 1 cm of soil into a clean test tube.

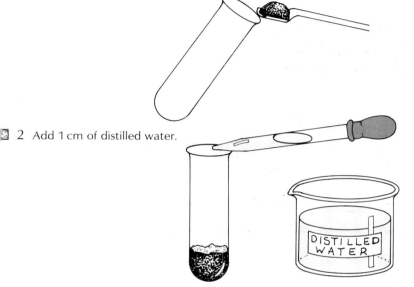

2 Add 1 cm of distilled water.

3 Put on a stopper and shake vigorously for a few minutes.

4 Allow to settle.

5 Dip a clean glass rod into the water and wet a piece of pH paper.

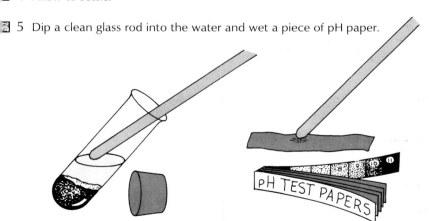

6 Compare with a pH colour card. Note the pH in your Student Record and the source and type of soil which produced it.

7 Obtain and record in your Student Record results for other soils.

Method B: Accurate method

1 Put between 1 and 2 cm of barium sulphate into a clean test tube. This will remove clay at the end to leave a clear suspension.

2 Add about 1 cm of soil.

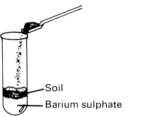

—Soil
—Barium sulphate

3 Add 10 ml of distilled water.

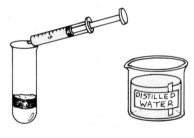

4 Add 2 ml of BDH soil indicator.

5 Put on a stopper and shake vigorously for a few minutes.

6 Allow to settle.

7 Compare the colour of the clear liquid with the pH colour chart. Select and note the pH it most matches.

8 Obtain and record in your Student Record results for other soils.

Think about it!

1 Why use distilled water instead of tap water in this experiment?
2 Various chemicals, including lime, can clear a clay suspension as well as barium sulphate, but are never used. Why might this be?
3 Why must all apparatus in this experiment be very clean?
4 Were the soils tested acid, neutral or alkaline?

▷ 12.5 Soil properties

▦ Method A: Water retention ───────────

▣ 1 You are supplied with 3 funnels containing equal volumes of *dry* clay soil, garden loam and sandy soil.

Line

Clay soil

Glass wool plug

Garden loam

Sandy soil

▣ 2 Put a 100 ml measuring cylinder under each funnel and pour 50 ml of water into each soil.

▣ 3 When each funnel has stopped dripping, measure how much water has collected in each cylinder. From this, calculate how much water has been retained by each soil. Record these results in your Student Record.

▣ 4 Keep the funnels for the next experiment.

▦ Method B: Drainage (permeability) ───────────

▣ 1 Use the 3 funnels of soaked soils from the previous experiment.

▣ 2 Put an empty measuring cylinder under the first funnel. Pour water into the funnel up to the line. Note the time in your Student Record.

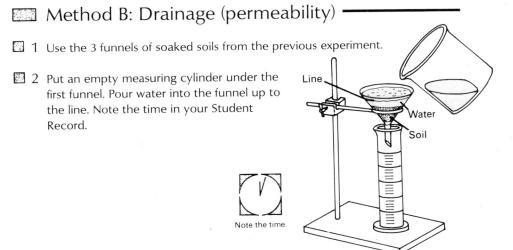

Line

Water

Soil

Note the time.

137

G

3 Keep the funnel topped up to the line for 1 minute, then measure how much water has collected in the measuring cylinder. Note this in your Student Record.

4 Repeat for the other two soils.

Method C: Capillarity

1 Stand a number of glass tubes of different bores (internal diameters) with one end in water.

2 Draw what happens in your Student Record.

3 Fill 3 long glass tubes with *dry* clay soil, garden loam and sandy soil and place the ends in water as shown.

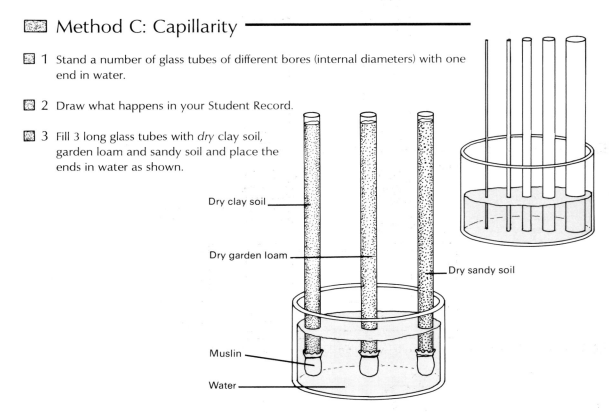

Dry clay soil

Dry garden loam

Dry sandy soil

Muslin

Water

4 Measure how far up each tube the water has risen after about an hour, then a few days later and, finally, about a week later. Note these measurements in your Student Record.

Think about it!
1 Which soil has:
   a the smallest spaces between particles?
   b the largest spaces between particles?
2 Which soil has:
   a the highest capillarity?
   b the lowest capillarity?
3 Which soil has:
   a the highest water retention?
   b the lowest water retention?
4 Which soil has:
   a the slowest drainage?
   b the fastest drainage?
5 How do the spaces between soil particles affect capillarity?
6 How does capillarity affect water retention and drainage?
7 Which soil has the best crumb structure?

▷ 12.6 The effect of lime on soil

☒ 1 Weigh out 1 g of powdered clay on a piece of paper. Put it in a large boiling tube. Repeat for a second tube.

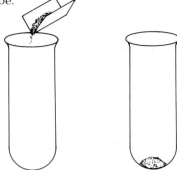

☒ 2 Three-quarters fill each tube with water. Put on stoppers and shake the tubes vigorously. Allow to stand.

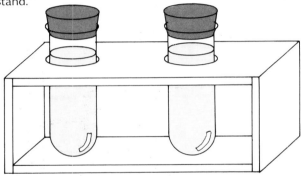

☒ 3 Put a small spatula-full of calcium hydroxide (lime) into *one* tube only.

☒ 4 Shake both tubes again. Allow to stand. Watch closely what happens to the clay particles.

☒ 5 In your Student Record, describe what you saw happening and draw the final appearance of the two tubes.

☒ 6 Dip a piece of pH paper into each liquid, compare it with a pH colour card and note the pH in your Student Record.

Think about it!
1 Why do clay particles not settle out by themselves?
2 What must lime do to cause them to sink?
3 Do you see signs of this happening?
4 How might this improve soil?
5 How might lime improve an acid soil?

12.7 Collecting soil animals

Various habitats can be investigated, for example garden, field, woodland, hedgerow, to compare the types and numbers of soil animals living there. Animals which live on or in the soil can be collected in a number of ways. These methods are described on the following pages.

Method A: From litter, etc

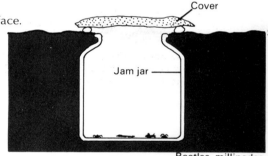

1 Look under stones, logs, twigs and leaves on the surface. Spread wet sacking on the ground overnight and look under it next morning.

2 Collect any animals you find. Catch them with a **pooter** if necessary.

3 Put each specimen in a specimen tube with a few damp leaves. Label the tube, saying where each specimen was found.

4 Use keys to identify them.

5 In your Student Record, note the numbers and types of organisms found.

Suck

Mus

Poo

Method B: Pitfall traps

Pitfall traps are used to catch small animals which move about on the soil surface.

1 Bury a jam jar so that its rim is level with the soil surface.

2 Cover the jar with a lid or flat stone to keep out the rain. Lift the cover clear of the ground with small stones or sticks.

3 Visit the trap each day and collect specimens.

4 Use keys to identify them.

5 In your Student Record, note the numbers and types of organisms found.

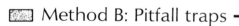

Cover

Jam jar

S

Beetles, millipedes, centipedes, etc, fall in.

Method C: Earthworms

✗ An idea of the earthworm population of a habitat can be obtained by bringing to the surface and counting all the worms in a single square metre.

Method

1 Collect a metre stick with a three-metre length of string attached to it.

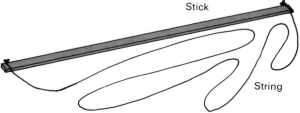

Stick

String

Randomly

2. Put the stick down on the area to be studied and straighten out the string to form a square metre. Peg it down if necessary.

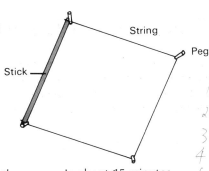

String
Peg
Stick

3. Pour 10 litres of 2% formalin (methanal) into the square. In about 15 minutes this should have brought all the worms to the surface.

   Note: Dilute potassium permanganate solution or dilute washing up liquid may be used instead of formalin.

4. As each worm emerges, pick it up gently with tweezers, dip it in water and put it in a beaker.

5. Count the worms which came up *inside* the square only and note the number in your Student Record. Release them in another place.

6. If a number of squares in the same habitat are sampled, a more accurate average number of worms per square metre can be calculated.

Method D: Tullgren funnel

A **Tullgren funnel** is used to collect very small animals which live in the air spaces in the soil. One design is shown here.

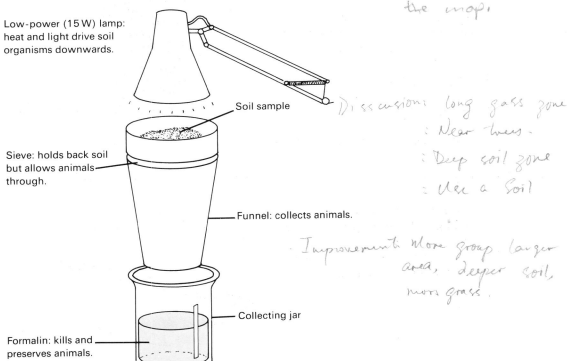

Low-power (15 W) lamp: heat and light drive soil organisms downwards.

Soil sample

Sieve: holds back soil but allows animals through.

Funnel: collects animals.

Collecting jar

Formalin: kills and preserves animals.

(handwritten table)

1	32	20	31
2	47	8	35
3	81	11	107
4	33	20	37
5	17	6	26
6	14	1	34
7	20	20	27
Average:	33.4	10.8	41.57
Average per square:	0.0334	0.0718	0.05981

b). the mass of the earthworms was also determined.

6. A map of the school grounds was drawn and the average no. of worms per squaremetre was inserted on the map.

Discussion: long grass zone
: Near trees.
: Deep soil zone
: Use a Soil

Improvement: More group larger area, deeper soil, more grass.

1 Break up the larger lumps in your soil sample and place it on the sieve mesh. Leave a space all round the sides.

2 Switch on the lamp and leave it on for several hours.

3 Using a hand lens or a microscope, examine the animals which have fallen into the collecting jar. Use keys to identify them.

4 In your Student Record, note the numbers and types of organisms found.

Method E: Baermann funnel

A **Baermann funnel** is used to collect very small animals which live in the soil water. In a way, they are aquatic animals. One design of Baermann funnel is shown here.

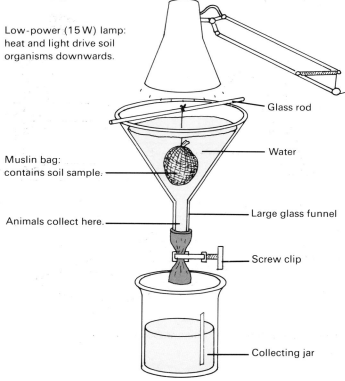

Low-power (15 W) lamp: heat and light drive soil organisms downwards.

Glass rod

Water

Muslin bag: contains soil sample.

Animals collect here.

Large glass funnel

Screw clip

Collecting jar

1 Tie the soil sample in a muslin bag and hang it inside the funnel as shown.

2 Switch on the lamp and leave it on for several hours.

3 Open the screw clip and run the water from the stem of the funnel into the collecting jar.

4 Examine the animals in the water with a hand lens or microscope. Use keys to identify them.

5 In your Student Record, note the numbers and types of organisms found.

▷ 12.8 Micro-organisms in the soil

Note: Sterile means free of germs (micro-organisms). The apparatus in this experiment is sterilised by heating to high temperature in an **autoclave** (pressure cooker).

1 Add a little fresh soil to a sterile test tube, half-filled with sterile water.

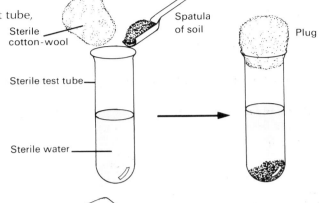

2 Shake the tube to mix the soil and water, then leave to settle.

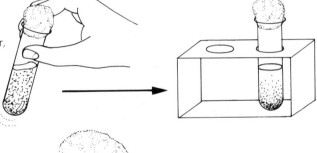

3 Pour half the water (not soil) into another sterile test tube. Remove the second test tube plug just enough to allow you to pour in the water. Replace it quickly.

4 Pour the rest of the water (not soil) into a third sterile test tube and boil it for a few minutes. Plug and leave to cool.

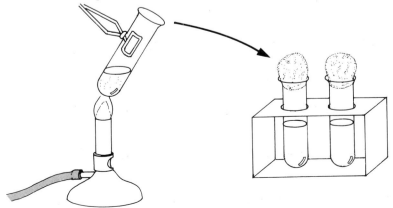

5 Collect 2 sterile Petri dishes containing nutrient agar. On the *bottom* of each write your name and the date. Mark one dish 'soil water' and the other 'boiled soil water'.

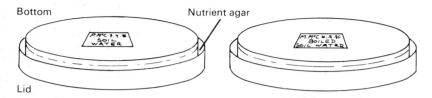

Bottom   Nutrient agar

Lid

Note: Agar is a clear jelly which is ideal for growing micro-organisms on. Before it sets, nutrients are added for them to feed on.

6 Lift the lid of the 'soil water' Petri dish a little – just enough for you to pour in a *small amount* of the soil water.

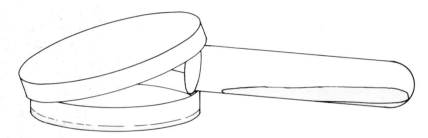

7 Replace the lid and swirl the liquid over the agar surface.

8 Similarly, put some boiled soil water into the other Petri dish.

9 Put the dishes upside down in an incubator at 23–30°C for 2 days.

SAFETY

10 Collect your Petri dishes. Do *not* open them! Do *not* touch the agar! Examine the agar for colonies (growths) of micro-organisms. Shiny growths are bacteria, fluffy growths are fungi.

11 Count the number of colonies of bacteria and fungi in each dish and note this in your Student Record. Draw the appearance of each Petri dish.

12 Place the Petri dishes in disinfectant. This will kill the micro-organisms, some of which may be **pathogenic** (disease-causing).

Think about it!
1 *Why must we raise the Petri dish lids just a little and for only a short time?*
2 *What effect does boiling have on soil micro-organisms?*
3 *Where could any colonies in the 'boiled' dish have come from?*
4 *Have the soil particles anything to do with the growth of colonies?*
5 *Without the nutrients in the agar, the micro-organisms can't grow. On what do they usually feed?*
6 *Why must you not touch the agar?*

SECTION 13

Micro-organisms

13.1 Food spoilage
(pupil's book page 228)
13.2 Culturing micro-organisms
(pupil's book page 228)
13.3 Bacteria and antibiotics
(pupil's book pages 20, 21, 229, 231)

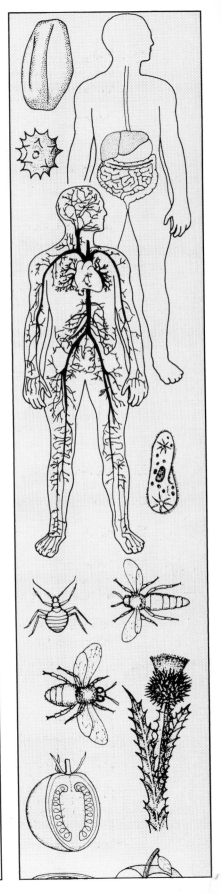

▷ 13.1 Food spoilage

1 Collect 5 small Petri dishes and 5 fresh foods. The foods should include bread, cheese, meat and fruit.

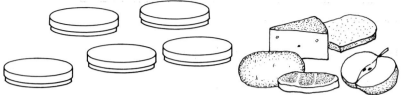

2 Cut a piece of each food small enough to fit into a Petri dish. It should not be more than half as thick as the Petri dish itself. Put the foods in the dishes.

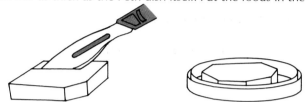

3 Leave the foods in the dishes with the lids off for 30–60 minutes.

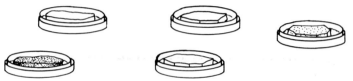

4 Add a drop or two of water to the surface of each food to moisten it.

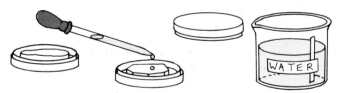

5 Put on the lids. Put your initials and the date on each lid and seal with clear tape.

6 Incubate in a warm place for a week.

7 Examine the dishes. In your Student Record, draw (and colour) how they appear.

8 Put them aside for another week. In your Student Record, describe how they look now.

9 Return the unopened dishes for hygienic disposal.

Think about it!
1 Are the foods being attacked by other organisms?
2 How many different organisms can you see?
3 Are they fungi or bacteria?
4 Are they consuming the food?
5 Where have they come from?

13.2 Culturing micro-organisms

> Micro-organisms can be dangerous.
> Always follow these safety rules when handling or culturing micro-organisms.

☐ 1 Wash your hands before and after each experiment.

☐ 2 Wipe the bench with disinfectant before and after each experiment.

☐ 3 Treat all micro-organisms as pathogens (disease-causing).

☐ 4 Never leave bottles or plates containing micro-organisms open.

☐ 5 Never leave Petri dish lids or culture bottle tops on the bench.

☐ 6 If a culture is spilled, flood it with disinfectant, then wash your hands.

☐ 7 Keep the bench clear during experiments.

☐ 8 Never remove a Petri dish lid when examining a culture.

☐ 9 Sterilise all cultures before disposal.

Method A: Bacteria ───────────────

☐ 1 Collect a bunsen burner, a clean white tile, an inoculating loop, a culture of
bacteria, a sterile Petri dish containing nutrient agar.

Note A: Sterile means free from germs (micro-organisms).

Note B: Agar is a type of clear jelly upon which micro-organisms are grown.
Before it sets, nutrients are mixed in to feed the micro-organisms.

☐ 2 Set out the apparatus before you as shown,
with the bunsen lit (opposite way round for
left-handers).

Culture of bacteria

BACTERIA CAREFUL

Tweezers

Petri dish

White tile

Inoculating loop

☐ 3 Take the inoculating loop in your right hand.
Hold it in the flame until it glows red, then
remove it. It is now sterilised. Keep it in your
hand.

☐ 4 Hold the bacteria culture bottle in your left
hand. Unscrew the cap with the little finger
of your right hand.

5 Pass the mouth of the bottle once through the flame to sterilise it.

6 Put the loop into the culture broth. Let it cool, then withdraw it.

7 Flame the bottle top again. Screw on the cap and put it aside.

8 Raise the lid of the Petri dish with your left hand, just enough to get the loop inside.

9 Rest the loop on the agar and very gently, draw it across the agar surface in a zig-zag pattern.

10 Lower the lid and flame the loop.

11 Seal the Petri dish with clear tape. Turn it upside down and write your name, the date and the bacteria used on the bottom.

12 Put the Petri dish, upside down, in an incubator at 37°C for 2 days.

Method B: Fungi

1 The fungus is supplied growing on an agar slope in a culture bottle.

2 An inoculating needle is used instead of a loop.

3 All operations are carried out as for bacteria except:
   (i) the surface of the agar slope is touched gently with the tip of the needle;
   (ii) the agar in the centre of the Petri dish is then touched with the tip of the needle.

4 After incubation, examine both dishes. Do not open or tilt them. In your Student Record, draw their appearance and write a short description.

5 Return your unopened dishes for safe hygienic disposal. Wash your hands.

Think about it!
1 Why should loop or needle be flamed before being put in a culture?
2 Why should they be flamed after inoculating the plates?
3 Why should the neck of the culture bottle be flamed?
4 Why are the Petri dishes sealed?
5 Why are Petri dishes stored upside down?
6 How do bacteria and fungi growing on agar differ in appearance?

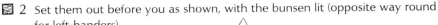

▷ 13.3 Bacteria and antibiotics

▣ 1 Collect a bunsen burner, a clean white tile, an inculating loop, a culture of bacteria, a sterile Petri dish containing nutrient agar, a pair of tweezers.

▣ 2 Set them out before you as shown, with the bunsen lit (opposite way round for left-handers).

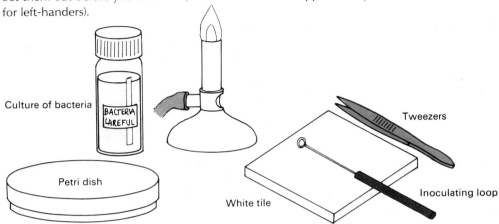

Culture of bacteria

BACTERIA CAREFUL

Petri dish

White tile

Tweezers

Inoculating loop

▣ 3 Take the inoculating loop in your right hand. Hold it in the flame until it glows red, then remove it. It is now sterilised. Keep it in your hand.

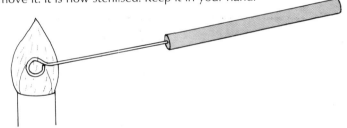

▣ 4 Hold the bacteria culture bottle in your left hand. Unscrew the cap with the little finger of your right hand.

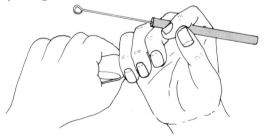

▣ 5 Pass the mouth of the bottle once through the flame to sterilise it.

▣ 6 Put the loop into the culture broth. Let it cool, then withdraw it.

▣ 7 Flame the bottle top again, screw on the cap and put it aside.

8 Raise the lid of the Petri dish with your left hand, just enough to get the loop inside.

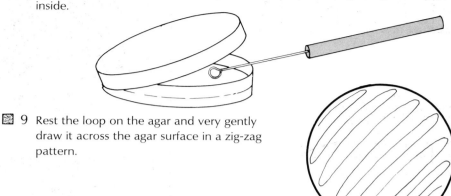

9 Rest the loop on the agar and very gently draw it across the agar surface in a zig-zag pattern.

10 Lower the lid and flame the loop.

11 On the white tile collect two antibiotic sensitivity discs – one penicillin and one streptomycin.

12 Flame the tweezers, then use them to place the discs on to the agar like this:

Penicillin sensitivity disc

Streptomycin sensitivity disc

Flame the tweezers after each disc.

13 Seal the Petri dish with clear tape. Turn it upside down and write your name, the date and the bacteria used on the bottom.

14 Put the Petri dish, upside down, in an incubator at 37°C for 2 days. Wash your hands.

15 Examine the dish. Do not open it or tilt it. In your Student Record, draw the appearance of the agar.

16 It may have been possible for you to do this experiment with other types of bacteria. If so, write your results as a table. If not, obtain the results of other groups who have used different cultures. Enter these in your Student Record.

Think about it!
1 Why should the loop be flamed before putting it into the bacteria culture?
2 Why should it be flamed after it has been used on the agar plate?
3 Why should the neck of the culture bottle be flamed?
4 Why should the lid of the Petri dish be lifted just a little?
5 Do antibiotics prevent the growth of bacteria? Explain.
6 Do antibiotics prevent the growth of all bacteria? Explain.
7 Might some antibiotics be more useful than others? Explain.

SECTION 14

Ecology and pollution

14.1 Investigating an ecosystem: collecting
(pupil's book pages 102–3)

14.2 Investigating an ecosystem: plant distribution
(pupil's book pages 102–3)

14.3 Monitoring water pollution
(pupil's book pages 234–5)

14.4 Air pollution: smoke on leaves
(pupil's book page 234)

14.5 Sulphur dioxide and plants
(pupil's book page 234)

▷ 14.1 Investigating an ecosystem: collecting

▦ Animals

The purpose of catching animals in an ecosystem is to identify them, count them and note where they were found. When this is done, they should be returned, as near as possible, to the exact spot where they were caught.

If it is absolutely necessary to remove an animal for further study, only one suitable specimen should be taken, placed in a numbered specimen tube and the number and location carefully recorded in your field notebook.

The equipment used to catch animals depends on the type of animal and its habitat. Some examples are described here.

1 **Air nets** are used to catch insects and other small land-living animals. They include:

a **insect nets** – lightweight nets used to catch flying insects.

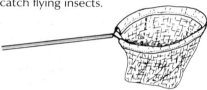

b **sweep nets** – used to brush through grass and other vegetation to catch insects and spiders.

c **beating trays** – placed underneath branches and bushes which are then shaken (not beaten); the small animals which fall out are caught in the tray.

2 **Water nets** are used to catch animals living in water. They include:

a **dip nets** for sweeping through water to catch invertebrates, fish, etc.

b **plankton nets** which are towed through water to catch plankton which collects in a specimen bottle at the bottom of the net.

Specimen bottle

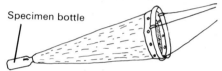

c **dredge nets** which sink to the bottom and are pulled along to collect animals living near the bottom.

3 **Pooters** are used to suck up and catch small arthropods from soil, under rocks, etc, or from other traps.

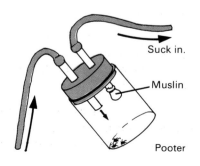

Suck in.

Muslin

Pooter

4 **Pitfall traps** are used to catch small animals which move about on the soil surface. A jam jar is buried with its rim level with the soil surface. A raised cover is put over it to keep out the rain. The trap can be baited with a small piece of raw meat to attract carnivorous animals. Pitfall traps should be inspected each day.

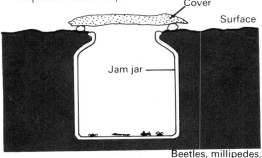

Beetles, millipedes, centipedes, etc, fall in.

5 **Light traps** are used to catch night-flying insects such as moths, which are attacted to the light inside them. These traps should be inspected every day.

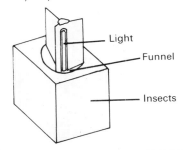

6 **Scoops and sieves** are used to collect organisms from soft mud and sand. The scoop is filled with sand which is washed through the mesh bottom, leaving the organisms behind.

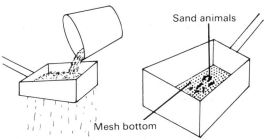

7 **Longworth mammal traps** will catch small mammals such as voles and field mice. Bedding and food are put in the nest box. To reach this the animal goes through the tunnel. As it does so, it treads on a wire which realeases the trapdoor. These traps should be inspected each day and the animals released. The animals must be handled with great care, using gloves. They are liable to bite and cause infection.

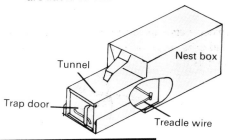

Plants

Plants can usually be identified where they are growing and should be disturbed as litle as possible. If it is essential to take a plant for identification, use a pen-knife to cut a suitable stem, leaves, flowers or fruit. *Never* uproot a plant. Only one specimen should be taken per class. *Never* take any part of a rare or protected plant.

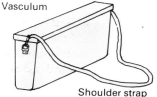

When a specimen is cut, a numbered label should be tied to it and the number and location recorded in your field notebook. The specimen can then be taken away in a polythene bag or a vasculum. If the plant is to be preserved, it is put between two sheets of absorbent paper in a plant press.

The plant is laid out flat and carefully arranged to display it at its best. It is numbered and its number, height, location, colour, scent, etc, are recorded. The straps are then buckled on as tightly as possible.

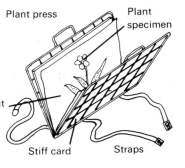

The press is kept in a warm place and the paper changed every few days. After a week or so the plant should be completely dry and flat. It can now be identified and properly mounted on white card.

14.2 Investigating an ecosystem: plant distribution

It would be impossible to map the position of every plant in a habitat. Instead, small sample areas are chosen and surveyed as shown below. Before starting, a map of the habitat, as large-scale and detailed as possible, is needed. This could be traced from an Ordnance Survey map and enlarged. A compass will give the direction of the areas sampled. These areas are chosen completely at random. Rough notes are taken in a field notebook and a fair copy made up later.

Method A: Quadrats

A **quadrat** is a frame, usually $\frac{1}{2}$ metre square, used for sampling small areas of short vegetation.

1 Place the quadrat frame on the ground. Note its direction with a compass.

$\frac{1}{2}$ metre $\frac{1}{2}$ metre

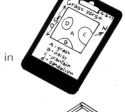

2 Use keys to identify all plants inside the quadrat.

3 Draw a square in your field notebook and note the position of each species in the frame. Use a letter to identify each species. Some quadrats can be subdivided with string into smaller squares to make mapping easier.

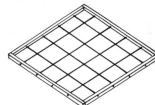

4 Back in the laboratory make a fair copy of the results. It may be possible to make a coloured diagram to show the distribution of each species.

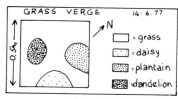

Method B: Line transects

1 Drive 2 stakes into the ground, 10 metres apart. Stretch a measuring tape on the ground between them. Note its direction with a compass.

Stake

10 m

Measuring tape

2 Use keys to identify those plants touching the tape at 25 cm intervals. Note their position and also their height.

3 Transfer the results to a piece of graph paper. Use symbols to represent the species you found.

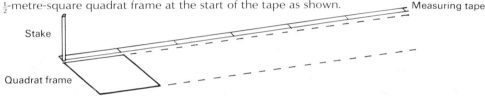

Method C: Belt transects

A **belt transect** will show up plants which might be missed with a line transect.

1 Drive 2 stakes into the ground, 10 metres apart. Stretch a measuring tape on the ground between them. Note its direction with a compass. Place a $\frac{1}{2}$-metre-square quadrat frame at the start of the tape as shown.

Measuring tape

Stake

Quadrat frame

2 Use keys to identify all plants inside the quadrat.

3 Draw a square in your field notebook and note the position of each species in the frame. Use a letter to identify each species. Note carefully the position of the quadrat along the tape, eg 0 to $\frac{1}{2}$ m.

4 Move the quadrat to the next location, note it, eg $\frac{1}{2}$ m to 1 m, and repeat.

Tape

Stake

Position of first sample (0 to $\frac{1}{2}$ m)

Position of second sample ($\frac{1}{2}$ to 1 m)

5 Repeat this for each quadrat along the tape. To save time, though, other groups may do some of the quadrats. Each group must note carefully the position of each quadrat it does.

6 Combine the results, to show the distribution of each plant species in the transect. It may be possible to do this in the form of a coloured diagram as shown.

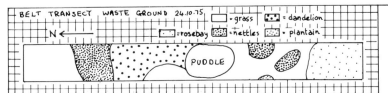

Method D: Profiles

A **profile** shows the shape of a piece of ground. It can be combined with a transect as here, to show how this affects the distribution of plants.

1 Drive 2 stakes into the ground, 10 metres apart.

2 Fix a measuring tape between the stakes so that it clears the vegetation. Note its direction with a compass.

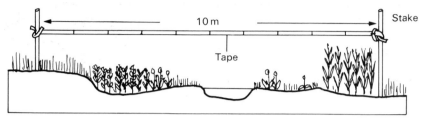

3 Use a spirit level to make sure the tape is perfectly horizontal.

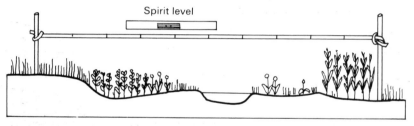

4 Every 25 cm, measure how high the tape is above the ground. Note this in your field notebook.

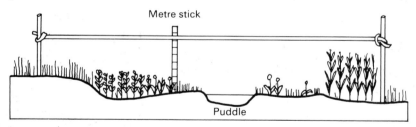

5 At each position, identify the plant growing there and measure its height. Note these in your field notebook.

6 Transfer the results to a piece of graph paper. Use symbols to represent the species you found.

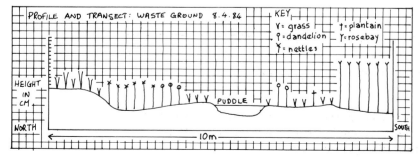

▷ 14.3 Monitoring water pollution

▱ Method A: Indicator animals ──────────

Note: Some organisms can tolerate only very low levels of pollution, while others can survive in very polluted areas. The presence of different species indicates the level of pollution. These are known as **indicator organisms**.

▱ 1 Select a stretch of water which you think may be polluted by organic waste. It could be a river, stream or pond.

▱ 2 Half-fill a white pie dish with cleanish water from the surface.

▱ 3 Sweep a fine plankton net through the mud at the bottom. Sweep against the flow.

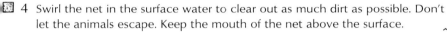

▱ 4 Swirl the net in the surface water to clear out as much dirt as possible. Don't let the animals escape. Keep the mouth of the net above the surface.

▱ 5 Dump the organisms into your dish by turning the net inside out under the water.

▱ 6 Use a hand lens to help identify any indicator animals present. The animals illustrated indicate various levels of pollution. Take several sweeps at the same spot to make sure which animals are there.

CLEAN WATER	SLIGHT POLLUTION	HIGH POLLUTION

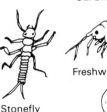
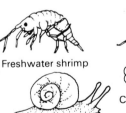

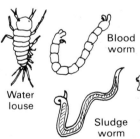
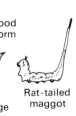

Mayfly nymph

Fish

Stonefly nymph

Freshwater shrimp

Water snail

Caddis fly larva

Water louse

Blood worm

Sludge worm

Rat-tailed maggot

▱ 7 In your Student Record, record the indicator organisms you identified and the numbers present. Write a short description of the area studied. Return all the animals.

▱ Method B: Bacteria in water ──────────

Important: Follow all the safety rules on page 147.

TY

▱ 1 Collect a bunsen burner, a clean white tile, an inoculating loop, a sterile bottle containing tap water, a sterile bottle containing polluted water, 2 sterile Petri dishes containing nutrient agar.

2 For each Petri dish, carefully follow Steps 2 to 10 on pages 147–8 , streaking one agar plate with tap water and the other with polluted water.

3 Seal both Petri dishes with clear tape. Turn them upside down. Write your name, the date and 'tap water' or 'polluted water' on them.

4 Put the Petri dishes, upside down, in an incubator at 37°C for 2 days.

5 After incubation, examine both dishes. Do not open or tilt them. In your Student Record, draw and colour the appearance of each dish. If any of the colonies are pink, they may be *E Coli*, a bacterium often in sewage.

6 Return your unopened dishes for safe, hygienic disposal. Wash your hands.

Method C: Oxygen in water

1 Collect 2 gas burettes. Label one A and the other B.

Suba Seal stopper

Tap

2 Fill burette A with tap water. Put on the stopper. The burette and tap must be completely filled, with no trapped air.

3 Submerge the tap end of the burette in a trough of water and open the tap.

SAFETY

4 Slowly and carefully inject 1 ml of potassium hydroxide solution from a syringe into the burette. (Take care – potassium hydroxide burns; syringe needles are dangerous.)

POTASS HYDRO SOLU

Water

SAFETY

5 Using a fresh syringe, inject 1 ml of pyrogallol solution into the burette. (Take care – pyrogallol burns.)

Oil to keep out air

PYROGALLOL SOLUTION

6 Close the tap, turn the burette upside down a few times to mix the contents.

The chemicals are turned black by oxygen. The more dissolved oxygen the water sample contains, the darker the colour.

A

7 Fill burette B with a sample of polluted water and repeat the procedure.

8 Compare the burettes. Colour the boxes in your Student Record to match the colour of the liquid in the burettes.

Think about it!
1 Why does organic waste encourage the growth of bacteria?
2 Why should water rich in bacteria be low in oxygen?
3 Why can fish not survive in water rich in bacteria, even if the bacteria do not cause them illness?
4 Blood worms have haemoglobin. Why should this allow them to live in polluted water?

> 14.4 Air pollution: smoke on leaves

Note: The leaves (needles) of the Scots pine last for 3 years. At the end of each branch there is a terminal bud. Each year's growth starts from this. When it starts growing in the spring, its protective scales fall off, leaving marks called a girdle scar. From the position of these, we can tell whether the leaves are 1, 2 or 3 years old as in this example.

1 From different locations obtain pine branches with leaves up to 3 years old. Note the locations in your Student Record with a description of each, especially any nearby sources of smoke.

2 Detach a 1-, 2- and 3-year-old needle from the first branch.

3 Take a needle (make sure you know how old it is), put it between 2 pieces of white paper and clamp it in the jaws of a wooden clothes peg, like this:

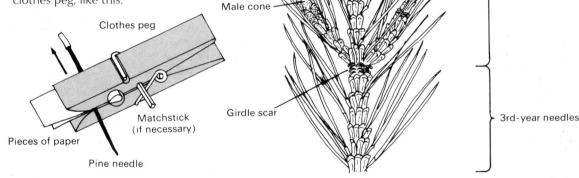

Clothes peg

Matchstick (if necessary)

Pieces of paper

Pine needle

Female cone

Girdle scar

1st-year needles

Male cone

Girdle scar

2nd-year needles

3rd-year needles

4 Pull the needle slowly and gently through the clothes peg. If the needle breaks, put in a matchstick as shown to loosen the spring.

5 The paper will wipe off any soot coating the needle. Cut out the marks, fix them to a strip of clear sticky tape and stick them in the correct year's position in your Student Record.

6 Repeat for the other two needles from that branch, then go on to branches from different locations.

Think about it!
1 How did leaves of different age compare? Why?
2 How did leaves from different places compare? Why?
3 Explain two ways in which soot could affect a leaf's ability to carry out photosynthesis.
4 Often leaves of the same age on a tree will have different amounts of soot on them. Can you think of any reasons for this?

▷ 14.5 Sulphur dioxide and plants

1 Label 2 Petri dish bases with your initials and A or B.

2 Cut blotting paper to fit the dishes and moisten it with water. Place cress seeds, about 1 cm apart, on the moist paper.

3 Leave for a few days until the first leaves open. Moisten again if necessary.

4 Put dish A in a polythene bag. Using tongs, soak a wad of cotton-wool in sodium metabisulphite solution. Put it on a watch glass, using tongs.

Cress seedlings

SODIUM META-BISULPHATE

Watch glass

Note: Sodium metabisulphite is a chemical which gives off sulphur dioxide gas.

5 Put the watch glass with the cotton-wool into the bag beside the cress seedlings. Seal the bag with an elastic band.

6 Prepare dish B in the same way but soak the cotton-wool in water instead of sodium metabisulphite.

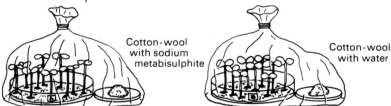

Cotton-wool with sodium metabisulphite

Cotton-wool with water

7 In your Student Record, note how the seeds appear at the start. Record their appearance again after 20 minutes, then 40 minutes, then after a day or so.

Think about it!
1 *Were seedlings B damaged? If not, why bother to set them up?*
2 *Is sulphur dioxide harmful to plants?*
3 *How does sulphur dioxide get into the atmosphere?*
4 *What does sulphur dioxide look like?*

MASTERING

MANAGEMENT

IN THE

CHURCH

ED ROEBERT

Sovereign World

Sovereign World
PO Box 777
Tonbridge
Kent TN11 0ZS
England

First published in 1986 by
Hatfield Christian Church
PO Box 33626, Glenstantia 0010
Pretoria
South Africa

All Bible quotations are taken from the New King James Bible unless otherwise stated, copyright © 1983, Thomas Nelson Inc., Nashville, USA

ISBN   1 85240 181 8

Printed in England by Clays Ltd, St Ives plc

CONTENTS

Foreword   v

OUTLINE OF THE COURSE

Section 1   Survey   11

Section 2   Planning   25

Section 3   Organizing   74

Section 4   Leading   114

Section 5   Managing or Monitoring   140

FOREWORD

Today, the cell movement has blanketed the earth. Those who say it can only exist in one culture are deceived. The cells which comprise Christ's body on earth today are not impacted by the kingdoms of this world, but by life in the Kingdom of God. Those who are veterans in cell church development have an obligation to share with pastors who are transitioning the principles they learned through the years. One of these men is Ed Roebert. He writes from the experience of growing a tiny community of Christians to one now numbering hundreds of cell groups and thousands of cell members.

Roebert's name has long been associated with the creative reconstruction of church life. Long before his fellow South African pastors saw the biblical basis for the cell church movement, the Hatfield Christian Church had formed dozens of 'Basic Christian Communities'. They were years ahead of the rest.

His careful blending of cells and congregations with a powerful celebration has drawn thousands into the Kingdom of God. The activity of the Holy Spirit is carried from public worship to the hundreds of living rooms where his cells meet weekly. Healings of bodies, minds, and emotions mark the ministry of the cell members whenever they meet. Learn the principles that made it happen in these pages.

Hatfield's growth began because the leader received anointing in the area of management and administration as a gift from God and used it to glorify Christ. This book is one of the few that describes the pastoral administration of a cell church and the way it must be built around biblical leadership principles.

Anyone serious about Spirit-guided management of a cell church will find this a handbook to be referenced over and over. For this reason, it is required reading for church workers enrolling in the *Year of Transition* training now being used to prepare hundreds of churches to leave behind traditional, building-bound activities and form clusters of cells.

I am delighted that this book has come into your hands, and trust it will mean as much to you as it has meant to others who were trained directly by Ed Roebert in seminars.

Dr Ralph W. Neighbour, Jr
President, Touch Outreach Ministries International

INTRODUCTION

THE MAJOR DIFFERENCE BETWEEN SMALL AND LARGE CHURCHES

Most churches have a membership of under one hundred. This is true worldwide! Unfortunately, many pastors have simply accepted this to be an irreversible situation. However, in the heart of most pastors there is a desire to grow their local congregations and to increasingly impact the community.

Then too, there seem to be barriers or ceilings that churches encounter, and unless these are broken the churches will remain enslaved to their current "small" mentality. Some churches reach a ceiling of one hundred and then level off in their growth. Others level off at three hundred, five hundred, one thousand, two thousand et cetera. Whatever the ceiling is, it seems to take a major move or a complete change of philosophy before that ceiling is penetrated.

There are many reasons why churches find it difficult to break through such barriers! One such reason is **"Parish Mentality."** Dr Ralph Neighbour in his excellent book, WHERE DO WE GO FROM HERE? says, "Another problem with Program Base Design churches is their "parish mentality." A Baptist, Methodist, or other brand of church planter will enter a portion of a city and mark off a "church field." He recognises the existence of "sister churches" (same brand) in neighbouring districts, and considers their "church fields" out of bounds. Each "local church" sifts through its limited territory seeking for "like-us people" until most are finally drawn into the membership. Stagnation finally sets in".

Parish mentality is only one of the reasons for placing a ceiling over a local church. Elmer Towns in his fascinating book, The Complete Book of CHURCH GROWTH, lists ten "Church Growth Methods":
1. Soul-winning Evangelism
2. Research and Scientific Analysis
3. Prayer
4. Bible Teaching and Edification
5. The Holy Spirit
6. Lay Involvement and Spiritual Gifts
7. Aggressive Leadership
8. Faith and Goal-Setting
9. The Sunday School [I would like to add, Cells].
10. Social Action

These methods help us to blow the ceiling off a local church and break through the barriers that inhibit growth. To pursue one of the above ten growth methods will undoubtedly make a difference, but I am of the opinion that they all need to be pursued in a balanced way.

The crux of the matter is that whenever a church breaks barriers and experiences growth **a new approach to the management of that church becomes essential! "Mastering MANAGEMENT IN THE CHURCH"** will be of assistance to you as your local church breaks through ceiling after ceiling. Simply reading this book will help you. Implementing what it suggests will change both your life and the life of your local church. This has happened to me! Perhaps the major difference between a small church and a large church is management. Unless you become a leader-manager you will never lead a large church.

CONTENTS OF INTRODUCTION

OUTLINE OF THE COURSE

Section 1   SURVEY
Section 2   PLANNING
Section 3   ORGANIZING
Section 4   LEADING
Section 5   MANAGING

INTRODUCTORY COMMENTS

1. ORIGIN OF THE COURSE

1.1   God - a God of order

1.2   Jesus - a leader-manager

2. THE AIMS OF THE COURSE

ACKNOWLEDGEMENTS

OUTLINE OF THE COURSE

Section 1: SURVEY

WHAT is Management?
WHY is Management Important for Christians?
WHAT is the Management Process?
The FOUR MAJOR STEPS in Management

Section 2: PLANNING

WHAT is Planning?
Biblical Reasons for Planning
Activities Involved in Planning
HOW to Plan
Remember the following when Planning!
Let's Do Some Planning!

Section 3: ORGANIZING

Definition of Organizing
The Importance of Organizing
The Basic Principles of Organizing
The Method to Follow
Two Major Aspects of Organizing:
      A. Job Descriptions
      B. Delegation

Section 4: LEADING

Definition of Leadership
NATURAL Leaders versus MANAGER Leaders
SITUATIONAL LEADERSHIP
ESSENTIAL INGREDIENTS of Effective Leadership

Section 5: MANAGING or MONITORING

A DEFINITION of Managing
WHY Manage?
PRACTICAL GUIDELINES for Managing
Managing as a Lifestyle

INTRODUCTORY COMMENTS

1. ORIGINS OF THE COURSE

During the late sixties and the early seventies, the church in South Africa experienced a wonderful wave of RENEWAL. This was climaxed in the thrilling 1980 HOLY SPIRIT CONFERENCE. Thereafter the renewed church went through even further changes, one of the major changes being the emergence of many "Independent" churches. These churches for the most part had little or no STRUCTURE and many of them were almost entirely without organisation. Some in fact thought that organisation was contrary to the move of the Spirit. Then, to add to the problem, a phenomenon emerged in the life of the South African Church that had never happened in the three hundred year history of the nation, namely, the emergence of mega-churches. All of a sudden, from out of the blue churches of a thousand, of two thousand, of three thousand and even up to five thousand began to emerge, and what is more as the years passed by they grew even bigger! Only those who were part of such a church understood the need for *"all things to be done decently and in order!"*

1.1 God - A God of order

It is a Biblical fact that God is not the author of confusion but rather the author of order. But how was this order to be applied to the life of the church?

This forced me into an in-depth study of the Bible to see what it had to say about the subject. I discovered that in both the Old Testament and the New Testament, the Lord always respected and required order, organisation and discipline.

There was perfect order in the creation and in the planets and stars! There was perfect order in the Temple building and in the temple ceremonies! There was order in the way in which the nation of Israel was positioned, tribe by tribe, around the Tabernacle in the Wilderness! When the Captain of the host of the Lord gave instructions for the children of Israel to take the City of Jericho, there was clear order in the way in which it was to be done!

The God of the Old Testament certainly is a God of order.

The same is true of the New Testament. **Jesus** was thorough and organised. The people said of Him, *"He doeth all things well!"*. When He fed the five thousand, He set them down in rows and fed them in an orderly manner. Jesus knew why He was on earth and what He wanted to accomplish on earth. When it came to the time for Him to face death at Calvary, *"He steadfastly set his face to go towards Jerusalem."* And even in the midst of the pain of death organised for John to take care of His mother, Mary.

As one moves on into the story of **the early church,** we see the Apostle **Paul** to be the champion of order, as he addresses the subject in 1 Corinthians 14, he says in verse 33,

> *"For God is not the author of confusion but of peace as in all the churches of the saints. "* Then he says in verse 40,

> *"Let all things be done decently and in order."*

As I went back and forth from Old Testament to New Testament and studied the life and work of Moses, Paul, Jethro, Nehemiah, Daniel and a host of others, I soon realised that organisation and the flow of the Spirit of God are compatible. This was a revelation to me. I had always thought that as soon as we organised anything the Holy Spirit withdrew. I have now come to the conclusion that because God is a God of order, the most well organised people should be the Holy Spirit controlled people of God. Of course, the crux of the matter is that we need to make sure that the plan and the order we are following, is HIS PLAN and HIS ORDER, and not our own.

We are therefore happy to present **MASTER MANAGEMENT as a guideline to assist in ascertaining GOD'S PLAN, STRUCTURE AND ORGANIZATION for our lives, with a view to following it**.

2. AIMS OF THE COURSE

The major aim of this course is **to equip men and women of God to be able to serve the Lord more effectively**. This involves learning to hear the voice of the Lord so as to ascertain His plan for our lives or for a particular project He has given us.

In addition, a further aim of this course is **to assist us in the practicalities of HOW to accomplish what the Lord has given them to do**. This involves the practical nuts and bolts of how to get the job done! In other words, our **AIMS** are:

1. To show that there is a **BIBLICAL BASIS** for MASTER MANAGEMENT.

2. To share the practical **NUTS AND BOLTS** of Management with particular emphasis on **HOW TO DO IT!**

3. To give a series of **WORKSHEETS** to assist us in our planning.

4. To **ASSIST THOSE IN LEADERSHIP** in and outside of the Church to more effectively do what God has called them to do.

5. To encourage and give guidelines to those who are yet to emerge into some form of leadership.

THE ULTIMATE AIM of the course is TWOFOLD
1. **TO BE MASTER MANAGED,** that is, to be managed by Jesus, and
2. **TO MASTER MANAGEMENT** - To learn and apply the principles of management.

ACKNOWLEDGMENTS

For years I have studied the subject of MANAGEMENT, gleaning from as many sources as possible, all the important and relevant information that I could gather. This took me through many books and several courses.

In compiling this course I endeavoured to summarise the approach that is generally followed in most courses. In the process I was amazed to see that all good management principles have a strong Bible base. This delighted me! Many of the secular writers may not be happy to hear that their courses have strong Biblical foundations, but whether they know it or not, that is in fact the truth.

The books in this field that made the greatest impact on my life I list below and happily acknowledge that I have leaned heavily on them in the preparation of this course.

CHARTING YOUR COURSE, an edition of Acts magazine [Vol. 9, Number 6] by Ralph Mahoney of World MAP, 900 North Glenoaks Blvd, Burbank, California 91502, USA.

MOTIVATION TO LAST A LIFETIME, written by Ted Engstrom and published by Zondervan Publishing House. ISBN 08-310-24251-7.

THE DYNAMICS OF LEADERSHIP, an excellent commentary on the book of Nehemiah by Cyril J. Barber. Loizeaux Brothers, Inc. ISBN 0-87213-021-5.

THE MINISTRY OF MANAGEMENT, Campus Crusade for Christ International. This Manual made a deep impression on me and inspired me to produce Master Management.

MANAGEMENT FOR THE CHRISTIAN WORKER by Olaf Hendrix. A clear, concise and practical book. ISBN 0-916608-01-8.

MARKETING THE CHURCH by George Barna, a book that challenged me to move out of my conservative mind set. ISBN 08910-92501. NavPress.

STRATEGIC PLANNING for ministry and Church Growth by R. Henry Migliore. ISBN 0-89274-513-4. Published by Harrison House.

THE SEVEN HABITS OF HIGHLY EFFECTIVE PEOPLE by Stephen R. Covey. Published by Simon and Shuster Ltd., ISBN 0-671-71117-2.

ELSA BROWN was responsible for all the drawings.

Most of the Scripture quotations are from the **New King James Version**.

Over the years, as I have read and studied these books and many others, certain things have become evident:

1.   There are general principles to management that flow through all.

2.   Many authors seem to borrow definitions from each other and seem to follow the general overall approach of others, and it is difficult to ascertain who produced the original work.

3.   Some books are far more refreshing to read than others but all have been valuable.

4.   Because some books seem to quote each other verbatim and yet do not always state their source it is difficult is give full recognition for such statements.

5.   In presenting Mastering MANAGEMENT IN THE CHURCH, I acknowledge that I have leaned heavily on many others who have pioneered the way in defining a Biblically based method of management. I have not tried to re-invent the wheel. As a matter of fact I am convinced that all good managerial principles have their origin in the Bible and so ultimate acknowledgement must go to the Holy Spirit, the Author of the greatest book ever written!

1. SURVEY

CONTENTS OF SURVEY

I. WHAT IS MANAGEMENT?

> Definition
> Difficulties

II. WHY IS MANAGEMENT IMPORTANT FOR CHRISTIANS?

> It helps Christians pursue EXCELLENCE
>
> It helps Christians FOLLOW THE EXAMPLE
> OF SUCCESSFUL MEN OF GOD, like
> > 2.1 Nehemiah
> > 2.2 Joseph
> > 2.3 Daniel
> > 2.4 Moses
> > 2.5 Paul
> > 2.6 JESUS
>
> It helps Christians FULFILL THEIR ROLE AS GOOD STEWARDS.

III. WHAT IS THE MANAGEMENT PROCESS?

> Step 1. **PLANNING**
>
> Step 2. **ORGANIZING**
>
> Step 3. **LEADING**
>
> Step 4. **MANAGING / MONITORING**
>
> - which includes supervising, regulating
>   and controlling

"His lord said to him, 'Well done, good and faithful servant; you were faithful over a few things, I will make you ruler over many things.' Matthew 25:21

I. WHAT IS MANAGEMENT ?

1. DEFINITION:

Lawrence A. Appley says,

"Management is getting things done through other people."

Many pastors know that this is part of their responsibility but still fail to manage. They have become so accustomed to carrying the total load that they never move into biblical management. Some even feel that this is the cross that they are called to bear. However, this is totally in conflict with the teaching of the Bible which clearly emphasises the fact that the Lord expects every member of the Body to be actively involved.

"[Jesus] From whom the whole body, joined and knit together by what every joint supplies, according to the effective working by which every part does its share, causes growth of the body for the edifying of itself in love." Ephesians 4:16.

Here we see that JESUS is the ultimate manager of the Body of Christ! According to Ephesians 1:22, He is the great HEAD of the church. He is its manager!

However, Jesus has delegated managerial authority to men. Acts 20:28 is an example of this. Here Paul speaks to the ELDERS of the church at Ephesus and he says,

"Therefore take heed to yourselves and to all the flock, among which the Holy Spirit has made you OVERSEERS, to shepherd the church of God ......".

A clearer MANDATE FOR MANAGEMENT could not be found anywhere in the Bible. If you are a pastor, a minister or a priest, YOU HAVE BEEN CALLED TO MANAGEMENT! Make no mistake about it! It's up to you to take up your responsibility. Obey the Holy Spirit! Become an OVERSEER - a MANAGER!

Naturally there are many different levels of management both inside and outside the church. For instance, in the church the following positions are of a managerial nature: a cell leader; an assistant cell leader; an assistant pastor; a team leader; a head usher, to name only a few. These are all assistant managers.

The sheer logic of the situation is that **it is not the pastor's task to do everything** in the church. He has been called to be a manager! He has been called to get the job done through other people - the people in his flock.

DEFINITION:
   MANAGING IS GETTING THINGS DONE THROUGH OTHER PEOPLE

2. DIFFICULTIES

The very thought of a minister being a manager is completely unacceptable to some. They feel that it compromises the position of a pastor and aligns him with the worldly system. That is not true at all! What we are running away from is the use of words. We associate the word MANAGEMENT with the world and therefore shun it. Actually it is simply another word for OVERSEER. Don't let the things that you associate with words hinder you from fulfilling your calling as a pastor or as a leader.

There are several **FEARS** that tend to grip the would-be manager-pastor:

2.1 THE FEAR OF LOOSING THE PERSONAL TOUCH WITH PEOPLE

This fear is understandable, especially in the light of the strong emphasis that the Bible places on relationships. Perhaps we need to take a look at Jesus in this regard. He ministered to the crowds but poured His life into a small group of twelve. As we become managers we are able to pour our lives more effectively into a few people, with better results. No, we do not loose personal touch, we actually move into deeper and more intimate relationships with our leaders and as a result they become more effective.

2.2 THE FEAR OF BECOMING A MAN HEAVILY EMBROILED IN ONE COMMITTEE MEETING AFTER THE OTHER

This too is a legitimate fear. No pastor, who has been called of God would like his ministry to degenerate into becoming a committee man. A pastor-manager who sits in committee meetings all day long has not understood the point that a manager is a person WHO GETS THINGS **DONE** THROUGH OTHER PEOPLE.

2.3 THE FEAR OF BEING A MAN INVOLVED IN NOTHING MORE THAN SECULAR EMPLOYMENT

Naturally, any anointed pastor would avoid this like the plague! But this is certainly not what is envisaged in becoming a pastor-manager. Perhaps we have wrongly differentiated between the secular and the spiritual.

For example, the leader of a Children's Church, who may not actually teach a class, but is responsible for the smooth running of the entire Children's Church is in no way inferior to any class teacher who actually gives the lesson.

And, by the way, the pastor-manager is still very much involved in sharing the Word of the Lord by preaching, be it to the congregation or to his leaders or on a one-on-one basis.

3. WAS JESUS A MANAGER?

He certainly was!   He managed the TEAM OF TWELVE.
He managed the TEAM OF SEVENTY that He sent out.

In the Book of the Revelation we see Jesus, in chapters 2 and 3, managing the seven churches in Asia Minor. Here we see Jesus speaking into the lives of these churches. He commends them. He rebukes them. He corrects them. He advises them and in so doing He leads and MANAGES them.

II. WHY IS MANAGEMENT IMPORTANT FOR CHRISTIANS ?

So often the church has presented a poor image. Mediocrity has dogged its footsteps. Many local churches are totally disorganised. This image has not been a credit to the Lord. The time has come for the people of God not only to be a people of prayer, holiness and integrity but also a people of discipline and example, especially in terms of excellence.

1. MANAGEMENT HELPS CHRISTIANS ACHIEVE EXCELLENCE!

JESUS achieved excellence!
> Mark 7:37 says, *"And they were astonished beyond measure, saying, HE HAS DONE ALL THINGS WELL."*

PAUL emphasised the importance of excellence in the following scriptures.
> Philippians 1:10, *"...that you may approve the things that are excellent".*
> Philippians 4:8, *"...if there be any virtue (NIV says, 'if anything is excellent') ..think on these things."*

Excellence is an attribute of God!
> Psalm 8:1 and 9 says, *"O LORD, our Lord, HOW EXCELLENT IS YOUR NAME in all the earth".*

We should therefore THINK excellence!
> Ecclesiastes 9:10 says, *"Whatever your hand finds to do, do it with your might."*

Ted W. Engstrom, in his outstanding book, THE PURSUIT OF EXCELLENCE, says "Striving for excellence in our work, whatever it is, is not only our Christian duty, but a basic form of Christian witness".

Therefore the aim of every man and woman of God should be -
I WILL DO AND BE MY BEST FOR GOD!

2. MANAGEMENT HELPS CHRISTIANS FOLLOW THE EXAMPLE OF SUCCESSFUL MEN OF GOD IN THE BIBLE!

It is one thing to be given a great task to accomplish for the Lord, but its altogether another matter to successfully complete it.

In both the Old Testament and the New Testament there are exciting examples of people who were called by the Lord to accomplish mammoth tasks for Him, and it is very exciting to see how the Lord inspired them with managerial abilities to accomplish the task. In the same way as the Lord anointed Bazaleel to be a craftsman [Exodus 31:1 - 5], He anoints leaders with managerial ability to successfully accomplish their calling.

Let's take a look at some of the examples in the Bible:

2.1 NEHEMIAH

This man above all others in the Old Testament has fascinated me. I would rate him as **perhaps the most successful manager of the Old Testament.**

His assignment?	To build the walls of Jerusalem!
His obstacles?	A demoralised people. A sparsity of materials. Opposition from within and without.
His attitude?	An indomitable spirit of faith in God!
His approach?	From beginning to end he demonstrated the dynamics of effective leadership!

He proved himself to be a manager par- excel lance!

I should like to highly recommend an excellent book written by Cyril J. Barber, entitled, **NEHEMIAH AND THE DYNAMICS OF EFFECTIVE LEADERSHIP**. Printed by Loizeaux Brothers, Neptune, New Jersey.
I would rate this book as "outstanding" and would say it is a must for any serious would-be pastor-manager.

2.2 JOSEPH

The story of Joseph is another example of a man being given supernatural ability to manage.
Think about his **TASK** for a moment: Gather grain from all the farmers of Egypt for a period of seven good years! Imagine the complaints when to all intents and purposes there wasn't even a sign of drought. Think of the logistics of gathering, storing and controlling the entire project. Think of the building projects that this must have included. Think of the "paper work". Imagine how difficult it was to gather twenty percent of each farmer's crop. Think of the transport problems. And then think of the controlling of the distribution of the food during the seven long years of drought.

And, in addition Joseph was only thirty years of age when he was given the responsibility of taking command over everything in Egypt!

That takes GOD-INSPIRED MANAGEMENT!

That is exactly what he possessed!

Joseph had to get all of these jobs done through people - and he succeeded.

2.3 DANIEL

The circumstances that surrounded his youth were far from ideal. As a young man he was deported together with his people. There seemed little hope of him ever accomplishing much, but God stepped in and in a very short while he was promoted to be the top man in the land.

Refusing compromise he became one of God's great managers.

2. 4 MOSES

He only learned the principles of management at a later stage in his life, when he was in danger of collapsing under the intense load he was carrying.

It was **Jethro, his father-in-law** who assisted him in moving into management. This vitally important story deserves our careful attention. It is found in EXODUS 18. The main part of this story is related in verses 13 to 26. If you are not familiar with this story, stop and read it right now.

It includes one of the most clearly defined systems of management in the entire Bible.

2. 5 PAUL

Paul was undoubtedly a LEADER OF LEADERS. He always had someone travelling with him, not only as a companion but as a trainee. This was a principle of Paul's life. He taught Timothy to do the same. In 2 Timothy 2:2 he says,

> *"And the things that you have heard from me among many witnesses, commit these to faithful men who will be able to teach other also."*

When one considers what Paul accomplished during his life and the way in which he gave oversight to so many churches, and the way in which he worked with teams of leaders and workers, one can clearly see him as a Holy Spirit anointed leader-manager.

Then, of course, the greatest example of all is the Lord Jesus Himself.

2.6 JESUS.

Jesus is to us the sum total and essence of perfect leadership!
He was and is the greatest leader ever!

Jesus came to earth to accomplish certain things, and two of the most important things that He aimed to achieve were:

A.   TO RAISE UP A TEAM!

This team He referred to again and again in His high-priestly prayer in John 17.

> "I have glorified You on the earth. I have finished the work which You have given Me to do.
> 5 "And now, O Father, glorify Me together with Yourself, with the glory which I had with You before the world was.
> 6 **"I have manifested Your name to THE MEN WHOM YOU HAVE GIVEN ME out of the world."**

He then goes on to say several things about these men, referring to them as THEM, THOSE, THEY etc. [capitalised]:

> 6 " .. **THEY were Yours, You gave them to Me**, and THEY have kept Your word.
> 7 "Now THEY have known that all things which You have given Me are from You.
> 8 "For **I have given to THEM the words which You have given Me**; and THEY have received them, and have known surely that I came forth from You; and THEY have believed that You sent Me.
> 9 **"I pray for THEM**. I do not pray for the world but for THOSE whom You have given Me, for THEY are Yours.
> 10 "And all Mine are Yours, and Yours are Mine, and I am glorified in THEM.
> 11 "Now I am no longer in the world, but THESE are in the world, and I come to You. Holy Father, **keep through Your name THOSE whom You have given Me, that THEY may be one as We are**.
> 12 "While I was with THEM in the world, I kept them in Your name. **THOSE whom You gave Me I have kept; and none of THEM is lost except the son of perdition** [here He was referring to Judas, who betrayed Him], **that the Scripture might be fulfilled.**
> 13 "But now I come to You, and these things I speak in the world, that THEY may have My joy fulfilled in THEMSELVES.
> 14 **"I have given THEM Your word**; and the world has hated THEM because THEY are not of the world, just as I am not of the world.
> 15 "I do not pray that You should take THEM out of the world, but that You should **keep THEM from the evil one.**
> 16 "THEY are not of the world, just as I am not of the world.
> 17 **"Sanctify THEM by Your truth**. Your word is truth.
> 18 **"As You sent Me into the world, I also have sent THEM into the world."**

19

Notice, as Jesus prays this prayer to His Father, He says in verse 4,

"I HAVE FINISHED the work which You have given Me to do".

Obviously He was not referring to the work that He was yet to accomplish on the cross of Calvary. He seemingly was referring to the work of glorifying His Father through being faithful to raise up the team of disciples that were going to continue the great work He had started!

Jesus therefore seems to have accomplished two great works on earth, which He declared to be "FINISHED" or accomplished. The first was the raising up of a team to whom He would hand over the work that He had initiated.

The second great work was,

B.   TO SECURE OUR SALVATION through His death on the cross.

With regard to this second task Jesus also said,
"IT IS FINISHED!" [John 19:30].

Before Jesus accomplished the second great work on the cross, He had already raised up the team that would make sure that the message of salvation would be carried to the ends of the earth.

Management is getting things done through others!

This was foundational in the ministry of Jesus.

May I dare to say that Jesus was, is and ever will be THE GREATEST MANAGER-LEADER IN THE ENTIRE UNIVERSE.

Let me quote an old song.

"HE'S GOT THE WHOLE WIDE WORLD IN HIS HAND".

3.   MANAGEMENT HELPS CHRISTIANS FULFILL THEIR ROLE AS GOOD STEWARDS!

Towards the end of His ministry Jesus told the parable of the TALENTS. (Matthew 25:14 - 30). In the story the Lord tells about a Master who went on a journey. When he left he gave to his three servants five talents, two talents and one talent respectively. Some have suggested that in terms of today's money a talent could have been worth up to $30,000. On his return the master expected his servants to give an account of their talents. Well, both the servant with the five talents as well as the servant with the two talents doubled their talents. The master rewarded them equally. Then the servant with the one talent came and returned his one talent. His master was far from pleased with him.

The **MAIN MESSAGE** of this parable is that **GOD EXPECTS US TO WISELY USE WHATEVER HE HAS GIVEN US.** And He has given us so much!

He has given us health, strength, our time, our education, our financial resources, our specific talents and so much more. He expects us to use all wisely. He will reward us accordingly.

The Lord has given to many of us ministries. Some have been given the responsibility of overseeing the ministries of others. To be able to effectively fulfill our responsibilities we must **learn to manage well.**

III. WHAT IS THE MANAGEMENT PROCESS ?

There are TWO AREAS of management that every good manager will need to carefully consider.

1. MANAGING OURSELVES AND OUR TIME

2. MANAGING OTHERS

We will now consider the second aspect of management - the managing of others.

THE FOUR MAJOR STEPS IN MANAGEMENT!

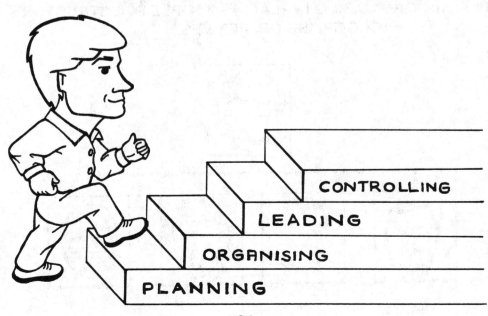

CONTROLLING

LEADING

ORGANISING

PLANNING

IV. THE FOUR MAJOR STEPS IN MANAGEMENT

STEP 1   PLANNING

Dictionary: "to arrange beforehand;
to design a way of proceeding."
Definition: **PLANNING IS PREDETERMINING A COURSE OF ACTION.**

STEP 2   ORGANISING

Dictionary: "to give a definite stricture; to arrange;
to put in order; to systematize."
Definition: **ORGANISING IS PLACING PEOPLE IN A STRUCTURE TO ACCOMPLISH OBJECTIVES**

STEP 3   LEADING

Dictionary: "to cause to go along with oneself; to guide, direct to a place; to indicate the way; to march at the head of and direct the movement of."

Definition :   LEADING IS CAUSING PEOPLE TO TAKE EFFECTIVE ACTION

STEP 4   MANAGING / CONTROLLING

Dictionary: "to control the affairs of; to take charge of; to administer; to succeed in accomplishing."

A dictionary of **synonyms** gave the following synonyms for the word "manage."
- conduct, direct, regulate, superintend, supervise, administer, carry on, guide, handle, order and transact.

Definition: MANAGING IS ASSURING
> **THAT PERFORMANCE CONFORMS TO PLAN;**
> **THAT WHAT WE HAVE PLANNED IS ACCOMPLISHED.**

If you are a good manager you will you will cover each of these **four major steps of management thoroughly.**   They follow a logical sequence!

Think about it for a while and then **list two reasons** for each of these important steps:

WHY SHOULD WE **PLAN**?

1.	
2.	

WHY SHOULD WE **ORGANISE**?

1.	
2.	

WHY SHOULD WE **LEAD**?

1.	
2.	

WHY SHOULD WE **MANAGE**?

1.	
2.	

When filling in the above be sure to refer to the definitions of these four words.

2. PLANNING

2. PLANNING
CONTENTS

I. WHAT IS PLANNING?

II. BIBLICAL REASONS FOR PLANNING

1. GOD IS A PLANNER

2. GOD COMMANDS US TO LIVE ORDERLY LIVES

3. JESUS TAUGHT US TO PLAN AHEAD

   3.1 The man who builds a tower
   3.2 The king who contemplates war

4. LACK OF PLANNING LEADS TO CONFUSION AND FRUSTRATION

5. PAUL THE APOSTLE WAS A MAN WITH A PLAN

   5.1 At the time of his conversion the Lord clearly stated the OBJECTIVES for his life
   5.2 Paul followed a definite pattern in each city where he evangelised

6. THE OLD TESTAMENT HAS SEVERAL WONDERFUL EXAMPLES OF ANOINTED MEN WHOSE PLANNING GOD DIRECTED AND BLESSED

III. ACTIVITIES INVOLVED IN PLANNING

1. HEARING FROM GOD

2. DETERMINING OUR OBJECTIVES

3. PLANNING OUR STRATEGY

4. BUILDING IN A TIME ELEMENT

5. MARSHALLING OUR RESOURCES

CONTENTS CONTINUED

IV. HOW TO PLAN

1. HEAR FROM GOD

SEVEN BASIC PRINCIPLES OF PRAYER

1. Become still before God
2. Get into communion with the Holy Spirit
3. Develop your visions and dreams
4. Take authority over the devil in your circumstances
5. Keep and accurate record of your requests to God
6. Praise God in advance
7. Pray without ceasing

2. DETERMINE YOUR OBJECTIVES

3. PLAN YOUR STRATEGY

3.1 Criteria for goals
3.2 Three important questions

4. BUILD IN A TIME ELEMENT

5. MARSHALL YOUR RESOURCES

5.1 Your MANPOWER resources
5.2 Your FINANCIAL resources
5.3 Other resources

V. REMEMBER THE FOLLOWING WHEN PLANNING!

1. Plan a little beyond your own strength
2. Be prepared to change your plan
3. Involve others in the planning process
4. Take cognizance of policies and procedures
5. Remember that planning is a process
6. Market your plan correctly
7. Always be sensitive to the leading of the Holy Spirit

VI. LET'S DO SOME PLANNING!

2.PLANNING

"For which of you, when he wants to build a tower, does not first sit down and CALCULATE THE COST, to see if he has enough to complete it? Otherwise, when he has laid a foundation, and is not able to finish, all who observe it begin to ridicule him, saying, "This man began to build and was not able to finish." Luke 14:28-30.

I. WHAT IS PLANNING?

Planning is a process that every one of us is involved in virtually all the time. Whether you are involved in building a house, taking the family on a holiday, going on an overseas business trip, or laying out your garden, the bottom line in each case is **PLANNING**.

Imagine the amount of **planning** that goes into a space probe!
Think about how much planning goes into a sky-scraper, or into the launching of a new type of fighter plane.

With all of these ventures it is of the utmost importance that the planning be thorough! When you consider the value of your life, your career or your ministry, it becomes imperative to **plan appropriately**.

Let's take another look at the definition we have already stated.

DICTIONARY: Planning is... "to arrange beforehand;
to design a way of proceeding."

DEFINITION: PLANNING IS PRE-DETERMINING A COURSE OF ACTION.

II. BIBLE REASONS FOR PLANNING

Christians should plan because...

1. GOD IS A PLANNER

* Creation is evidence of this.
* The human body is evidence of this.
* A snow-flake is evidence of this.
* The plan God gave Moses for the Tabernacle in the wilderness is evidence of this.
* The plan of salvation is evidence of this

God certainly is a PLANNER!

2. GOD COMMANDS US TO LIVE ORDERLY LIVES

That He sets the example for us is clear from what Paul, the apostle says in 1 Corinthians 14:33,

"For God is not the author of confusion but of peace, as in all churches of the saints."

He also says to us in Ephesians 5:1,

"Be ye therefore followers of God, as dear children."

God's COMMAND that we should live orderly lives comes through clearly in 1 Corinthians 14:40,

"Let all things be done decently and in order."

Have you ever gone down town with a view to doing or buying certain things, only to be unable to recall everything you had made a mental note of?
As a result you did not accomplish all you set out to do. Adequate planning would obviate such disorganisation and frustration! Next time be sure to draw up a list!

30

3. JESUS TAUGHT US TO PLAN AHEAD

This is the clear message of the parables in Luke 14:28 - 32.

3.1 THE MAN WHO BUILDS A TOWER

Luke 14:28 "For which of you, intending to build a tower, does not sit down first and count the cost, whether he has enough to finish it -
29 "lest, after he has laid the foundation, and is not able to finish it, all who see it begin to mock him,
30 "saying, 'This man began to build and was not able to finish."

3.2 THE KING WHO CONTEMPLATES WAR

Luke 14:31 "Or what king, going to make war against another king, does not sit down first and consider whether he is able with ten thousand to meet him who comes against him with twenty thousand?
32 "Or else, while the other is still a great way off, he sends a delegation and asks conditions of peace".

Both builder and king are advised to **plan ahead.**

4. LACK OF PLANNING LEADS TO CONFUSION AND FRUSTRATION

It has often been said that **"If we fail to plan we plan to fail."**

From my personal experience I have seen that those who do not work according to a plan, often:

        ... have little or no direction,
        ... live life in a "hum-drum" way,
        ... very seldom show lasting enthusiasm,
        ... accomplish very little and
        ... more often than not are dictated to by circumstances.

For example, they are ruled by the telephone or by one or two people in their church or organisation. Often they spend much of their time with problems and have little time to get involved in doing constructive things.

This, of course, results in frustration for the leader and confusion for the followers.

Paul suggests that we should know what we are aiming at and plan accordingly!

> *"Do you not know that those who run in a race all run, but only one receives the prise? **Run in such a way that you may obtain it.** And every one who competes for the prise is temperate in all things. They then do it to obtain a perishable crown, but we for an imperishable crown. **Therefore I run thus: not with uncertainty [AV: not without aim];** Thus I fight; not as one who beats the air." 1 Corinthians 9:24 - 26.*

5. PAUL THE APOSTLE WAS A MAN WITH A PLAN

5.1 AT THE TIME OF HIS CONVERSION THE LORD CLEARLY STATED HIS OBJECTIVES FOR HIS LIFE

Acts 26:16 - 18, says,
*'But rise and stand on your feet; for **I have appeared to you for this purpose**, to make you a minister and a witness both of the things which you have seen and of the things which I will yet reveal to you.*
17 'I will deliver you from the Jewish people, as well as from the Gentiles, to whom I now send you,
18 'to open their eyes and to turn them from darkness to light, and from the power of Satan to God, that they may receive forgiveness of sins and an inheritance among those who are sanctified by faith in Me.'

I am strongly of the opinion that **God has clear objectives for each of our lives.** He does not want us to simply drift from day to day. **He has a specific plan for each of us. Yes, for YOUR life!**

If we wait on the Lord, He will communicate His OBJECTIVES for our lives, to us.
It would be better to spend a week waiting on God for His clear-cut instructions, than to spend the rest of our lives muddling through, and battling all the time to find out what **think** He wants us to do.

Paul **knew** what God wanted him to do, and he did it. As a result he could say at the end of his life, *"I have finished the course.."*.

5. 2 PAUL FOLLOWED A DEFINITE PATTERN IN EACH CITY WHERE HE EVANGELISED

A. He always **started in the synagogue** where he did two things:
   a. Preached the gospel (Acts 19:8) and,
   b. Performed miracles (Acts 19:11).

B. He then **gathered a leadership group** and gave them special attention and input. (Acts 19:10). Obviously it was during these two years that he raised up the elders at Ephesus.

C. Often Paul would in addition to the leadership group, **leave behind him a special person to take up the responsibility of being THE leader.**

   Note Titus 1:5 in this connection.

D. He would then be sure to **encourage them by subsequent visits and or letters.**

   This was the PATTERN or the PLAN that Paul followed. He did not simply drift from one day to the next, claiming to be under the control of the Spirit. No, he was a man with a God-given strategy who followed this strategy under the control of the Holy Spirit.

E. **Paul's strategy also included STRATEGIC CITIES.**
   He specifically aimed at setting up churches in cities like Rome, Ephesus, Corinth and Philippi. These cities were either capital cities or on major trade routes. It was from these KEY cities that the gospel spread rapidly.

6. THE OLD TESTAMENT HAS SEVERAL WONDERFUL EXAMPLES OF ANOINTED MEN WHOSE PLANNING GOD DIRECTED AND BLESSED

For example:
            Moses............ Exodus 18
            Nehemiah...... Nehemiah chapters 1 to 3.

III. ACTIVITIES INVOLVED IN PLANNING.

To the Christian PLANNING is of vital importance and includes the following exciting procedures:

1. HEARING FROM GOD

This involves going before the Lord in prayer, and in total dependence on the Holy Spirit, so as to receive from the Lord His directions for our lives, and this could include:

A. **HIS VISION FOR OUR LIVES**, that is, His OVERALL OBJECTIVES for us.

B. **HIS INSTRUCTIONS FOR A SPECIFIC PROJECT** we may be launching.

We cannot do without His advice! We desperately need it in every project or undertaking. We ALWAYS need God's help in EVERY WAY.

BUT, how does one hear from God?

The answer is given in the section on HOW TO PLAN that follows a little later.

2.   DETERMINING OUR OBJECTIVES

To hear from God is fundamental to our successful planning. Once we have heard from Him, we need to write down His instructions in terms of **OBJECTIVES**.

We also need to understand that there is a difference between an **objective** and a **goal.**

An OBJECTIVE is a LONG-RANGE GOAL.

GOALS are stepping-stones or mile-stones along the road leading to our objectives.

It is very important to define our objectives clearly.

Think about it, and then write down what you feel are

YOUR MAJOR OBJECTIVES IN LIFE.

As you define your objectives a sense of destiny will begin burn in your heart!

You have been destined for greater things!

3. PLANNING OUR STRATEGY

This involves defining **HOW** objectives should be reached.

Here we define **the steps that need to be taken** in pursuit of our objectives.

It is the establishing of **A STEP BY STEP PLAN,** which is often called **A CRITICAL PATH.**

4. BUILD IN A TIMETABLE

Here we answer the question, **WHEN?**

* When will we reach point A, B, C, and D?
* When do we plan to reach our objective?
* Here we are establishing a time schedule.
* Here we are relating our plan to the Calendar.

5. MARSHALLING OUR RESOURCES

This answers the question, **HOW MUCH?**

Three of the most important resources that are always used in a project are:

5.1 MANPOWER

How much manpower do I need?

What manpower is available?

5.2 MONEY

How much will it cost?

What financial resources do we have?

5.3 MATERIAL

What do I need?

What computers, photostat machines, office space, letterheads, office furniture et cetera do I have?

These questions all need to be asked and all these items need to be budgeted.

Marshalling our resources is often referred to as **budgeting.**

All successful planning covers these five points thoroughly.

IV. HOW TO PLAN

Let's take a deeper look at this planning process.

1. HEAR FROM GOD

To many Christians this is a major problem!
"HOW do you hear from God?" is the question they are asking.

Well, obviously, the person must be a born-again child of God, otherwise he will not have the Spirit of God living in him.

If he has been filled with or baptised in the Holy Spirit this certainly will be to his advantage. What is of great importance is that each Christian should be actively seeking to establish a relationship with the Holy Spirit. The Holy Spirit has come to be our friend and has promised to LEAD us into all truth. Having developed such a relationship the Christian leader, or doctor, or lawyer, or foreman, or artisan is at a distinct advantage over the person who does not know the Lord. Through the Holy Spirit we have a supernatural advantage over others. This is especially so when we realise that God's word says,

"He that is joined unto the Lord IS ONE SPIRIT."
[KJV] 1 Corinthians 6:17.

But, still the question remains, **HOW DO WE HEAR FROM GOD?.**

I have looked for the answer to this question for years and feel that one of the best method I have ever come across is that suggested by Dr Paul Yonggi Cho, in his book, MORE THAN NUMBERS. On pages 111 to 117 he gives his

SEVEN BASIC PRINCIPLES OF PRAYER

I. GET STILL BEFORE GOD

So often we fail to hear from God because we are too busy speaking to Him, and never give Him an opportunity to speak to us. To hear from God **we need to learn to be still before Him.**

If I need direction from the Lord, what I usually do is to go into the lounge of our home and sit down in the most comfortable chair. Of course it is important that I am not tired and exhausted, otherwise I may fall asleep. As I sit there in complete comfort I decide not to talk a lot. I may say to the Lord, "Lord, I've come to be still before You for a while. I want to relax before You and hear You speak to me again. I need Your wisdom and insight on the following matter!" I would then tell the Lord about the particular area in which I need His wisdom and direction.

Then I Would specifically discipline myself to **stop speaking.**

The time has come **just to listen and think on the Lord.**

THINK about
* the greatness of God,
* the wonderful ministry of Jesus and
* how special the Holy Spirit is.
* the fact that the Holy Spirit still speaks to us today
    - usually through the "still small voice."
* the fact that the Bible says,
"Call to Me and I will answer you and show you great and mighty things...". Jeremiah 33:3.

ii. GET INTO COMMUNION WITH THE HOLY SPIRIT

2 Corinthians 13:14 speaks about the **"communion"** of the Holy Spirit. Now the word "communion" can also be translated as the **"partnership"** of the Holy Spirit.
In other words, the Holy Spirit, our senior partner is waiting to for us to enter into communion with Him.

To put it into very practical terms we need to understand that the Father is in heaven, as is the Son. Therefore our point of contact is the Holy Spirit. We have been brought into partnership with Him. Therefore we should expect that **He will communicate with us.**

Dr Cho says, "I begin by speaking directly to the Holy Spirit." He further develops this all-important subject of the **Importance of Fellowship With the Holy Spirit,** in chapter 12 of his challenging book, SUCCESSFUL HOME CELL GROUPS. You ought to get this book and read this chapter.

As we recognise the presence of the Holy Spirit and by faith anticipate hearing Him speak, the channel of our spirit begins to open up. This prepares the way for step three.

iii. DEVELOP YOUR VISIONS AND DREAMS

At first I did not understand what Dr Cho was speaking about. But as I read further, it became evident that he was suggesting that in the same way as many people in the Bible heard from God in different ways, such as through dreams and visions, we should expect God to speak to us too. Daniel, Peter, Joseph, Abraham, Paul, Ananias, John and a host of others also received revelations from God. God is a communicator. He still speaks today! He wants to speak to **you** and impart to you His vision and dream for your life and for every project or problem you face.

For example, if you are launching an evangelistic thrust or a prayer thrust in your church, it is always best to do it because you have received an instruction from God. And then, why not wait on Him for the smallest details in terms of HOW to plan it? Such instructions and details are part of the visions and dreams that Dr Cho speaks about.

As you hear from the Holy Spirit you are able to do it God's way and so success is guaranteed. Remember, God never sponsors any flops!

Once you have His dreams and visions, His instructions and details, you are ready for action in terms of ...

> * of spiritual warfare
> * of specific requests
> * and of launching the project.

The best plans and strategies that have ever been embarked upon are those that were birthed by the Holy Spirit in the "inner room."

iv. TAKE AUTHORITY OVER THE DEVIL IN YOUR CIRCUMSTANCES

The devil hates any and all of God's plans and will undermine them whenever he can. If he can steal them out of your mind before they ever get off the ground, he will do so. If he can fowl them up once they are underway, he will do that too.

BUT, WE HAVE BEEN GIVEN AUTHORITY OVER ALL THE POWER OF THE ENEMY AND NOTHING SHALL BY ANY MEANS HURT US! HALLELUJAH!

> *Luke 10:19 "Behold, I give you the authority to trample on serpents and scorpions, and over all the power of the enemy, and nothing shall by any means hurt you."*

From our position of being seated in HEAVENLY PLACES with Jesus we can resist all of the enemy's plans. This involves taking authority over the enemy so that we can move ahead in victory.

> *James 4:7 "Therefore submit to God. Resist the devil and he will flee from you."*

v. KEEP AN ACCURATE RECORD OF YOUR REQUESTS BEFORE GOD.

Many people have prayed themselves into total unbelief. This is a tragedy. To avoid this pitfall and against the backdrop of what the Holy Spirit has revealed to you, go before God with specific prayers. Don't be vague! Write down the specific things you request from God. Don't rely on your memory. Have a special book in which you record you requests. Go back to these requests again and again, and when a specific request has been granted, give the Lord the praise He deserves.

vi. PRAISE GOD IN ADVANCE

This is in line with the teaching of Jesus in Mark 11:24. In this verse Jesus says,

> "Whatever things you desire, **when you pray, believe** that you receive them (or more literally, have received them), and you shall have them." [KJV].

Remember that God sets the example for us in Romans 4:17, where we read,

> "Even God, who gives life to the dead, and calls those things which do not exist as though they were."

It all boils down to the fact that a dimension of **faith** needs to be added to our prayer lives.

vii. PRAY WITHOUT CEASING

Constantly seek fellowship with the Lord - never let up! At home, abroad or wherever you may be, seek to be in communion with the Lord.

Become friends with God! Abraham did! So can you!

If possible go through these seven steps on a regular basis. We need His constant input for all those appointments we face each day. He is available. How marvellous of God to totally identify Himself with His creatures and to be completely available to each of us, at all times.

2. DETERMINE YOUR OBJECTIVES

Many people meander aimlessly through life. They have no sense of destiny. They tend to regard themselves as another one of the crowd. Consequently, a kind of hopelessness comes over them, and their theme tune is, 'Whatever will be, will be.'

This certainly is not God's plan for our lives. He has placed us on the earth and deposited in us potential far beyond our wildest dreams, and longs for us to establish relationship with Him so that He can impart to us **HIS OBJECTIVES** for our lives.

Pursuing these objectives will result in us living a full and meaningful life.

So, in establishing our objectives we are **determining WHAT should be accomplished through the instrumentality of the people working with us.**

Determining objectives involves far more than drawing up a BUDGET or filling in a YEAR PLANNER.

Let's do an **exercise** together that will assist us in understanding what objectives are, and remember that objectives are the **RESULTS we wish to accomplish.**

Fill in the following:

WHAT ARE YOUR PERSONAL OBJECTIVES for your life?

WHAT ARE YOUR FAMILY OBJECTIVES?

IF YOU ARE A PASTOR OR A LEADER, WHAT ARE YOUR CHURCH OBJECTIVES?

We see that to establish objectives is no simple matter, but it's certainly very important!

Clearly defining our objectives generally stirs up considerable enthusiasm within us. We suddenly realise that there is a great task to accomplish, and that the Lord will help us to accomplish it through others.

3.   PLANNING OUR STRATEGY

OBJECTIVES help us clarify WHERE we are going and WHAT we plan to accomplish. GOALS and STRATEGY define HOW we are going to get there.

PLANNING OUR STRATEGY involves setting out the STEPS we plan to take and the GOALS we plan to reach in pursuit of our OBJECTIVES.

In other words, GOALS = STEPS.

Different authors use different words. Some refer to GOALS as the ultimate end of the plan, whereas we have chosen to use the word OBJECTIVE which seems to be the most widely used word.

Let us take a simple illustration:

| My OBJECTIVE? | to buy a house for my family. |
| My STRATEGY ? | deals with the HOW of securing the house. |

Many people have great intentions but never see them realised, simply because their intentions never reach the nitty-gritty stage of **planning a strategy.**

Working on the basis of our already established objectives, we need to trust the Lord to give to us the WAY in which our objectives can be realised.

3.1   CRITERIA FOR GOALS

In defining goals there are certain criteria that need to be considered:

[1]   **Goals must be REALISTIC**!
One must be able to achieve them within a specified period of time, otherwise they are not goals - they are only WISHES!

[2]   **Goals must be COMMUNICABLE**!
They must be FULLY UNDERSTOOD by those who set them and be easily communicated to all who will be involved in pursuing them. Fuzzy goals are frustrating, confusing and demotivating.

[3]   **Goals must be MEASURABLE**!
If the achievement of a goal cannot be measured how will you ever know that the goal has been achieved? If the goal is not measurable, it can also never be controlled!

[4]   **Goals must be DEFINITIVE**!
They must clearly define what specific action must be taken! People respond to specific action! If they know exactly what must be done, they find it far easier to do it.

[5]   **Goals must have THE FULL COMMITMENT OF ALL INVOLVED!**
If your team is not committed to the goals that have been set, then the desired results will never be obtained.

This is perhaps the most difficult part of goal setting, but involvement in the setting of the goals and corporately experiencing the leading of the Holy Spirit in setting the goals will inspire commitment. Praise God for the Holy Spirit!

3.2   THREE IMPORTANT QUESTIONS

Dr Howard Hendricks suggests three important questions, the answers to which will assist you in determining your strategy:

[I] What must exist at the target date in order for our objective to be accomplished?
To answer this question you need to do two things:

* 1. **Write down your objective or objectives in summary form.**
OBJECTIVE:
To build a rowing boat and trailer for the family in time for the Christmas holidays.

* 2. **Elaborate in detail what will exist at target date**.
DETAILS AT TARGET DATE:
A boat completed; painted; licenced; fitted out with life jackets oars and anchor.
A trailer with tail lights; treated against rust; roadworthy and registered.
A trailer hitch fitted to the family car .

[ii] How far along the road are you toward what must exist at the target date?
What has already been accomplished by **yourself**?
    I have a plan of the boat.
    I have a garage in which to do the project.
    I have seventy five percent of the money.
    I have the support of my family and the help of my son.
What has already be accomplished by **others**?
    My wife has already priced a new set of oars and rowlocks.

[iii] What specific activities will take you from where you are now to your objectives?
* Draw a detailed list of all the activities that need to be pursued.
* These items can be ticked off on completion.

4. BUILD IN A TIME ELEMENT

That means,
"DETERMINE *WHEN* THE DIFFERENT STEPS OF THE PLAN SHOULD BE ACCOMPLISHED."

Obviously, if you are planning for the next year you should consider dividing your project up into quarterly steps or monthly steps or even into weekly steps.

You may be planning to call on 1200 homes during the year. This means that by the end of February you should have already called on 200, by the end of June on 600 etc. **OR,** you are maybe trusting God for a growth in membership of 120 during the year. Therefore you should goal for 20 by February. However, the month of July may be a month in which you expect little or no growth, consequently your projected growth would possibly be as follows:

Month	Monthly Figure	Total
January	10	10
February	10	20
March	10	30
April	10	40
May	12	52
June	12	64
July	4	68
August	10	78
September	10	88
October	12	100
November	10	110
December	10	120

5.   MARSHALL YOUR RESOURCES.

This important phase of planning answers the question, **HOW MUCH?**

5.1   YOUR **MANPOWER** RESOURCES

Here you answer the following questions:
   HOW MUCH manpower do I need?
   HOW MANY people will it take to get the job done?
   HOW MANY people do I have available to assist me?
   HOW MANY of them are trained?
   HOW MANY of them can I train?

At this stage you need to get down to the nitty-gritty of drawing up lists of names of people who fall into the various categories implied in the questions above. Every good manager not only depends tremendously on the people he has available to assist him but also knows what they can do best and how to motivate them to do it.

As you begin to draw up these lists of names you will be surprised to see what resources you have available. Long before I was ever introduced to the idea of management I always used to keep lists of names in the back of my Bible under the following headings:

* Prospective leaders
* Prospective pastors
* Prospective cell leaders
* Prospective deacons.

Very often the people on these lists would actually be appointed to these positions in a matter of months. This exercise ought to be a constant part of a leaders planning.

Keep on marshalling your resources.

5.2   YOUR FINANCIAL RESOURCES

Financial resources are of great importance! The gospel is free but the task of spreading the gospel costs money.

Remember the following:

[i]   God holds us accountable, therefore we must be responsible.

[ii]   God is our source therefore we must not be unbelieving.

[iii]   God finances every project He launches, so be sure that the project you are involved in comes from God.

[iv]   Remember that many of the projects we can launch in the church do not demand a lot of finance.

For example, the launching of cells, or a visitation programme or a neighbourhood friendship evangelism thrust could be undertaken at minimal expense.

Be careful about finances but never let finances stop you from fulfilling God's plan for your life. Remember that faith is a necessary ingredient for serving the Lord, but presumption has no place in the kingdom of God.

5.3   OTHER RESOURCES.

These include...
* Buildings/ Office space
* Typewriters/ computers
* Office Furniture
* Public address systems
* Computer programmes
* Vehicles etc.

List:
A. What resources you have
B. What resources you need

This concept of marshalling our resources is often referred to as **BUDGETING.**

ALL SUCCESSFUL PLANNING COVERS THESE FIVE POINTS THOROUGHLY.

V. REMEMBER THE FOLLOWING WHEN PLANNING!

The whole planning process must done against the backdrop of the following important considerations:

1.   PLAN A LITTLE BIT BEYOND YOUR OWN STRENGTH!

If you plan within your own limitations then the dimension of FAITH is not needed.

If you plan a little beyond yourself, your sense of dependance on God is heightened. This provides a faith platform from which God can operate and thus provide a miracle. Remember that, *"Whatsoever is not of faith is SIN."*

There are many Biblical examples of this principle, but perhaps one of the most outstanding is that is that of

GIDEON'S ARMY OF THREE HUNDRED!

Judges 7:
1 "Then Jerubbaal (that is, Gideon) and all the people who were with him rose early and encamped beside the well of Harod, so that the camp of the Midianites was on the north side of them by the hill of Moreh in the valley.
2 And the LORD said to Gideon, "<u>The people who are with you are too many for Me</u> to give the Midianites into their hands, <u>lest Israel claim glory for itself against Me, saying, 'My own hand has saved me.'</u>
*3 "Now therefore, proclaim in the hearing of the people, saying, '**Whoever is fearful** and afraid, let him turn and depart at once from Mount Gilead.' "And twenty-two thousand of the people returned, and ten thousand remained.*
4 And the LORD said to Gideon, "<u>The people are still too many</u>; bring them down to the water, and I will test them for you there. Then it will be, that of whom I say to you, 'This one shall go with you,' the same shall go with you; and of whomever I say to you, 'This one shall not go with you,' the same shall not go."
5 So he brought the people down to the water. And the LORD said to Gideon, "Everyone who laps from the water with his tongue, as a dog laps, you shall set apart by himself; likewise everyone who gets down on his knees to drink."
*6 **And the number of those who lapped, putting their hand to their mouth, was three hundred men**; but all the rest of the people got down on their knees to drink water.*
*7 **Then the LORD said to Gideon, "By the three hundred men who lapped I will save you, and deliver the Midianites into your hand**. Let all the other people go, every man to his place."*
8 So the people took provisions and their trumpets in their hands. And he sent away all the rest of Israel, every man to his tent, and retained those three hundred men. Now the camp of Midian was below him in the valley.
*9 And it happened **on the same night that the LORD said to him, "Arise, go down against the camp, for I have delivered it into your hand.***
*10 "**But if you are afraid** [sometimes even leaders are afraid!] **to go down, go down to the camp with Purah your servant,***
*11 "and you shall hear what they say; and afterward your hands shall be strengthened to go down against the camp." **Then he went down with Purah** his servant to the outpost of the armed men who were in the camp.*
12 <u>Now the Midianites and Amalekites, all the people of the East, were lying in the valley as numerous as</u>

locusts; and their camels were without number, as the sand by the seashore in multitude.

13 And when Gideon had come, there was **a man telling a dream** to his companion. He said, "I have just had a dream: To my surprise, a loaf of barley bread tumbled into the camp of Midian; it came to a tent and struck it so that it fell and overturned, and the tent collapsed."

14 Then his companion answered and said, "<u>This is nothing else but the sword of Gideon the son of Joash, a man of Israel;</u> for into his hand God has delivered Midian and the whole camp."

15 And so it was, <u>when Gideon heard the telling of the dream and its interpretation, that</u> **he worshipped**. He returned to the camp of Israel, and said, "Arise, for the LORD has delivered the camp of Midian into your hand."

16 Then **he divided the three hundred men into three companies**, and he put a trumpet into every man's hand, with empty pitchers, and torches inside the pitchers.

17 And he said to them, "Look at me and do likewise; watch, and when I come to the edge of the camp you shall **DO JUST AS I DO**:

18 "When I blow the trumpet, I and all who are with me, then you also blow the trumpets on every side of the whole camp, and say, 'The sword of the LORD and of Gideon!' "

19 So Gideon and the hundred men who were with him came to the outpost of the camp at the beginning of the middle watch, just as they had posted the watch; and they blew the trumpets and broke the pitchers that were in their hands.

20 Then the three companies blew the trumpets and broke the pitchers - they held the torches in their left hands and the trumpets in their right hands for blowing - and they cried, **"The sword of the LORD and of Gideon!"**

21 And every man stood in his place all around the camp; and the whole army ran and cried out and fled.

22 When the three hundred blew the trumpets, the LORD set every man's sword against his companion throughout the whole camp; and the army fled to Beth Acacia, toward Zererah, as far as the border of Abel Meholah, by Tabbath."

If you have to begin to trust God for something then the stage is set for the Lord to be glorified through His miraculous intervention and provision.

2.   BE PREPARED TO CHANGE YOUR PLAN!

Many a project has ended up on rocks because of an unwillingness to change. Some have refused to change their plan, believing that they received it from God and God doesn't change His mind!

The crux of the matter is that sometimes we only hear half of what God wanted us to hear - *"For we know in part and we prophesy in part"* [1 Corinthians 13:9], and then when He needs to say something more to us, we are unable to receive it simply because we feel that God has already said all that needed to be said!

Let me remind you of an amazing story from the Old Testament in 2 Samuel 5:19 - 23

Any person who is not willing to change or adjust their plan is in for a hard time. Circumstances alter. Additional information may necessitate dramatic changes. Remember that planning is not done " according to the law of the Medes and Persians that altereth not." Planning is a guideline that needs to be revised as often as necessary.

But, perhaps you ask,

How must one go about CHANGING a plan of action?

The following guidelines may be useful:

* Anticipate revising your plan at least every six months

* Compare the difference between the plan and the actual results.

* List new problems and new opportunities

* Gather all the relevant information

* Assess what needs to be revised

* Institute the change.

* Avoid changing your plan too often.

3.   INVOLVE OTHERS IN THE PLANNING PROCESS

Remember that two heads are always better than one. Be prepared to learn from others. If planning is not one of your strong points then delegate this responsibility to someone who will be able to assist you. I have realised that on my staff I have men who are more competent at planning than I am. I am constantly asking them for input. Perhaps the following procedure could be followed:

* Give him an idea of the way you are thinking.

* Ask him to draw up a "first draft" plan for your approval.

* From this "first draft" draw up your actual plan of action.

The more people you can involve in the planning process, the greater will be their commitment to the plan of action!

The trend today is towards "PARTICIPATIVE MANAGEMENT" in which more and more management responsibilities can be shared with subordinates - "doing it together and coming up with the best solutions". This can work well until one or two of the group become obstinate and demand that their opinion must be followed.

In the Christian context, the direction to be taken is often given to the leader by revelation, but then, of course, he can include others in the planning process.

4.   THE IMPORTANCE OF POLICIES AND PROCEDURES

4.1   POLICIES

Every church or organisation has policies and procedures. Without these there would be much confusion. For instance, in our local church we have certain policies when it comes to the matter of our involvement in the launching of a new branch church, which we normally call a FELLOWSHIP.

1.   It is our policy to help as many such emerging fellowships as possible.

2.   Each of these fellowship we would help with a set amount of finances, on a monthly basis, for a period of six months and then this assistance would be reviewed. Often we would make the same amount available for a further six months, but our policy is not to financially support a new church for more than a year. This policy was decided on after we had experimented and seen that it was valid.

Now, it is the responsibility of our man, to whom we have delegated the task of assisting new churches to see to it that he operates within the framework of our policy. Naturally, if he were to offer assistance to a Fellowship for more than a year, it would have to be referred back to the Steering Committee for authorization. For him to act without this authority he would be neglecting to implement our policy.

All churches and institutions have such policies that must be taken into consideration when drawing up a plan of action.

4.2   PROCEDURES

Most organisations would never employ a man until he had filled in the official "Work Application Form". Then too, all organisations have specific procedures with regard to handling cash or opening mail. A new PLAN of action does not replace these procedures unless a specific decision is made in this regard.

These policies and procedures are **standard methods or ways of doing certain things** that need to be done again and again.

A new plan of action must take cognisance of these policies and procedures.

5.   REMEMBER THAT PLANNING IS A PROCESS

It is not an event that takes place once or twice a year. Rather, it is an on-going process that takes place daily. Actually a good manager-leader will plan each month, each week and each day.

Naturally, he will also plan each new project or challenge.

As changes are made to the original plan, to line it up with the existing set of circumstances, the planning process is carrying on.

6.   MARKET YOUR PLAN CORRECTLY

After days and days of planning the time comes to present your plan. This is a crucial moment. This is an extremely important task that demands the most thorough preparation.

At times this may be an easy task, especially if you have involved most of your people in the planning process. But, often you will need to "sell" your product to people who could well choose not to flow with you. This could be a rather rough road to travel, and that is all the more reason why you should adequately prepare yourself for the presentation.

I'm reminded of the time when Dr Paul Yonggi Cho wanted to present to his church, bathed in Eastern culture, the concept of using women in the church. He wanted to use them as cell leaders, for he was convinced that he had been given the idea by the Lord. However, before he presented the matter to his board he spent a lot of time in the Bible establishing the fact that the Lord had liberated women to minister. He listed all the appropriate texts and all the relevant facts and then systematically and enthusiastically presented it to them. By the time he had his say, all they could say was that he had a rather good case for what he was presenting. His project has certainly been very fruitful.

Practical suggestions!

* Pray much about it.

* Let the plan captivate you personally.

* Thoroughly prepare yourself and any visual aids you use.

* Begin by presenting the objectives.

* Briefly explain your strategy. (Your plan of action).

* Mention some important target dates.

* Mention how many people this project could involve.

* Holy Spirit inspired enthusiasm is vitally important.

In presenting your plan, attempt to not only give *your* thinking, but also to stir up your audience by way of positive response.

7.   ALWAYS BE SENSITIVE TO THE LEADING OF THE HOLY SPIRIT

In serving the Lord it is of paramount importance that we should **ALWAYS** be open to the Holy Spirit. He should always have the right to step in and order whatever changes He may desire.
54

You will recall that on one occasion David enquired of the Lord as to whether he should engage his army in battle or not. The occasion was the anointing of David as king over Judah and Israel. The reaction of the Philistines to this announcement was that they determined to come up against Israel in battle. The story which is recorded for us in 2 Samuel 5:17 - 25, reveals that, *"David enquired of the Lord, saying, Shall we go up to the Philistines? Wilt Thou deliver them into my hands?"* The Lord's response to this is positive, He says, *"GO UP."* Victory followed!

At a later stage the Philistines came up against them again so once again, *"David enquired of the Lord."* This time God gave them a completely different strategy. (See verses 23 and 24). Again, victory followed!

Years ago I heard a preacher say, "Yesterday's anointing is not good enough for today." Allow me to coin another expression:
"Yesterday's plan is not good enough for today and last years plan is not good enough for this year."

Always be sensitive to the leading of the Holy Spirit.

Any plan that we follow we MUST be prepared to change as soon as the Lord requires it of us. To change our plan does not mean defeat. To stick to the old plan could. The basic secret is to constantly keep in touch with the precious Holy Spirit, and don't forget that He is not static but dynamic. The Holy Spirit is always full of surprises.

VI. LET US TAKE A LOOK AT AN EXAMPLE

Pastor James Walker has recently been called to pastor a congregation of 150 people. He has already been with them for nine months and the people have been greatly blessed by his ministry. There is a real warmth of love between pastor and people. The church is situated in a town with 15,000 inhabitants and needs to make a greater impact on the town for the Lord. To add to this, the pastor recently had a dramatic encounter with the Lord during which He said to the pastor, "I am giving to you and to your flock the responsibility of taking the gospel to the people of your town."

If you were Pastor James Walker how would you go about fulfilling this commission from the Lord?

A PRACTICE RUN IN PLANNING!

PLANNING WORKSHEET.

1. Quietly sit in the presence of the Lord and **ask Him to speak to you about your PURPOSE in life**. Ask the following questions and then write down what you feel the Lord says to you.

A. "Dear Lord, what are Your major objectives for my life?
    What do You want me to accomplish? What is my purpose in life?"

It may not be easy initially to fill in this section, but if you will persist and do it a deep sense of purpose and destiny will begin to rise up in you.

B. "Dear Lord, are there any of the objectives that I have so far been following
    that need to be adjusted, totally changed or up-dated?"

C. Write down any other things that you feel the Lord has said to you, even if they appear a little way-out, or even if you don't actually understand what they mean. (These revelations could make a lot of sense in a couple of weeks or months time.)

PLACING A SPECIFIC PROJECT BEFORE THE LORD.

For example, launching of a Bible School, or holding of an evangelistic crusade, or launching cells in your church, or starting a new business, or planning the purchase of or the building of a home, or planning the next year, term or the next five years etc. Settle what your PROJECT is and then do the following:

1. In a few simple sentences place before the Lord the project in which you are going to get involved.

2. Stop praying and listen!
Remember that God speaks in your spirit, often in a spontaneous way, and then what is in your spirit comes up as THOUGHTS in our mind.

3. As soon as these thoughts begin to spontaneously arise in your mind **be sure to write down what you receive from the Lord.**
Remember that our thoughts are not all evil and that God speaks to us in this way.
Write down any Scripture verse, vision or revelation that the Lord may give you.
And now be sure to LISTEN!

Write down in the place provided below what the Lord says to you:

Spend some time **SUMMARISING** what the Lord has said:

ESTABLISH THE OBJECTIVES FOR YOUR LIFE

A. WRITE DOWN WHAT YOU HOPE TO ACCOMPLISH. Be sure to be SPECIFIC!

B. WHERE will it be done?
Clearly state where you intend pursuing these objectives.

C. BY WHEN must you have accomplished these objectives?
In other words, set your **'target dates'**.

	OBJECTIVE	DATE
1		
2		
3		
4		
5		
6		
7		
8		

ESTABLISH OBJECTIVES FOR A PROJECT

NAME PROJECT:	

A. WRITE DOWN WHAT YOU HOPE TO ACCOMPLISH. Be sure to be SPECIFIC!
YOUR OBJECTIVES ARE:

1	
2	
3	
4	
5	
6	
7	
8	
9	
10	

B. WHERE WILL THIS PROJECT TAKE PLACE? State parameters.

C. BY WHEN must you have accomplished your objectives?
Set your '**target dates**'.

Objective:	Date:	Objective:	Date:
1		5	
2		6	
3		7	
4		8	

PLAN YOUR STRATEGY

You will now consider the objectives that you have already written down, one by one. The questions you will need to ask as you consider each objective, are:

1. What already exists?

2. What activities do I need to begin NOW?

OBJECTIVE 1:	
What already exists?	What **activities** do I need to begin NOW?
1	1
2	2
3	3
4	4
5	5
6	6
7	7

OBJECTIVE 2:	
What already exists?	What **activities** do I need to begin NOW?
1	1
2	2
3	3
4	4
5	5
6	6
7	7

OBJECTIVE 3:	
What already exists?	What **activities** do I need to begin NOW?
1	1
2	2
3	3
4	4
5	5
6	6
7	7

OBJECTIVE 4:	
What already exists?	What **activities** do I need to begin NOW?
1	1
2	2
3	3
4	4
5	5
6	6
7	7

OBJECTIVE 5:	
What already exists?	What **activities** do I need to begin NOW?

Each objective must be processed as the above.

ADD A TIME ELEMENT TO EACH OF THE ACTIVITIES

1. Place a TARGET DATE next to each activity.

	LIST ACTIVITY FROM PW 5 BY NAME OR NUMBER	TARGET DATE
1		
2		
3		
4		
5		
6		
7		
8		
9		
10		
11		
12		
13		
14		

Continue on reverse side of paper.

2. With the use of your DIARY, a CALENDAR or a YEAR PLANNER begin to document the dates you have now set.

[Be sure also to clearly mark in you DIARY or YEAR PLANNER, the dates of all important events like your Annual Convention, all school holidays, etc., and then start to write in your specific target dates.]

MARSHALL YOUR RESOURCES

A. LIST RESOURCES AVAILABLE NOW:

1. **MANPOWER** RESOURCES [Names or groups of people]

2. **MONEY** RESOURCES

3. **OTHER** RESOURCES

B. ESTIMATE RESOURCES NEEDED TO ACCOMPLISH OBJECTIVES:

C. LIST IMMEDIATE ACTION NECESSARY TO PROVIDE NEEDED RESOURCES

ADDITIONAL FINANCIAL WORKSHEET

If your project is going to involve considerable expense, then it is essential to approach this matter in a far more professional manner. It is therefore advisable that you enlist the assistance of your accountant or bookkeeper or Bank Manager, so that you may be able to handle the financial side of your project with excellence. This cannot be over emphasised!

He could assist you in carefully assessing:

1. What kind of expenses you could anticipate

2. What amount of finances you have immediately available

3. What sources of income you can draw on

4. What kind of income your project could possible generate.

Remember that any project launched that does not get off the ground because of lack of finances tends to bring discredit on the kingdom of God. Therefore it is imperative that you plan your finances thoroughly and responsibly. The assistance of those more qualified is always helpful, so long as they are also able to appreciate the importance of the element of FAITH.

Set dates NOW for appointments with your financial advisors:

Name:		Date:	
Name:		Date:	

3. ORGANIZING

3. ORGANIZING

CONTENTS

I. DEFINITION of ORGANIZING

Definition
Key Words

II. The IMPORTANCE of ORGANIZING

Its BIBLICAL basis
Its LOGICAL basis

III. BASICS of ORGANIZING

IV. THE METHOD TO FOLLOW WHEN ORGANIZING

V. TWO MAJOR ASPECTS OF ORGANIZING

JOB DESCRIPTIONS

DELEGATION

VI. INTERPERSONAL RELATIONSHIPS

VII. AN EXERCISE IN ORGANIZING

3. ORGANIZING

I. A DEFINITION OF ORGANIZING

Here we will endeavour to answer the question, **WHAT IS ORGANIZING?**

DICTIONARY: "Organizing is
>   to give a definite structure to;
>   to arrange systematically; to order;
>   to bring together or form as a whole or combination, for a common objective;
>   to systematically unite a number of individuals for some end or work."

DEFINITIONS: Dr Howard Hendricks says,

ORGANIZING IS THE PROCESS OF PLACING PEOPLE INTO A STRUCTURE TO ACCOMPLISH OBJECTIVES

Louis A. Allen, in The Allen Management Action Program says,

ORGANIZING IS THE WORK A MANAGER PERFORMS TO IDENTIFY AND GROUP THE WORK TO BE   DONE SO THAT IT CAN BE PERFORMED EFFECTIVELY BY PEOPLE

From these definitions it can be seen that ORGANIZING includes a variety of activities. Let us focus in on FOUR of these:

1.   "TO GIVE A DEFINITE STRUCTURE TO.."

Most people see structure in terms of an ORGANIZATIONAL CHART.

Every combined effort needs some form of STRUCTURE.

As a skyscraper needs a very strong structure to reinforce it to be able to stand up to strong winds and storms, so every team, business or committee also needs some form of structure.

This concept of ORGANIZATION or STRUCTURE reaches its zenith

in an ARMY!

> Brigadiers,
> Colonels,
> Commandants,
> Majors,
> Captains,
> Lieutenants,
> Regimental Sergeant Majors,
> Sergeants,
> Corporals and
> Troops.

In a UNIVERSITY!

> Deans,
> Professors,
> Lecturers etc.

In a GOVERNMENT!

> Prime Minister,
> Ministers,
> Senators,
> Members of Parliament,
> Directors etc.

ALL OF THESE STRUCTURES HAVE AS THEIR BASE THE DIVINE ORDER THAT GOD GIVES US IN HIS WORD! GOD IS A GOD OF ORDER!

This is evident from....

A. The Order among the heavenly beings whom God has created.

Archangels, cherubim, seraphim, angels etc.

B. The Divine order God has established in the FAMILY UNIT.

The father is the head of the home, and the children relate to him through the mother.

C. The Divine order God established in the Old Testament PRIESTHOOD

High Priest, Priests and Levites.

D. The Divine order God established in the New Testament CHURCH.

Apostles, prophets, evangelists, pastors, teachers, elders, deacons etc.

Although a man's office may give to him a certain level of authority, God still sees all men as being equal.

Our definition further suggests that ORGANIZING INCLUDES.....

**2.   "THE PLACING OF PEOPLE....or
        THE UNITING OF A NUMBER OF INDIVIDUALS."**

This gives **dignity, direction and distinctiveness** to different people.

It also suggests TEAMWORK or UNITY of action.

**3.   "TO ACCOMPLISH OBJECTIVES..."
        "FOR A COMMON OBJECTIVE....."
        "FOR SOME END OR WORK......."**

Organizing involves placing common OBJECTIVES before a group of people so that they can unitedly strive toward these objectives.

A well organized and motivated team can always accomplish more than an individual.

An outstanding Biblical illustration of this is the concept of the church as the BODY OF CHRIST. It has many parts which together form an incredible unity that can accomplish

objectives as broad as taking the gospel to the whole world!
Romans 12:4 - 5

> 4 *"For as we have many members in one body, but all the members do not have the same function,*
> 5 *so we, being many, are one body in Christ, and individually members of one another."*

Every organization must PRE-DETERMINE ITS OBJECTIVES and then constantly keep these objectives before it. The more people they can involve in the pursuit of these objectives the sooner they will reach them. There is often an optimum number of people needed for a given task.

Organizing without clearly defined objectives is a waste of time. It's like going to university and studying any subject you like without pursuing a specific degree or diploma that will equip you for some useful task.

4.   "TO IDENTIFY AND GROUP THE WORK TO BE DONE..".

This is essential to the smooth running of any organization.

It is in this area that the church often flounders. Let me illustrate this :

A certain church begins to grow! As a result it develops various departments to give emphasis to its various objectives. It launches a Youth Department, an Evangelism Department and a Children's Church. This all sounds good until one day they consider the staff situation that has become top-heavy and realise that some changes need to be made. For instance, they now have three secretaries that are not being fully used, and what's more they have three computers and actually only need one. And besides this they have spent so much on printing only to realise that their printing bill is draining them financially. This means that the **time** has come **for the manager to step in and make some needed changes.** He then launches another department, a Printing Department and places one of the other secretaries in this department. In the mean time he sends back one of the leased computers and secures a photostat machine that covers most of their printing needs.

In so doing he groups together the work that needs to be done and organizes it into the correct groupings, where it can be done by those who are more qualified to do that specific kind of work.

This is an on-going responsibility of a manager. It's called ORGANIZING.

SUMMARY

From the above we see that **ORGANIZING IS NOT**....

..... putting people in a box
..... forcing people into a heavy structure
..... restricting the creativity of people.

NO, rather **ORGANIZING IS** ....

..... giving a definite structure to,
..... the placing of people,
..... establishing common objectives and
..... identifying and grouping work to be done.

One thing remains to be said,
ORGANIZING IS A PROCESS WHICH NEVER ENDS AND IS ALWAYS TAKING PLACE!!

II. THE IMPORTANCE OF ORGANIZING

This can be very clearly seen by taking a brief look at the results of not organizing and at the results of organizing.

1.   IF WE DON'T ORGANIZE

* Many things we could do, would be left undone!

This often takes place when a church experiences exceptional growth - important things are neglected. Acts 6:1 to 3 is an example of this. When they realised what was actually happening the church "RE-ORGANIZED" itself.

> Acts 6:1 *"Now in those days, when the number of the disciples was multiplying, there arose a murmuring against the Hebrews by the Hellenists, because their widows were neglected in the daily distribution.*
> *2 Then the twelve summoned the multitude of the disciples and said, "It is not desirable that we should leave the word of God and serve tables.*
> *3 "Therefore, brethren, seek out from among you seven men of good reputation, full of the Holy Spirit and wisdom, whom we may appoint over this business;"*

* Many things are done badly and by people who are not adequately equipped for the task!

In many situations a worker has to be jack of all trades and master of none.
This results in work that does not have the stamp of excellence.
The expression "every man to his trade" applies here.

2. IF WE DO ORGANIZE

* We will be able to accomplish far more!
 - "many hands make light work."

* We will be able to pursue excellence!

* We will be able to involve more people!
 - and this is a Biblical principle, namely to involve all of God's people.

An outstanding modern example of ORGANIZATION is Dr Paul Yonggi Cho.

III. THE BASIC PRINCIPLES OF ORGANIZING

1. ESTABLISH YOUR OBJECTIVES AND PLAN, BEFORE YOU ESTABLISH YOUR STRUCTURE

Always determine what you want to do and how you are going to do it before you set up a big organisation to do it.

NEHEMIAH is a perfect Biblical example of this. God gave to him the task of rebuilding the walls of the city of Jerusalem. Before he ever delegated any of the work he first of all thoroughly inspected the walls and obtained a first hand idea of the project. Then he began to organize accordingly. Nehemiah 2:12 -17.

> *12 "Then I arose in the night, I and a few men with me; I told no one what my God had put in my heart to do at Jerusalem; nor was there any animal with me, except the one on which I rode.*
> *13 And I went out by night through the Valley Gate to the Serpent Well and the Refuse Gate, and viewed the walls of Jerusalem which were broken down and its gates which were burned with fire.*
> *14 Then I went on to the Fountain Gate and to the King's Pool, but there was no room for the animal that was under me to pass.*
> *15 So I went up in the night by the valley, and viewed the wall; then I turned back and entered by the Valley Gate, and so returned.*
> *16 And the officials did not know where I had gone or what I had done; I had not yet told the Jews, the priests, the nobles, the officials, or the others who did the work.*
> *17 Then I said to them, "You see the distress that we are in, how Jerusalem lies waste, and its gates are burned with fire. **Come and let us build** the wall of*

> *Jerusalem, that we may no longer be a reproach.""*

2. BE SURE TO AVOID EXTREMES

Some people when they begin to organise get bitten by the organisation bug and OVER-ORGANIZE. This leads to so much confusion. The person who says, "I'm going to get organized and so I'm going to do it thoroughly", tends to go too far and develops far too many levels in their organizational structure. This in turn brings in so much frustration, because one has to respect all of these levels of authority and this tends to choke up the flow of things.

Then too, to be UNDER-ORGANIZED also results in frustration because one person must then relate to too many on a given level. The following organizational charts represent these two forms of extreme.

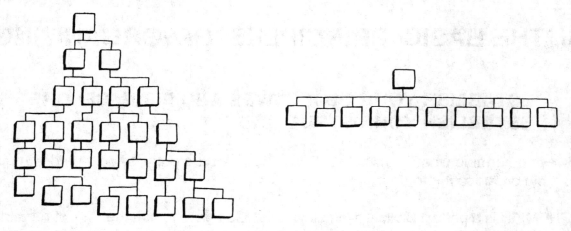

The multi-storied hierarchy.   The flat organization.

3. ORGANIZE AROUND BASIC GIFT OR TRAINING GROUPINGS

Certain people are gifted in different ways and it is essential that they be channelled along the avenue of their gifting if they are to enjoy job satisfaction.

This implies **two important things:**

3.1 ASCERTAINING WHAT THEIR BASIC GIFT IS

God has built into every one of us basic "giftings". These BASIC GIFTS He has distributed to every human being. Paul writing to the Romans lists them for us in Romans 12:6 - 8.

Selwyn Hughes, in is excellent book, DISCOVERING YOUR PLACE IN THE BODY OF CHRIST, (Printed by Marshall, Morgan and Scott. ISBN 0 551 00946 2) lists these SEVEN BASIC GIFTS as follows:

THE SEVEN BASIC GIFTS

LET'S TAKE A LOOK AT WHAT THE BIBLE SAYS!

Romans 12:4 *"For as we have many members in one body, but all the members do not have the same function,*
5 so we, being many, are one body in Christ, and individually members of one another.
6 Having then gifts differing according to the grace that is given to us, let us use them:
[1] *if* **prophecy**, *let us prophesy in proportion to our faith;*
[2] *7. or* **ministry**, *let us use it in our ministering;*
[3] *he who teaches, in* **teaching**;
[4] *8. he who exhorts, in* **exhortation**;
[5] *he who* **gives**, *with liberality;*
[6] *he who* **leads**, *with diligence;*
[7] *he who* **shows mercy**, *with cheerfulness".*

Selwyn Hughes suggests that everyone has been gifted in one or more of the above seven ways. What is important is to be able to ascertain in which areas each person is gifted.

In his book he includes a very interesting test which assists one to understand what is ones basic gifting. In preparing your team for action it would be to your advantage to acquire this book and assist your team members to identify their basic giftings.

We now include, with permission, the test Selwyn Hughes uses, for your convenience.

A CHART TO HELP YOU DISCOVER YOUR BASIC GIFT

Before we focus on a simple but practical exercise to help us identify our basic gift or gifts, here are some important points to consider:

1. Approach the issue in a spirit of prayer and dedication.
When you consider that Paul's listing of the seven basic gifts in Romans 12 follows hard on the heels of his earnest appeal for every Christian to *'present your bodies as a living sacrifice'* it suggests we ought to approach the whole subject in an attitude of prayerful expectancy. Dedication always precedes revelation. When you dedicate your body to God as a living sacrifice then you will discover where you fit into His Body.

2. Recognise that the following practical guide to discovering your basic gift is simply a tool and must not be over-rated.
As you follow the subsequent instructions keep in mind that the statements together with the chart are designed to focus on the inner motivation of your spirit, or the inner drive that God has given you to function in a certain way within His Body. Such an important exercise needs further confirmation by those in your local church or

fellowship. In fact, other Christians often see a gift in us long before we ourselves are aware of it. Discuss the outcome with other believers, particularly with those who know you well and who are mature Christians.

3. Absolute honesty with yourself will give you the most useful result!

4. Write down the answer without trying to produce a desired result!

INSTRUCTIONS

Thirty-five statements follow which may help you discover your basic gift or gifts. Rate yourself with the following scale by writing the appropriate number in the corresponding number square.
Ask yourself, **'Is this statement true in my spiritual life and experience?'**
Then indicate your score in the appropriate number square on the following scale.

Greatly	3
Some	2
Little	1
Not at all	0

After you have completed the test by rating yourself for each of the 35 statements, add the scores in each horizontal row. Record the number in the Total column. Your total score for each row indicates your level of interest in that particular gift. The highest score may lead you to a clearer understanding of the basic spiritual gift or gifts which God has deposited in your life. After you have completed the test fill in the name of each gift in the appropriate column.

										TOTAL	GIFT
		DISCOVERING YOUR BASIC GIFT									
A	1		8		15		22		29		
B	2		9		16		23		30		
C	3		10		17		24		31		
D	4		11		18		25		32		
E	5		12		19		26		33		
F	6		13		20		27		34		
G	7		14		21		28		35		

Greatly	3	Some	2	Little	1	Not at all	0

Ask yourself 'Is this statement true in my spiritual life and experience?'

1. I enjoy presenting God's truth in an inspired and enthusiastic way.

2. I am always ready to overlook my personal comfort in order that the needs of others may be met.

3. I find great delight in explaining the truth within its context.

4. I am able to verbally encourage those who waver and are spiritually troubled.

5. I am able to manage my financial affairs efficiently so that I can give generously to the Lord's work.

6. I find it easy to delegate responsibility and organise others toward spiritual achievement.

7. I readily find myself sympathising with the misfortunes of others.

8. I am conscious of persuasiveness of speech when encouraging people to examine their spiritual motives.

9. I have the knack of making people feel at home.

10. I delight in digging out facts concerning the Bible so that I can pass them on to others.

11. I have a deep concern to encourage people towards spiritual growth and achievement.

12. I am cheerful about giving material assets so that the Lord's work can be furthered.

13. I am able to effectively supervise the activities of others.

14. I enjoy visiting those in hospital, or the shut-in's.

15. I am able to present the Word of God to a congregation of people with clarity, and conviction.

16. I am happy when asked to assist others in the Lord's work, without necessarily being appointed to a leadership position.

17. I am concerned that truth should be presented in a clear fashion with proper

attention to the meaning of words.

18. I am at my best when treating those who are spiritually wounded.

19. I have no problem in joyfully entrusting my assets to others for the work of the ministry.

20. I am able to plan the actions of others with ease and supply them with details which will enable them to work effectively.

21. I have a great concern for those involved in trouble.

22. I find myself preaching for a verdict whenever I present the truths of the Word of God.

23. I delight in providing a gracious haven for guests.

24. I am diligent in my study of the Bible

25. I am able to help those who need counselling over personal problems.

26. I am concerned over the question of financial assistance being available to all sections of the Church.

27. I am deeply sensitive to the need of a smooth running administration so that every phase of activity is carried out decently and in order.

28. I work happily with those who are ignored by the majority.

29. I find that my preaching brings people to a definite point of decision.

30. I enjoy taking the load from key people so that they can put more effort into their own particular task.

31. I am able to explain well how the Bible hangs together.

32. I am acutely aware of the things that hold people back in their spiritual development and long to help them overcome their problems.

33. I am careful with money and continually pray over its proper distribution in the work of the Lord.

34. I know where I am going and am able to take others with me.

35. I am able to relate to others emotionally and am quick to help when help is needed.

Now do four important things:

[1] Add up your totals horizontally.

[2] Write in the names of the gifts.
        Row A. PROPHECY
        Row B. SERVING
        Row C. TEACHING
        Row D. ENCOURAGING / STIMULATING THE FAITH OF OTHERS
        Row E. GIVING
        Row F. LEADING, RULING or CO-ORDINATING
        Row G. SHOWING MERCY / SYMPATHY

[3] Spend a little time meditating about your results!

[4] Discuss your results with someone you know, or with another person in the same room with you.

We need to acquaint ourselves with the meaning and purpose of each of the seven basic gifts. We will be able to flow in our own gift or gifts much more easily if we take time to examine and understand each one.

1. PREACHING / PROPHECY
Public exposition or presenting truth with force, hence the idea of communicating.

2. SERVING / MINISTERING
A deep concern and desire to help other in practical ways.

3. TEACHING
A deep desire to search out and share truths with others.

4. ENCOURAGEMENT / EXHORTING
Stimulating the faith of others.
The ability to come alongside someone who is struggling.

5. GIVING
A high degree of wisdom in relation to material giving.
Possibly also involves the giving of oneself as well.

6. LEADING / RULING / CO-ORDINATING
The ability to be able to preside over the activities of others and be able to co-ordinate other people's labours.

7. SYMPATHY
An ability to be able to show a deep sympathy and understanding towards the misfortunes of others.

As we now return to the subject of ORGANIZING we see that we need to organize people according to their natural giftings and as a result they will find a far greater degree of fulfilment in their work.

Once you have ascertained what their basic gift or gifts are, then the next important task is

3.2 TRAINING THEM IN THE AREA OF THEIR BASIC GIFT OR GIFTS

Teaching may be natural to a person in your team, but without adequate training in the principles of teaching that person may only reach forty percent of their potential as a teacher. We can all, always learn and improve.

Whether it be in the church or in any organization **training is very important.**
If **you** are able to train your team, then DO SO. But, if you are unable, see to it that you appoint someone to train them, either from inside or from outside of your organization. Don't be threatened by people in your team who know more about a given subject than you know. Actually you should expect to have such people in your team. They can be a great help to you. Don't rate them as competing with you but rather as being complementary to you.

Another way of training your team is to arrange for them to attend a course that covers the area in which they need to be trained. Over many years of ministry I have found that training members of my team only assists the team.

The training of your team and leaders is of paramount importance. It is undoubtedly one of the most important keys to success.

4. AVOID FUZZINESS AND GO FOR CLARITY

If you plan well you will begin to see that the overall task can usually be divided in distinct 'bite-size' tasks. It is the manager's responsibility to clearly detail these tasks and then to assign them to the various members of his team.

If a person knows exactly what they are responsible to do, then they can tackle their part of the project with certainty and enthusiasm.

A beautiful Biblical example of this is to be found in the story of NEHEMIAH chapter 3. This entire chapter is given over to explaining how Nehemiah gave to those working on the wall around Jerusalem **specific assignments.** They knew precisely what they were to do and so with confidence could get on with the job.

The application of this to us is clear!

IV. THE METHOD TO FOLLOW

This answers the question, **HOW** must I go about organising?

STEPS IN ORGANIZING

To be able to organize well, you need to do the following:

STEP 1:   LIST AND GROUP ACTIVITIES

To do this you must go back to your Planning Worksheets, [PW - 5] and take note of the ACTIVITIES you wrote down on these Worksheets.

Now work through two very important and practical steps:

A.   LIST THE ACTIVITIES YOU WROTE DOWN DURING YOUR PLANNING ON YOUR FIRST ORGANIZING WORKSHEET: [OW - 1]

ADD any additional activities that may have occurred to you since you worked on your planning.

B.   GROUP THE ACTIVITIES THAT ARE RELATED

As these groups of activities begin to emerge, write down a heading to describe the group. For example, you may have the following headings:

1.   Initial action
2.   Training
3.   Administration
4.   Finance
5.   Printing etc.
6.   Team (Personnel)

Allow the creativity of the Holy Spirit to flow through you!

STEP 2: DRAW UP AN ORGANOGRAM
for your ministry, business or project.

An ORGANOGRAM is also called an **FUNCTIONAL OR ORGANIZATIONAL CHART**.

Such a chart shows HOW an organisation functions.

For example, my local church functions as follows:

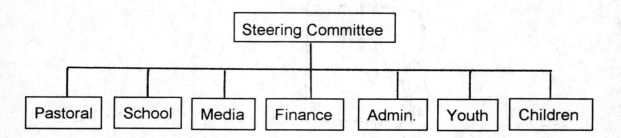

An organogram gives an overview of what the organization looks like and how it functions. When the organization is small, a basic organogram will paint a fairly complete picture, but as it grows, it soon becomes evident that several DEPARTMENTAL or SECTIONAL ORGANOGRAMS are necessary.

PRACTICAL APPLICATION:

Turn now to ORGANIZING WORKSHEET NO 1 [OW - 1] at the end of the section on organization and do a rough draft of an organogram of your life, your work situation, your business, or of whatever aspect of your life you are re-organizing.

STEP 3: LIST NAMES OF THE PEOPLE WHO CAN ASSIST YOU

* List the names of people who are available to help you.

If you are planning the future of your CELL you have every member available to help you. If you are a pastor you most likely have eighty percent of your people waiting to get involved and if you go about it the right way, you will be surprised to see how committed they will be. If you are involved in a business your staff are available to assist you and where necessary you may have to hire additional staff.

* Assess them in terms of STRENGTHS and WEAKNESSES.

We all have strengths and weaknesses. Being involved in the areas of our strengths will always result in job satisfaction. Being forced to operate in the areas of our weaknesses will always bring frustration. However, with adequate training weaknesses can become strengths.

* List the groups of activities they are good at!

Giving them such responsibilities will always bring out the best in them and will result in performance that will result in early achievement of goals and objectives.

STEP 4:   NOW PLACE PEOPLE INTO YOUR ORGANOGRAM

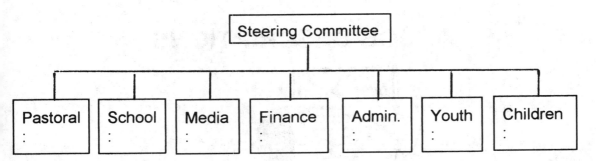

In the above I would place the names of the District Pastors under Pastoral; the School Principal under School; the Manager of the media under Media; the Accountant under Finance; the Administrator under Admin; the Youth Pastor under Youth and the Children's Pastor under the Children.

Remember the definition of Dr Howard Hendricks?

ORGANIZING IS THE PROCESS OF PLACING PEOPLE INTO A STRUCTURE TO ACCOMPLISH OBJECTIVES

PRACTICAL:

Place the names of the people in your organogram who will become the responsible people for the respective tasks.

Once you know WHO is in your organisation and WHERE they fit into the overall scheme, the next step is to define their JOB DESCRIPTIONS.

V. TWO MAJOR ASPECTS OF ORGANIZING

There are two major aspects of organizing:

A.   JOB DESCRIPTION

B.   DELEGATION

A. JOB DESCRIPTIONS

In any organisation JOB DESCRIPTIONS are of vital importance, for in a job description clarity is given regarding the specific responsibility of each person in the organization.

1.   DEFINITION OF A JOB DESCRIPTION

A job description is a document that describes four things:

1.   MY RESPONSIBILITIES
2.   MY AUTHORITY
3.   TO WHOM MUST I LOOK FOR DIRECTION
4.   WHO LOOKS TO ME FOR DIRECTION

1.1   JOB DESCRIPTIONS ARE BIBLICAL!

* God gave a job description to MOSES.   Exodus 3:1 - 10.

* God gave a job description to JOSEPH.   Genesis 37:5 - 11.

* God gave a job description to ABRAHAM.   Genesis 12:1 - 3.

* God gave a job description to THE DISCIPLES.   Matthew 28:19 - 20.

* God gave a job description to THE APOSTLE PAUL.   Acts 26:16 - 19.

*Acts 26:16 'But rise and stand on your feet; for **I have appeared to you for this purpose**, to make you a minister and a witness both of the things which you have seen and of the things which I will yet reveal to you.*
17 'I will deliver you from the Jewish people, as well as from the Gentiles, to whom I now send you,
18 'to open their eyes and to turn them from darkness to light, and from the power of Satan to God, that they may receive forgiveness of sins and an inheritance among those who are sanctified by faith in Me.'
19 "Therefore, King Agrippa, I was not disobedient to the heavenly vision,"

1.2   THERE ARE THREE FOUNDATION STONES TO A JOB DESCRIPTION!

RESPONSIBILITY:	AUTHORITY:	ACCOUNTABILITY:
AN ACTIVITY TO BE INVOLVED IN	THE RIGHT TO CARRY OUT THE RESPONSIBILITY	LIABILITY TO GIVE AN ACCOUNT

2. THE FUNDAMENTALS OF A JOB DESCRIPTION

2.1   A JOB DESCRIPTION SHOULD BE RATED AS A FORMAL AGREEMENT

It is an agreement between an employer and an employee which amounts to a legal contract. Each party agrees to put something into it with a common goal in mind.

In many Christian organisations and in Churches we face the additional problem of people holding honorary positions. These people hold down positions for which they do not receive remuneration and as a result they do not tend to give their full co-operation.

2.1.1 Voluntary workers

Against this backdrop we need to keep in mind that most church workers are volunteers and this situation will never change. We therefore need special grace to enlist the full co-operation of our church people. But HOW?

To obtain full commitment from these voluntary workers will place extra demands on us and we will need to constantly take note of the following:

1. Never take them for granted.

2. Always give them V.I.P. treatment.

3. Major on encouraging them.

4. Rather involve more people who have fewer responsibilities.

5. Be sure to make the road easy for them by giving them adequate training and guidelines on how to do the job.

6. On-the-job training gives then not only the ability to do the job, but also the happiness of working with a person whom they respect - of working with you.

7. Never grumble in front of your workers about other, less committed workers.

8. Show them by your example that you love serving the Lord.

9. Never pick them out publicly or refer to the uncommitted people you have in your team from the pulpit or any other platform.

10. Publicly honour those who do a good job of work.

11. Teach them the Biblical principles of serving the Lord.

12. Remember that some of the seemingly most insignificant often are the most reliable and faithful.

13. Pray for your team - it works wonders.

14. Pray for yourself in this regard, for special ability to be able to lead a team of voluntary workers with God's special grace on you.

15. Tell God in prayer that you believe the two of you can successfully pull it off together.

For these reasons a job description for a voluntary worker needs to be prepared with extra care.

Remember that irrespective of whether this is a job description for a remunerated or voluntary worker, it nevertheless remains a contract.

2.2 HOW TO COMPILE A JOB DESCRIPTION

STEP 1: Suggest that the person reporting to you draws up his own job description as an original draft.

STEP 2: Spend some time together discussing this draft, endeavouring to agree on the contents, adding and deleting whatever is necessary.

STEP 3: Have the final job description typed and filed in the employee's file.

This process could take several discussions but the outcome is vital to your working relationship. These discussions will develop a commitment to and an understanding of what is expected of the person.

It is important to note that the job description can only be viewed as a formal agreement after both you and the person reporting to you have agreed on its specific contents..

3. WRITING A JOB DESCRIPTION

In writing out a job description SIX IMPORTANT POINTS need to be covered:

1. The TITLE
2. The PURPOSE
3. The SCOPE
4. The RESPONSIBILITIES
5. The LEVEL OF AUTHORITY, and
6. The RELATIONSHIPS

3.1 The TITLE

This should explain WHAT the person does and WHAT THIS IS THEIR POSITION in the organisation, e.g: Cell Leader, or Sales Manager or Janitor, etc.

3.2   The PURPOSE

This should be a concise summary of the job. For example, The Cell Leaders purpose is to care for a small group of church people; OR, The Sales Manager should manage the Sales Department; OR The Janitor is to be caretaker of the building.

3.3   The SCOPE

The scope refers to the boundaries or parameters of the job. For example, The Cell Leader is appointed over four or five blocks in a suburb or over a block of flats; OR The Sales Manager is given the responsibility for the sales of a company in a province or in the entire nation; OR The Janitor is responsible only for the buildings or for the grounds as well.

3.4   The RESPONSIBILITIES

Here the specific responsibilities are listed. For the sake a clarity, first the *broadest groupings of responsibilities* should be listed, and then under each of these _detailed responsibilities_, explaining what must be done within that grouping, must be given.
Because each responsibility calls for a degree of authority, the next thing that needs to be described is :

3.5   The LEVELS OF AUTHORITY

In a job description there are usually THREE LEVELS OF AUTHORITY:

Level 1:   ACT

Here the individual can fulfil his responsibility on his own initiative. He does not have to inform his superior nor seek approval for his actions.

Level 2:   ACT AND INFORM

Here the individual can fulfil his responsibility on his own initiative, but he should inform his superior of the results of his actions.

Level 3:   ACT AFTER APPROVAL

Here the individual does not act until approval has been given. He may have to do some research or preliminary planning, for example, of a building, but actions may only be taken after approval.

KEEP IN MIND!

1.   The more experienced a person is, the more authority should be given them TO ACT.

2.   All managers should aim at increasing the number of responsible people who have authority TO ACT.

3.6   WORKING RELATIONSHIPS

In this regard three matters need to be clarified:

1.   To whom do I report?

2.   Who reports directly to me?

3.   With whom must I work closely?

EXAMPLE

JOB DESCRIPTION

NAME:	REV. I. M. A. PREACHER

1. TITLE:	Pastor
2. PURPOSE:	To shepherd a specific flock
3. SCOPE:	suburbs of Brooklyn and Hatfield

4. AREAS OF RESPONSIBILITY:	
A. To shepherd the flock (This is the *broad* responsibility)	
1	Visitation (house and hospital visits.)
2	Counselling.
3	Conduct marriages, dedications and funerals.
4	To promote youth and children's activities.
5	To develop the congregation into a family.
6	To encourage evangelism.
7	To prepare new contacts for membership.
AUTHORITY: Authority **TO ACT**.	
These are *detailed* responsibilities. See 3:4 above.	

B. To develop a leadership team. (A *broad* responsibility.)	
1	Identify potential leaders in his flock.
2	Give them specific training and input.
3	Blend them into a leadership team.
4	Release them into leadership at the appropriate time.
5	Train them to train others.
These five points are the detailed responsibilities.	
AUTHORITY: In points 1, 2, 3 and 5, AUTHORITY TO **ACT**. In point 4, AUTHORITY TO **ACT AND INFORM**.	

98

	C. To run the Children's Church. *(A broad grouping.)*
1	Restructure and appoint additional staff
2	Plan and construct one additional meeting place.

Authority: For 1 and 2: **ACT AFTER APPROVAL**

3	Hold monthly teachers meetings and give them input.
4	Enlist children for evangelism training
5	Organise an annual "Fun Run".
6	Keep up to date records of attendance and offerings.
7	Supervise and supply teaching materials.

These seven points are detailed responsibilities.

AUTHORITY: For points 3 to 7 authority is given **TO ACT**.

---

5. WORKING RELATIONSHIPS:

1	**To whom do I Report?**	
	> To the District Pastor	
2	**Who reports to me?**	
	In terms of SHEPHERDING:	> My Cell Leaders
	In terms of LEADERSHIP DEVELOPMENT	> My Shepherds
	In terms of CHILDREN'S CHURCH	> My Departmental Heads
3	**With whom must I work closely?**	
	> With the rest of the pastoral team	
	> With the Youth Pastor	
	> With the Children's Cell Leaders	

JOB DESCRIPTION

NAME:	

1. TITLE:	
2. PURPOSE:	
3. SCOPE:	

4. AREAS OF RESPONSIBILITY:

A. (This is the *broad* responsibility)

DETAILED RESPONSIBILITY

1	
2	
3	
4	
5	
6	
7	

AUTHORITY:

B. (A *broad* responsibility)

DETAILED RESPONSIBILITIES

1	
2	
3	
4	
5	

AUTHORITY:

C.		(A *broad* responsibility)
DETAILED RESPONSIBILITIES		
1		
2		
3		
4		
5		
6		
7		
AUTHORITY:		

5. WORKING RELATIONSHIPS:	
1	**To whom do I Report?**
2	**Who reports to me?**
3	**With whom must I work closely?**

B. DELEGATION

1. WHAT IS DELEGATION?

The Oxford Dictionary says that to delegate is "to send or commission a person as a deputy or representative, with power to act for another," OR "to entrust or commit authority to another as an agent or deputy."

According to the British Institute of Management, "delegation is the process of entrusting authority and responsibility to others in a way which enables them to make the decision their superior would otherwise make as opposed to merely carrying out the superior's detailed instructions. The subordinate is responsible to his superior for the results he achieves, while the superior in turn is accountable to his own boss for what the subordinate does. Delegation is not the same as abdication. It does not mean giving a man a task, with the minimum of guidance and leaving him to sink or swim".

Howard Hendricks says, "Delegation is the on-going process by which a manager assigns additional responsibilities and authority. These are assigned in such a way that a degree of burden or personal accountability is produced within the individual".

Delegation is not merely assigning routine tasks to anyone who happens to be available.

When delegation is properly done, it will always stir up within the person to whom the task has been delegated a sense of responsibility and a feeling of privilege.

2. WHY DELEGATE ?

2.1 Advantages of delegating

1. Delegating helps you to concentrate on those special aspects of your job that need your personal skill, experience and "know-how".

2. Delegation relieves you of burdens that can be shouldered by others.

3. Delegation builds the morale of your people. It develops their self-confidence AND their ability to assume more responsibility.

4. Delegation helps you to spend more time planning for the future.

5. Delegation will result in an increase of the total amount of work accomplished.

2.2   Results of not delegating

1.   Those who do not delegate are eventually overwhelmed by their jobs. The load becomes far too big. This is particularly true in a growing organisation.

2.   If you do not delegate, you tend to carry all the burdens, and make all the decisions, and so load yourself that there is the possibility of developing an ulcer as well.

3.   If you do not delegate, your people become staid and dormant and as a result they lose their motivation.

2.3   Difficulties of delegating

1.   Delegating involves risk - the risk that the person to whom the task is delegated cannot cope.

2.   Delegating involves a threat, for the person to whom you are delegating may be able to do it better than you are able to do it.

3.   Delegating may tend to make you feel as though you are losing touch with the task. This need not be the case.

4.   Delegating is often avoided because of an attitude that says, "He could never do the job as well as I do it." Only time will tell!

5.   Delegating never releases the manager from carrying the ultimate responsibility.

Delegation is not without setbacks but in the long run it is an essential activity.

3.   THE BIBLICAL BASIS FOR DELEGATING

There are many examples of delegation in the Bible, but the story of MOSES and how he followed the advice of his father in law, Jethro, is perhaps the most outstanding example of all.

This story is recorded in Exodus 18:14 - 27. Jethro saw that Moses was inundated with work. The people were coming to him from morning until night - it was an impossible situation, and so Jethro said,

> *"The thing that thou doest is not good. Thou wilt surely wear away, both thou and this people that are with thee; for the thing is too heavy for thee; thou art not able to perform it thyself alone."*

Jethro then proceeded to give his advice in verses 19 - 23.

> *Exodus 18:19 "Listen now to my voice; I will give you counsel, and God will be with you: Stand before God for the people, so that you may bring the difficulties to God.*
> *20 "And you shall teach them the statutes and the laws, and show them the way in which they must walk and the work they must do.*
> *21 "Moreover you shall select from all the people able men, such as fear God, men of truth, hating covetousness; and place such over them to be rulers of thousands, rulers of hundreds, rulers of fifties, and rulers of tens.*
> *22 "And let them judge the people at all times. Then it will be that every great matter they shall bring to you, but every small matter they themselves shall judge. So it will be easier for you, for they will bear the burden with you.*
> *23 "If you do this thing, and God so commands you, then you will be able to endure, and all this people will also go to their place in peace."*

Moses took his advice and implemented it according to verses 24 to 26, after which Jethro was able to return home (verse 27).

Jethro's suggestion was to place rulers over thousands, over hundreds, over fifties and over tens. They would handle the small cases but the major cases would still be brought to Moses.

This partially solved the problem.

But in Numbers 11 the same problem emerges, especially when the people began to moan and complain. In the circumstances Moses goes so far as to ask God to take his life. (Numbers 11:10 - 15).

The LORD had a solution! God tells Moses to appoint 70 men who are elders to stand with him. God then undertakes to come down personally and take of the spirit that is upon Moses and place it upon these men,

> *"and they shall bear the burden of the people with thee, that thou bear it not thyself alone"* (Numbers 11:16, 17 and 25).

Unless the person to whom the task has been delegated assumes the burden or feels personally responsible, the delegation process cannot take place.

In this case God placed the burden on the 70 elders and in so doing, clearly endorsed the idea of delegation. Yes, it has a definite Biblical base.

This is also true in the New Testament. Not only did Jesus send out the twelve and the seventy, delegating to them His authority, but when He was about to return to heaven, He delegated to His disciples the responsibility of evangelising the entire world.

We may therefore draw the following conclusion:

GOD'S WORD SUPPORTS DELEGATION. GOD IS A DELEGATOR.

4. DELEGATION TECHNIQUES

1. Delegation + motivation = success!
   What baby would learn to walk if every time it stumbled and fell it received a beating?

2. Delegation of responsibility must be accompanied by the delegation of AUTHORITY. Responsibility without authority is very demotivating.

3. Delegation must include FOLLOW-THROUGH.
   Once the task has been delegated, the process has only begun. Initially, you will have to spend some time with the persons to whom the task has been delegated to assist them and, if necessary, walk with them through the process in an attempt to train them. Naturally, once they have been trained they will be able to handle the task without constant attention. But even when they have been trained, the manager always will have to spend some time controlling the system and monitoring the progress.

4. Delegation must avoid all actions and attitudes that negate the delegation process. These include:

   A. Undermining a man's position by giving instructions to men under him.
   B. Insisting on making all the important decisions yourself.
   C. Giving responsibility without giving authority.
   D. Contradicting decisions by a subordinate that are well within the range of his authority.
   E. Deciding an issue for a subordinate when he only came to discuss it with you, etc.

Therefore,

RESPONSIBILITY
+ AUTHORITY
+ MOTIVATION
+ FOLLOW-THROUGH
+ AVOIDANCE OF THAT WHICH NEGATES
_____

= SUCCESSFUL DELEGATION.

5. HOW TO DELEGATE

In working through this section, you will need to make use of the Worksheet D 1.

STEP 1:   PREPARING TO DELEGATE

1.   List your activities.
2.   Prioritise in numerical order.
3.   Is it delegatable ? (Yes/No)

STEP 2:   PEOPLE TO WHOM YOU CAN DELEGATE

1.   Write down their names.
2.   Write down their strengths.
3.   Write down their weaknesses.

STEP 3:   DELEGATE AND SET FOLLOW-THROUGH DATE

1.   Match a person to each assignment.
2.   Record date of delegation.
3.   Record follow-through (report-back) date and DIARISE.

STEP 4:   TRAINING

1.   List delegated activities that need training.
2.   Set a date for training and DIARISE.

DELEGATION WORKSHEET

1. ACTIVITIES:

	LIST YOUR ACTIVITIES:	PRIORITISE:	IS IT DELEGATABLE?
1			
2			
3			
4			
5			
6			
7			
8			
9			
10			

2. ACTUAL DELEGATION AND FOLLOW-THROUGH:

	PERSON TO WHOM DELEGATED:	DATE:	FOLLOW-UP DATE:
1			
2			
3			
4			
5			
6			
7			
8			
9			
10			

STEP 1: LIST ACTIVITIES

1		11	
2		12	
3		13	
4		14	
5		15	
6		16	
7		17	
8		18	
9		19	
10		20	

2. GROUP ACTIVITIES

1		2	

3		4	

DRAW UP YOUR OWN ORGANOGRAM
    A. For your SPECIFIC PROJECT
                   OR
    B. For your BUSINESS, MINISTRY or LIFE

4. LEADING

4. LEADING

CONTENTS

I.   DEFINITION OF LEADING

1.   GOD WORKS THROUGH LEADERS

    1.1   In the Old Testament
    1.2   In the New Testament
    1.3   In Modern Times

II. NATURAL LEADERS VERSUS MANAGER-LEADERS

1.   PHASES OF LEADERSHIP

2.   CHARACTERISTICS OF THE NATURAL LEADER

3.   CHARACTERISTICS OF A MANAGER-LEADER

III. SITUATIONAL LEADERSHIP

1.   DEFINITION OF SITUATIONAL LEADERSHIP

2.   MATURITY OF THE FOLLOWERS OR GROUP

3.   BASIC CONCEPTS OF SITUATIONAL LEADERSHIP

    Style 1: Telling

    Style 2: Selling

    Style 3: Participating

    Style 4: Delegating

4.   APPLICATION OF SITUATIONAL LEADERSHIP

5.   COMPONENTS OF MATURITY

CONTENTS CONTINUED

IV. ESSENTIAL INGREDIENTS OF EFFECTIVE LEADERSHIP

1. VISION

1.1   Clear vision
1.2   Bible men had clear vision
1.3   Some important facts about vision
1.4   Vision is key no. 1 in effective leadership

2. COMMUNICATION

2.1   Seven steps in effective communication

3. MOTIVATION

3.1   Definitions
3.2   What motivates you to serve God?

4. DECISION-MAKING

4.1   General guidelines on decision-making
4.2   Suggested decision-making routine

5. SERVANT-HEARTEDNESS

4. LEADING

I. DEFINITION OF LEADING

"To aspire to leadership is an honourable ambition".
(1 Timothy 3:1, New English Bible)

DICTIONARY:
To "LEAD" is to go before; guide; direct; precede; tend to.
To be a "LEADER" is to be one who leads; chief of a party; principal wheel.

DEFINITION:
"Leading is causing people to take effective action." (Hendricks)

Once you have PLANNED and ORGANISED your situation or project, the next essential step is to stir up your people or your team to take action. The task of motivating your people to action is what we call LEADING.

There is a logical progression :

PLANNING	ORGANISING	LEADING

>>

1. GOD WORKS THROUGH LEADERS

The Bible clearly confirms this fact.   History clearly confirms this fact.

1.1   In the Old Testament

God always worked through leaders!

When God wanted to bring the people of Israel out of Egypt, He first appointed Moses to lead the people out, and then effected their deliverance.

When Moses died on the brink of the promised land, the Lord did not take them across the river Jordan until He had appointed JOSHUA as their leader in the place of Moses.

Before the Lord brought the people back from exile, He first of all saw to it that there was an EZRA and a NEHEMIAH to be their leaders.

And what is more:
WHENEVER THE PEOPLE OF ISRAEL HAD GOOD LEADERSHIP, THEY

EXPERIENCED GOD'S BLESSING.

A good king or prophet who turned their attention and hearts back to God and His Word, saw the nation experiencing God's blessing, His provision, His protection, His plenty and His prosperity.

WHENEVER THE PEOPLE OF ISRAEL HAD BAD LEADERSHIP, THAT LED THEM INTO SIN AND DISOBEDIENCE, THEY BEGAN TO LIVE UNDER THE CURSE.

Time and time again, a wicked king, who did that which was right in his own eyes, would cause the nation to suffer drought or ultimately to become subject to a conquering heathen king.

The stories of the JUDGES in the Book of Judges illustrate this again and again. Generally speaking, the nation was as good or as bad, as strong or as weak as its leaders.

This principle is equally true of the nations of the world today !

1. 2   In the New Testament

God always worked through leaders!

The TWO MAJOR TASKS that Jesus came to perform were:

1.   To redeem us through His DEATH on the cross.
      When HE had accomplished that HE said, *"It is finished . . ."*

2.   To raise up a team of leaders.
      When He had accomplished that HE said,
      "I have finished the work that You gave me to do . . ."

When He returned to heaven He handed over the entire responsibility for the leadership of the church to the apostles. They were to be the human leaders. He had no other plan. He has always chosen to work through leaders.

His leaders are varied. They include the fivefold ministry:
                    Apostles
                    Prophets
                    Evangelists
                    Pastors and
                    Teachers.

In many cases He has given the responsibility of leading local congregations into the hands of ELDERS who may or may not be in the fivefold ministry.

Naturally, He holds these leaders accountable!

1.3   In Modern Times

God still works through leaders.

Every local congregation that experiences the blessing of the Lord either will have a strong leader or leaders. Churches generally do not progress beyond the spiritual level of their leaders. Spiritually dead leaders lead spiritually dead churches. Strong leaders who are spiritually dead strongly lead spiritually dead churches. God even battles to gain entry into such churches.

Praise God that we are living in days when many good, spiritual leaders are emerging who pioneer many virile churches!

*   What is the condition of your local congregation?

*   What quality of leadership do you have in your church?

*   What kind of leader are you? God holds you responsible!

II. NATURAL LEADERS VERSUS MANAGER-LEADERS

LEADERSHIP IS NOT a handsome looking man radiating certain personality traits. It is not a charismatic person who has the ability to sweep people off their feet. That person may have the potential to be a leader and would be able to lead certain people but he would most likely be very far removed from a consistent and effective leader.

LEADERSHIP IS a definite set of activities that can be listed, learned and lived out. In other words, leadership is something that can be studied and applied.

1.   PHASES OF LEADERSHIP

A person usually becomes a leader because he acquired EXPERT ABILITY in a given field.
For example, the expert in Greek becomes an authority and therefore a leader in the field,
OR, the expert in finances automatically gets the top job and his advice is often sought because he is recognised as a leader in that field.

Take for instance the expert motor mechanic. His expertise soon opens up the way for him to be a foreman. *If*, at that stage, *he is prepared to build into his life certain managerial abilities*, he may well be appointed the general manager over several workshops. As a result he graduates from being a "grease-monkey" to being a leader.

The typical evolution is from NATURAL LEADERSHIP because of expertise, into MANAGER-LEADERSHIP. But, of course, he then needs to acquire certain abilities in this new area and aim at becoming an expert in this area.

2.   CHARACTERISTICS OF THE NATURAL LEADER

1.   He continues to operate in the field of his expertise.

2.   He continues to make all the decisions he's the expert !

3.   His decisions often are impetuous and subjective.

4.   He communicates by telling and instructing. He does not listen.

5.   He is always breathing down people's necks to inspect their work.

6.   There tends to be a selfishness about him.
He protects his interests to the neglect of others or of the organisation.
As a result **HE RUNS INTO PROBLEMS**.

7.   His staff becomes restless. They, too, desire to develop into making decisions and managing their own work.

8.   Because he is afraid to release other leaders and give them any authority, he begins to appoint "assistant to" positions and establishes other "blocking devises" such as committees.

9.   As a result morale begins to fade and in turn

    *   production falls, and
    *   expenses rise.

10.   Then good people begin to leave the organisation, because they see the writing on the wall.

However, if this natural manager is prepared to reprogramme himself, he can graduate with reasonable comfort to become a MANAGER-LEADER.

Olan Hendrix in his excellent book MANAGEMENT FOR THE CHRISTIAN WORKER, says in pages 11 and 12,

"Another reason why we neglect this subject [referring to Management] is that our traditional concept of leadership in the church is the *Strong Natural Leader*.

A student came along one time when I was in college, looked at my library such as it was, and said, "Look, all you have is Greek, Hebrew, apologetics and philosophy. Where are your biographies?" I replied, Why do I need them? I'M going to preach." He said, "You need to read biographies." So I went out and bought some biographies and autobiographies. You know, most biographies are written about Strong Natural Leaders. They did not help me. Reading those biographies hindered me. I found myself spending some nights in prayer, asking God to make me one of them. I did not know the term Strong Natural Leader then but I had Wesley, Taylor, Studd, Whitefield, Edwards, Spurgeon and others in mind. I wanted to be like them.

That is bondage. You have to accept yourself as you are. It was like getting out of jail when I awakened one day to discover that God wants me just as I am. I am not talking in a moral sense but in the sense of personality and capacity. God has made me as I am. God has equipped me as I am equipped. He has divided these gifts to every man according to His wisdom. Well, this is wonderful! But how slow we have been to recognise this.

The Strong Natural Leader is often successful - highly successful - *but usually only over a short period of time*. Unless he dies or is displaced, he often becomes his organisation's worst enemy. I was glad to discover that I was not a strong natural leader.

There is an alternative, and *the alternative is the professional leader*, the *scientific leader* or the *developed leader*. I mean, the man that does not have the dominating personality to draw people to himself automatically, to cause them to do what he wants them to do. But instead he is a person who is an ordinary human being like you or me who develops leadership skills and engages in this management work.

Now, I am not concerned with the Strong natural Leader. He seldom attends a leadership conference or reads a management book like this. He feels he does not need to. Ordinary persons like you and me who are in positions of leadership can develop extensive leadership skills."

3.   CHARACTERISTICS OF A MANAGER-LEADER

1.   He develops to the point where he acknowledges the need to develop TEAM MENTALITY. Obviously, he cannot do the entire job by himself. He needs others through whom he can get results.

2. As a result he DELEGATES responsibilities WITH the relevant AUTHORITY to make decisions to carefully-chosen men of his staff.

3. He begins to INVOLVE THEM IN THE PLANNING sessions.

4. He begins to ORGANISE and GROUP THE WORK to be done into logical groupings instead of around personalities.

5. He is careful to develop good, interpersonal relationships with his staff, majoring on COMMUNICATION by both LISTENING and TELLING.

6. He MANAGES BY EXCEPTION. Here the manager handles problems but keeps the greater machine running with the assistance and supervision of his subordinates.

7. At this stage he has reached the more mature position where the needs of the group and the organisation are above his own.

What rating would you give yourself in terms of these two phases :

| |
| |
| |

In what specific areas would you need to make changes soon?

| |
| |
| |
| |
| |
| |
| |

III. SITUATIONAL LEADERSHIP

A variable range of job maturities exists among workers in any work situation.

A successful manager must be able to discern the job maturity level of each individual reporting to him AND be able to adapt accordingly in his relationship to these people, taking cognizance of their different levels of job maturity.

1.   DEFINITION OF SITUATIONAL LEADERSHIP

Situational leadership is based on an interplay of several factors:

1.   The amount of guidance and direction a leader gives.

2.   The amount of support (relationship) a leader provides.

3.   The readiness (maturity level) that followers exhibit in performing a specific task or in pursuing an objective.

2.   MATURITY OF THE FOLLOWERS OR GROUP

Maturity is defined as the ability and willingness of a person to take responsibility for directing his personal behaviour.

Different people obviously are at different levels of maturity but these different levels should be taken into consideration only in terms of a specific task to be performed.

For example, a pastor may be excellent in visiting his flock but casual about completing the paperwork necessary for report back to his superior. Therefore it is appropriate for his superior to leave him alone in terms of visitation but to supervise him closely in terms of his paperwork until he can effectively cope with that area as well.

3.   BASIC CONCEPTS OF SITUATIONAL LEADERSHIP

According to situational leadership, there is NO ONE BEST WAY to lead people. The leadership style a person should use with an individual or a group depends on the maturity level of the people the leader is endeavouring to lead. This is illustrated as follows:

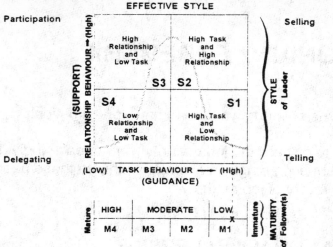

EFFECTIVE STYLE

Four Leadership Styles are related to Four Levels of Maturity

In this diagram FOUR LEADERSHIP STYLES are related to FOUR LEVELS OF MATURITY.

STYLE 1: TELLING

This is a HIGH TASK and LOW RELATIONSHIP leadership style in which the leader TELLS the subordinate what to do, when to do it, where to do it, and how to do it.

This line of leadership is adopted because the task force (the subordinates) are at a LOW MATURITY level (M1).

People at a low maturity level are defined as those who are unwilling and unable to take responsibility to do something through lack of confidence or competence.

STYLE 2: SELLING

This leadership style is to be used with people who have a LOW to MODERATE MATURITY level. This class of person is willing, but unable to take responsibility (M2). They are confident but lack skills AT THIS TIME and therefore direction is still needed. Through two-way communication and explanation the leader tries to "sell" to the follower the desired patterns of behaviour and action.

Followers at this maturity level usually will go along with a decision if they understand the reason for the decision and if their leaders also offer some help and direction.

STYLE 3: PARTICIPATING

Participating is for people who have a MODERATE to HIGH maturity level. Often people at this level are ABLE, BUT UNWILLING to do what their leader wants. Usually their unwillingness is due to a lack of confidence or a sense of insecurity.

The best leadership style for this situation is the PARTICIPATING style. This style opens the door for two-way communication and active listening and thus supports the follower's efforts to use the ability he already has.

This is a supportive, non-directive participating style.

STYLE 4: DELEGATING

This style of leadership is to be used for people who have a HIGH MATURITY level. People at this level are able and willing to take responsibility. Thus a low profile DELEGATING style that provides little direction or support has the highest probability of being effective.

Although the leader still may be involved in identifying problems, the responsibility for carrying out the plans is given to these mature followers. As a result, they are permitted to run the show and decide on the how, when and where.

This kind of follower has needs that tends more and more towards autonomy.

4. APPLICATION OF SITUATIONAL LEADERSHIP

The KEY to situational leadership is to ASSESS THE MATURITY LEVEL of the follower and to relate to him as the model suggests or prescribes.

Implicit in situational leadership is the idea that THE LEADER SHOULD HELP HIS FOLLOWERS GROW in maturity as far as they are able and willing to go.

Regardless of the maturity level of an individual or group, change may occur. Whenever the follower's performance begins to slip, the leader should reassess his maturity level and move backward through the curve, providing appropriate relational support and direction.

5. COMPONENTS OF MATURITY

According to David McLelland's research, achievement-motivated people have certain characteristics in common, including the capability to set high but obtainable goals, the concern for personal achievement rather than the rewards of success and therefore the desire for task-relevant feedback: "How well am I doing?" rather than "How much do you like me?"

- - oOo - - -

RESOURCE LIST:
Management of Organizational Behaviour, by Paul Hersley and Ken Blanchard.
Organizational Psychology, by Edgar H. Schein.
The Achievement Motive, by David C. McLelland.

IV. ESSENTIAL INGREDIENTS OF EFFECTIVE LEADERSHIP

1.   VISION

VISION has been called the KEY TO ACHIEVEMENT! Without it, confusion reigns. With it, the future is filled with excitement. The Bible says, (Proverbs 29:18)

"Where there is NO VISION the people perish".

Another translation puts it this way, *"Where there is no REVELATION or WORD FROM GOD, the people LIVE CARELESSLY". "Living carelessly"* means that they live recklessly, unlawfully and unrestrained. This verse suggests several things:

* God wants to speak to us.
* We can hear from God.
* God has a revelation for us.
* God has a special plan for each of our lives.
* Failure to know His plan for our lives results in our living a lifestyle that lacks purpose. It could end in living recklessly.
* Knowing God's plan for our lives will give us direction.
* His direction in our lives will cause us to become people of destiny.

Many adults have no vision for their lives. Many children, by the time they reach school-leaving age, have no vision for their futures. Many pastors have no vision for their lives. Many churches have no vision for their future. Having no purpose in life results in frustration, lack of motivation and a growing sense of futility.

BUT give a man a reason for living, give a man a sense of destiny, and all of a sudden his entire lifestyle is transformed.

1.1   CLEAR VISION

Ralph Mahoney in his Acts magazine, vol. 9, no. 6 says:

"Coming from a background of abstract theological values, we who are preachers frequently have a lot of illogically structured concepts. We express ourselves in AMBIGUOUS TERMS that have broad definitions, meanings and interpretations. When someone asks what OUR GOAL IN LIFE is, we say, "My goal is to glorify God." Doesn't that sound spiritual? Doesn't that sound wonderful ? How many of you realise that it is a totally ambiguous statement, especially to the average men in the street? His response would be, "What's that clown talking about ?"

If I were to ask you to define what it means "to glorify God", I most likely would get as many answers as there are readers. There is no precision to a statement like that.

I agree with this statement. We need clarity of vision. If we fail to come to this clarity, then the modern proverb will be true of us: "Blessed is he that runneth about in circles continually, for he shall be called a BIG WHEEL". Without clarity of vision we will virtually be visionless.

God certainly didn't plan it that way.

1.2   BIBLE MEN HAD CLEAR VISION

A brief survey of the Bible soon reveals this.

A.   JOSEPH received the vision for his life in two dreams.

Those dreams certainly influenced his thinking and his planning. In a word, this vision that he received at the tender age of seventeen made it clear that he was to become a ruler among men. His father, mother and brothers one day would bow down and serve him.

When he shared his vision, he was rebuked and hated for it. (Genesis 37:8, 10). People still respond similarly to visions today. As a matter of fact, sharing your vision can get you into deep trouble.

B.   MOSES was given a vision for his life at the burning bush.

C.   ABRAHAM was given a vision for his life by God showing him two important pictures:

* God showed him the sand upon the sea shore
* God showed him the stars in the heavens

and declared that his offspring would be as plentiful as the sand and the stars.

127

D.   PAUL was given a clear-cut vision by the Lord in Acts 9:15.

Later on, in Acts 26:19 Paul says to King Agrippa,
"I was not disobedient to the heavenly vision."

Vision is extremely important. We need to learn from these Biblical examples.

1.3 SOME IMPORTANT FACTS ABOUT VISION

A.   Vision Must Be Divinely Initiated

A true vision must have a divinely initiated purpose, that comes from God, to your spirit. It may not come through a dream or a blinding light; it usually comes by way of a deep conviction from God that there are certain things He wants you to accomplish. Often a sense of destiny comes with it!

What do you feel is the most important thing the Lord wants you to accomplish in your life?

| |
| |
| |
| |

B.   Vision Will Be Tested

The vision God gave to Joseph went through years of testing; testing that seemed as though it would permanently block the vision from ever being fulfilled.

David, anointed to be king went through untold testings before the vision was fulfilled.

People will test your vision, question your vision and try and convince you that it is not from God. You had better make sure that it is from God, and if you are certain that it is from God you must ensure that no one sidetracks you from pouring your everything into it.

C.   Vision Has its Limits

When the Lord communicates His vision to us, it is so easy to presume that it includes certain things that others are doing, but that may not be in the mind of God.

For instance, a local church may be sovereignly blessed and anointed by God. As a result it may develop into a mega-church. Now, because many mega-churches have a television ministry, this particular church automatically could gravitate in this direction but in the process go beyond the limits that God has planned for it.

Stay within the limits of the vision God has given to you !

D. Vision Needs to Be Incubated

Once a person has received a vision from the Lord an instinctive desire to run ahead with the vision so often begins to control that person. This often leads him into trouble. One needs to be able to discern between zeal and impatience.

Incubating the vision is essential to it being planted deeply into our spirits. We incubate a vision through times of fasting, prayer and meditation. As we meditate on it in openness to the Holy Spirit, He begins to clarify for us the details, the strategy, the timing and the people who are to assist us in implementing and fulfilling the vision. This phase of the vision also will protect us from beginning in the Spirit and then slipping over to the flesh.

Yonggi Cho says that the impartation of a vision is like fertilizing an egg. The hen must sit on it and brood over it until it breaks forth in an expression of life.

Everybody knows Genesis 1:1, but verse 2 says,

> "And the earth was without form and void; and darkness was upon the face of the deep and the Spirit of God was hovering (brooded) over the face of the waters".

God had a vision for His world, and it was brought forth by the Spirit of God brooding over the darkness that was upon the face of the deep and out of it burst forth the great creation that God had visualised.

Brood! Brood! And brood some more! By the power of the Holy Spirit something wonderful will be birthed.

E. The Vision Needs to Be Written

Habakkuk 2:2 - 3 says,

> "Then the Lord answered me and said: WRITE THE VISION, and make it plain on tablets . . .".

In committing the vision to writing we are doing several things :

a. We are expressing it.
b. We are "concretising" it. The devil will do his best to sidetrack us from the original details of the vision; writing it down helps us to keep to the original vision.
c. We are preparing ourselves to share it with others.
d   It helps to clarify the vision. *"Write . . . and make it plain"*.

Write down your vision!

F.   We Are Then to Run with the Vision

Habakkuk then goes on to show WHY it needs to be written. He says,

> *"Write the vision, and make it plain on tablets THAT HE MAY RUN WHO READS IT . . .".*

The moment you share the vision you have received from the Lord, the Lord will begin to call certain people to assist you in the fulfilment of the vision.

A "lone ranger" will not accomplish much. But a man who has a vision AND who can organise others by giving to them clearly-defined responsibilities and tasks to perform, that support such a vision, will soon be blessed with people who will "RUN WITH THE VISION".

A man who can build a team and impart a common vision, can do a significant work in the Lord's kingdom. The Bible speaks of ONE putting A THOUSAND to flight and TWO putting TEN THOUSAND to flight. That's quite a jump! Think about the following for a moment!

1 puts to flight	1,000
2 puts to flight	10,000
What about 4 putting to flight	100,000?
8 putting to flight	1,000,000?
16 putting to flight	10,000,000?
And 32 putting to flight	100,000,000?

One thing that these figures show us is that God honours unity!

Not only will sharing your vision result in people being willing to run with the vision in terms of working alongside of you, but others will be called by God to SUPPORT the vision FINANCIALLY.

One thing remains to be said: God requires from us that we use the resources He provides with wisdom and integrity.

1.4   VISION IS KEY NO. 1 IN EFFECTIVE LEADERSHIP!

2. COMMUNICATION

Once a vision has been received from the Lord, it is of the utmost importance that it be correctly COMMUNICATED. It is therefore vitally important that a leader should learn the art of communication and consistently use it.

Someone has said, "Communication is the name of the game", and there is definitely some truth in that statement.

Communication is absolutely essential in:

* marriage relationships
* family relationships
* team relationships
* church relationships
* an army
* a factory
* flying an aircraft
* running a nation
* running anything!

Communication therefore cannot be overemphasised.

DEFINITION:

Communicating is the work of a leader whereby he helps people to clearly understand, so that they can effectively complete the specific task that has been given to them.

2.1 Seven steps in effective communication

1. Be sure about what you wish to communicate.

2. Familiarise yourself with the people with whom you are to communicate. Get to knowing them and what makes them "tick"; it will help considerably in the communication process.

3. Be sure to gain their full attention.
   This can be done by focusing in on things that will interest them. Be sure to be human and to handle the present situation before moving to the future.

4. Aim at simplicity. Follow the KISS method: Keep It Simple Stupid!
   Use simple words. Start at a point that is understood by all before communicating the next point step by step in simple language.

5. Make sure they have recorded your communication.
Here we are speaking primarily of having received it; having almost "bought it".

    * To make sure they have "got" it , use repetition.

    * Giving them a written memo to reinforce the verbal communication will help.

6. Ask for feedback and questions. This always lends clarity to all.

7. Major on application.
Applying the communication always will improve the ability to understand and remember it. People tend to forget so soon; application welds it into the memory.

One of the major problem areas in communication is the loss or distortion of the message as it passes from level to level. Therefore direct communication is most effective.

3. MOTIVATION

Have you ever wondered what makes you do the things you do?

Why are you doing the job you are presently employed to do?

How would you go about motivating a group of TEN people who have submitted themselves to your leadership?

3.1 DEFINITIONS:

MOTIVE :

"that which moves or induces a person to act in a certain way."
"Motives are the mainspring of action in people."

MOTIVATION:

"That which creates a willingness to expend energy to achieve a goal or a reward."

3.2 What motivates you to serve God?

Love? Heaven? Prosperity? - What would you say are the greatest motivating factors of your life?

1	
2	
3	
4	

For a man called by God to the ministry perhaps some of the following points should be major motivating factors:

1. His CALL
2. The VISION he has received from the Holy Spirit
3. His DESIRE TO PLEASE GOD placed in his regenerated heart
4. A PASSION for souls
5. The Holy Spirit's friendship, fellowship and daily instructions.

What motivation!

As leaders we are involved in MOTIVATING OTHERS !

"Motivating is the work that a leader does TO ENTHUSE, TO ENCOURAGE and TO ACTIVATE people to action."

ENTHUSE:

To impart enthusiasm to people! An enthusiast is a dreamer or a visionary who stirs up a passion or a zeal or an enthusiasm in a person causing him to take effective action. People generally are inspired by a leader's personality, example and accomplishments.

ENCOURAGE:

This involves awaking people to action by praising them and helping them especially through giving them approval. This is one of the most important , and often neglected, aspects of effective leadership.

ACTIVATE:

This involves getting people going! Getting them involved in DOING the thing!
It includes action, involvement, diligence, energy, work and results.

Some leaders feel that it is quite in order to activate people through compulsion, coercion and fear, if necessary. Perhaps this is going a little too far, but maybe we all need to operate in the fear of the Lord! A little threat over our jobs now and again will help to activate us, but no one likes to live under this kind of pressure.

There are many different THINGS THAT MOTIVATE people and as leaders we need to be aware of these things and use of them to motivate people. The following list of NEEDS, although seemingly very selfish, touch all of our lives.

* Physiological needs
* Safety
* Belonging
* Esteem
* Purpose in life

Our physiological needs are most important.

These are the needs of our physical body, such as food and clothing.

Then there are the safety needs.

These are the needs for housing and protection against violence and violation.

The belonging needs are also very important!

The ideal place for these needs to be met is in the family. The church also provides a sense of belonging, as do cell meetings, sports clubs and a host of other social activities. The team feeling in the work situation can also provide the feeling of belonging.

Generally speaking, most people living in our normal modern-day society have the above three needs met to a greater or lesser degree.

However, when it comes to the following two needs, many people are deeply lacking:

The need for ESTEEM.

Unfortunately the Christian message has tended to add to the problem instead of to the solution. The emphasis on "we are worms" and "we are unworthy servants" has only served to put us down and as a result to make us less productive. I grew up in an environment where we were taught not to praise a person for something they had done well, because it may give them "a swollen head" - it may make them proud!
And yet it is from the Bible that the following expression comes,
"Well done, good and faithful servant; you have been faithful over a few things, I will make you ruler over many things. Enter into the joy of your lord."'
[Matthew 25:23.]

In the Book of the Revelation [chapters 2 and 3], where Jesus addresses the seven Churches, He on several occasions commends them for the good things they had done.

The need to FULFIL OUR PURPOSE IN LIFE!

Many people are purposeless! Such lack of purpose can completely remove the zest for living from us. As a matter of fact, a lack of purpose has often resulted in suicide. But, God has a plan and a purpose for each of our lives. He longs to give each of us a valid reason for living. As we surrender ourselves to the Lord and to the control of His Holy Spirit, we can learn what our purpose is for life!

There is no greater fulfilment than knowing God's purpose for our lives and fulfilling it!

So we see that the needs that God has built into us, He is able to fulfil! In so doing God becomes the greatest of all motivators. Our task is to help others find their purpose for living and as a result fulfil all of their deepest needs.

In the light of who we are and what God has planned for us we can say, CHRISTIAN, STAND TALL! STAND TALL! STAND TALL!

* You are in Christ and Christ is in you!
* You are the child of the King!
* To you has been delegated all authority over the devil!
* You have the mind of Christ!
* All His wisdom is available to you!
* He has a specific purpose for your life!
* He wants to meet all your needs in life!
* He is able to make all grace abound to you so that you can have all sufficiency in all things and so that you can abound in every good work.

HAVING REAL PURPOSE IN LIFE becomes a reality only when we fully submit ourselves to God and abandon our plans in favour of pursuing His plan for our lives. As we do this, we experience the greatest sense of fulfilment, for now we are fulfilling the purpose for which we were born.

On the human level a sense of self-esteem can be cultivated in our lives when managers or people whom we esteem compliment and encourage us. Major on encouraging others!

Finding purpose and esteem in life, in a non-Christian, context tend towards the "self life", whereas in the Christian context they bring us into our full inheritance in Christ.

Leaders should go out of their way to encourage subordinates to experience self esteem and purpose in life through Christ!

Dr Howard Hendricks in an outline on HOW TO MOTIVATE suggests nine ways of motivating:

1. Create a need through personal exposure to reality. In other words, help people understand what their real needs are in contrast to their conscious needs.
2. Feed responsibility to and develop responsibility in your subordinates.
3. Provide encouragement and recognition.
4. Show them how.
5. Convey personal enthusiasm.
6. Intensify interpersonal relations.
7. Dissolve emotional blocks.
8. Demonstrate unconditional love.
9. Believe that God can make them significant people.

4. DECISION-MAKING

All leaders are constantly involved in decision-making. There are generally two types of decision we are involved in :

1. A decision between right and wrong, and
2. A decision that involves making a choice between two or more alternatives.

Most times we are faced with this second type of decision.

Two of the most frustrating things that a subordinate faces is the indecision of his leader and the problem of having a leader who constantly vacillates. That does not mean that a leader will never change his mind. Of course he will, if further information comes to hand that indicates that a decision needs to be changed. Sometimes a subordinate will furnish information that could well result in a decision being changed, but it is of the utmost importance that a situation should not emerge where the "tail wags the dog."

4.1   General guidelines on decision-making

To enable us to make sound decisions we need to note the following :

1. Ask yourself, What am I trying to achieve?
2. Understand that in making a decision you usually will be choosing one of several possible solutions.
3. A decision should be seen as a satisfactory solution and not as an ideal solution.
4. Remember that making a satisfactory decision is better than making no decision at all.
5. Be sure to communicate your decision clearly to those whom it will affect.

DEFINITION:

DECISION-MAKING IS THE TASK OF A LEADER TO ARRIVE AT A CONCLUSION SO THAT PEOPLE CAN ACT ACCORDINGLY.

There are two ways of making a decision :

1. One made on the spur of the moment!
    These can often be right but they can also be wrong.
    Decisions should involve a knowledge of as many of the facts as possible.

2. Enlightened and judicious decisions.
    These are made with a full knowledge of the facts, and after careful consideration.

4.2   A suggested decision-making routine

1.   Clearly assess the problem.
2.   Gather all the facts.
3.   Endeavour to identify the "real" problem.
4.   List the alternatives.
5.   Opt for the "best" solution.
6.   Initiate action.

Christian leaders have the added advantage of the help of the Holy Spirit in making decisions and when we really ask Him for wisdom, He certainly gives it. (James 1:5)

If you are having difficulty in making decisions perhaps you need to take a good, long look at the subject of "Hearing God's Voice." To be able to hear from God is essential in the decision-making process.

5.   SERVANT-HEARTEDNESS

Jesus, the greatest leader of all time, said, *"I am among you as one who serves."* The servant-heartedness of Jesus won Him a place in the hearts of the people. Although He was God He humbled Himself, taking on Himself the form of a servant.

Perhaps one of the clearest examples of this can be seen in the washing of the disciples' feet in John 13.

Many leaders are unable to humble themselves to become servants. To many, humbling themselves would be a threat to their leadership role, but of course this is true only if the person is insecure and uncertain of his position.

Jesus was totally secure in His position ! This is the clear implication of John 13:3 - 5:

"Jesus, KNOWING
1.   *that the Father had given all things into His hands,*
2.   *and that He had come from God,*
3.   *and was going to God;*
rose from supper and laid aside His garments, took a towel, and girded Himself. After that, He poured water into a basin, and began to wash the disciples feet, and to wipe them with the towel . . ."

Here, the God of eternity, the greatest Leader of all time, because He knew who He was, where He had come from, and where He was going, found it completely comfortable to change roles. The Master became a Servant!

And in addition we hear Him say,
"For I have given you an example, that you should do as I have done to you."
(John 13:15).

This is a call to SERVANT-HEARTEDNESS.

The New Testament has a lot to say about this subject and presents servant-hood as a stepping-stone to greatness.

Matthew 20:27: *"And whoever desires to be first among you, let him be your slave."*

Matthew 23:11: *"But he who is greatest among you shall be your servant."*

Philippians 2:7: *"(Jesus) made Himself of no reputation, taking the form of a servant, and coming in the likeness of men."*

One of the characteristics of servant-hood is FAITHFULNESS.

Matthew 25:21:
"And the Lord said unto him, 'Well done, thou good and faithful servant: thou has been FAITHFUL OVER A FEW THINGS, I will make thee ruler over many things: enter thou into the joy of thy lord.'"

In a word, to be servant-hearted is to be like Jesus.

Servant-heartedness is a fundamental ingredient of leadership.

5. MANAGING

5. MANAGING

CONTENTS

I. A DEFINITION OF MANAGING

    1.   JESUS AND MANAGING

    2.   THE HOLY SPIRIT IS THE MANAGER

**II. THE IMPORTANCE OF MANAGING
    WHY MANAGE?**

    1.   MANAGING / MONITORING IS PERHAPS THE MOST VITAL LNK IN THE MANAGEMENT CHAIN

    2.   MANAGING HELPS US TO MAINTAIN THE INITIAL MOMENTUM

    3.   MANAGING HELPS US MAKE ANY NECESSARY CHANGES IN TIME

    4.   MANAGING HELPS A MANAGER TO FULFIL A TWOFOLD ROLE

        4.1   Each Level Deals with its Own Problems

    5.   MANAGING INVOLVES CONFRONTATION OF A PROBLEM BEFORE IT BECOMES A MAJOR ISSUE

        5.1   The Act and Attitude of Confrontation
        5.2   Jesus Taught Us to Confront Problems
        5.3   The Apostle Paul Confronted Peter

III. PRACTICAL GUIDELINES FOR MANAGING

    1.   ESTABLISH EFFECTIVE METHODS FOR OBTAINING REGULAR FEEDBACK

        1.1   How Does One Gather this Information?

    2.   EFFECTIVE REPORT BACK MUST BE RELATED TO JOB DESCRIPTION

CONTENTS

3. CAREFULLY PLAN HOW YOU WISH TO MEASURE YOUR
    RESULTS

    3.1   Jesus is Interested in Results!
    3.2   The Holy Spirit Also is Interested in Results!
    3.3   What Do You Want to Measure?

           3.3.1 The PROGRESS of your PLAN
           3.3.2 The DEVELOPMENT of your PEOPLE

4. MUTUALLY SETTLE WHAT ARE REASONABLE STANDARDS
    OF PERFORMANCE

    4.1   How is this Done?

5. ESTABLISH A METHOD OF MAKING CORRECTIONS

    5.1   How Does One Go About Making Corrections?

A PARENTHESIS ON BRAINSTORMING

1. WHAT TO DO AND HOW IT WORKS

2. FACILITATE YOUR MANAGING

    2.1   The Correct Use of Our Diaries
    2.2   Effective Use of Your Secretary
    2.3   Using Guidelines and Check Lists
    2.4   Regular Meetings with Key People

IV.   MANAGING AS A LIFESTYLE

5. MANAGING

"I want to suggest that you finish what you started to do a year ago, for you were not only the first to propose this idea, but the first to begin doing something about it. Having started the ball rolling so enthusiastically, you should carry this project through to completion just as gladly, giving whatever you can out of whatever you have. Let your enthusiastic idea at the start be equalled by your realistic action now." 2 Cor. 8:10 - 11. (Living Bible.)

I. A DEFINITION OF CONTROLLING OR MANAGING

In this chapter we will use the two words MANAGING and CONTROLLING interchangably!

DICTIONARY: to "CONTROL" is the power to govern, and
a "CONTROLLER" is an officer who checks other officers by a counter register of accounts.

That clearly indicates that controlling involves a person checking others on an established basis.

DEFINITION:

MANAGING OR CONTROLLING IS THE ACTION A MANAGER TAKES TO ASSURE THAT PERFORMANCE CONFORMS TO PLAN.

1. JESUS AND MANAGING

Jesus was not a one-man band, He operated with a team. Sometimes His team consisted of the twelve disciples, and at another time he sent out a team of 70 workers. Jesus constantly followed up on what He sent His disciples out to do.

The sending out of the 70 is documented in detail in Luke 10:1 - 24. The managing aspect of the ministry of Jesus is clearly seen in verses 17 to 20 and in verses 23 - 24.

1. They Reported Back

Luke 10:17 "Then the seventy returned with joy, saying, "Lord, even the demons are subject to us in Your name."

2.   The Reaction of Jesus is the Input He Gives

18 "And He said to them, "I saw Satan fall like lightning from heaven.
19   "Behold, I give you the authority to trample on serpents and scorpions, and over all the power of the enemy, and nothing shall by any means hurt you.
20 "Nevertheless do not rejoice in this, that the spirits are subject to you, but rather rejoice because your names are written in heaven."

3.   The Progress the Team Had Made Brought Jesus Pleasure!

21 "In that hour Jesus rejoiced in the Spirit and said, "I praise You, Father, Lord of heaven and earth, that You have hidden these things from the wise and prudent and revealed them to babes. Even so, Father, for so it seemed good in Your sight.
22 "All things have been delivered to Me by My Father, and no one knows who the Son is but the Father, and who the Father is but the Son, and the one to whom the Son wills to reveal Him."
23 And He turned to His disciples and said privately, "Blessed are the eyes which see the things you see;
24 "for I tell you that many prophets and kings have desired to see what you see, and have not seen it, and to hear what you hear, and have not heard it."

2.   THE HOLY SPIRIT IS THE MANAGER

As the paraclete, the Holy Spirit comes alongside us to monitor our every move constantly. As the executive of God's will, He desires to control our every word, action and attitude so that our lives may bring maximum glory to God.

He also is with us to guard us against wrong actions, attitudes and words.

*   There is no greater friend than the Holy Spirit!

*   There is no better manager in the church than the Holy Spirit!

*   There is no better manager of our personal lives than the precious Holy Spirit! He is the zenith of creativity, the source of power and the mainspring of the gifts and fruit of the Spirit.

*   We cannot live without Him. We need His controlling influence in our lives. He alone can bring us ultimate success.

When we think of the work of CONTROLLING or MANAGING, and that "it insures that performance conforms to plan", we soon discover that the Holy Spirit is constantly busy with the will of God (His plan), and that He is seeing to it constantly that our performance (way of living) conforms to God's plan.

Managing is therefore a Biblical concept!

It is important to note that the managing of the Holy Spirit is not forced on us. On the contrary, it is offered gently and lovingly to our advantage. It is therefore not domination.

Domination often is Satanic in origin and is frequently experienced in the occult. It lasts for a while but ultimately it backfires. Domination emerged strongly in communism.

The control of the Holy Spirit in our lives always brings forth the best in us, making us more productive than we ever could have been in our own strength and wisdom, and produces in us a sense of gratifying fulfilment.

The scripture reference from 2 Corinthians 8:10 - 11, quoted at the beginning of this chapter, clearly demonstrates the idea of managing:

> "I want to suggest that you finish what you started to do a year ago, for you were not only the first to propose this idea, but the first to begin doing something about it. Having started the ball rolling so enthusiastically, you should carry this project through to completion just as gladly, giving whatever you can out of whatever you have. Let your enthusiastic idea at the start be equalled by your realistic action now." 2 Cor. 8:10 - 11. (Living Bible.)

The church at Jerusalem was facing the problem of drought. As a result the church at Corinth launched a programme to assist them, obviously using all sorts of promotions. Enthusiasm was stirred up and there were great expectations. HOWEVER, a year later, when Paul returned to visit them he realised that very little had been accomplished and so he wrote to them, saying that they should revive this project and see it through to completion.

This is a common problem in virtually every area of life. Many individuals launch something and fail to see it through. How many students start a study course and fail to complete it? How many business men launch a thrust and fail to see it through?

IS THIS ONE OF YOUR PROBLEMS?

This all accentuates the need for CONTROLLING and MANAGING!

Having studied the subject of management for years, I have personally come to the conclusion that controlling is undoubtedly the most neglected link in the management chain. It is also interesting to note that most books or manuals give adequate information on the subjects of PLANNING, ORGANISING and LEADING, but when it comes to MANAGING, it seems as though it is inadequately dealt with. Often the PRINCIPLES of managing are stated clearly but the PRACTICALITIES are not presented.

I would like to share some of the practicalities that I have discovered. I fully acknowledge that I am still very much in the learning process and invite you to assist me with any further information you may have on the subject of controlling cr managament.

THE MANAGEMENT TRAIN

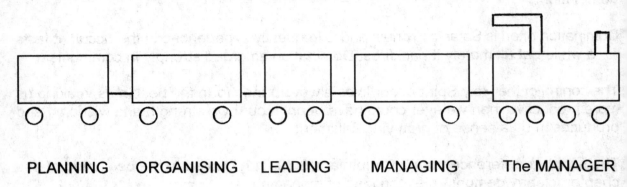

PLANNING   ORGANISING   LEADING   MANAGING   The MANAGER

If the link between the manager and the rest of the train is weak the manager will lose his coaches.

II. THE IMPORTANCE OF MANAGING WHY MANAGE?

1.   MANAGING OR MONITORING IS THE MOST VITAL LINK IN THE MANAGEMENT CHAIN

Controlling holds everything together. Planning, organising and leading are all a wasted exercise if they are not followed up by controlling. A team that has a planner as its leader but an organiser who fails to control, ends up demotivated and frustrated. This, of course, emerges even more clearly when the leader calls on the team to plan the next year and the previous year's planning was not correctly managed.

In a sense MANAGING is the master-link that keeps the contact between the leader and his team.

2.   MANAGING HELPS US TO MAINTAIN THE INITIAL MOMENTUM

A team that spends time planning and organising usually is delighted to be involved in launching the project. The excitement of the planning, the prospect of the goals, together with the motivation of the leader, ignite a flame of expectation, and everyone is enthusiastic about the project. BUT, as the weeks and months slip by and there is little or no feedback, and the dreary reality of hum-drum activity settles over the entire project, it is almost certain to fail.

This can be counteracted by the action of a manager through CONTROLLING.

Through control he can keep the project alive. Through feedback he can maintain the level of enthusiasm and readjust the goals, compliment the team on their successes and perhaps promote even more enthusiasm by establishing A SERIES OF INTERMEDIATE GOALS.

This will do wonders for the team in terms of maintaining the initial momentum.

3. MANAGING HELPS US MAKE ANY NECESSARY CHANGES IN TIME

No manager has the ability to make every decision a perfect decision. No manager has the ability to draw up a plan that never needs to be adjusted. Time will tell as to whether the decision was correct or the plan workable.

There are always many variables. A given plan may work for a specific staff member but it may not work for another.

Managing makes it possible to see, at an early stage, whether a plan needs to be changed. Through accurate feedback a manager is able to make the right adjustments to the plan of action as he compares the actual results with the planned results.

In making adjustments there are two major issues that need to be settled:

A.   WHEN Should the Adjustment Be Made?

If the adjustment is not made soon enough, then valuable time will be wasted and productivity lost. In addition people will become demotivated and frustrated. When these adjustments are made, they are not always popular and therefore there is a tendency to delay the change. This could be detrimental to the whole exercise. A good manager will know WHEN to adjust things, IF he is given accurate feedback in time.

B.   WHAT Adjustment Should Be Made?

To know WHAT adjustments should be made is not easy. There is the tendency among Christian groups to say that if adjustments are made then the leader did not hear from God in the first place - what hope is there that he heard from God in making the adjustment?

Of course, this is a complete misunderstanding of the whole issue of revelation and hearing from God. The Bible says *"we know in part and we prophesy in part."* No one hears one hundred percent accurately ALL THE TIME, and, what is more, conditions change and staff changes, and instructions from God change, especially when wrong attitudes emerge; changes therefore are essential. To illustrate this, we need to take note of what happened in Israel when Israel was involved in battle with the enemy. On one occasion God said, "Go up and fight with them", and on another, He said they were not to go up and fight with them. 2 Samuel 5:17 - 23.

An instruction received from God in November could well be changed in March. The crucial issue is to stay in tune with the Lord all the time.

Changing a plan is not a sign of instability but of progression in God, and of progression in His will for us. Refusal to change often is a sign of spiritual stagnation.

4.   MANAGING HELPS A MANAGER TO FULFIL A TWOFOLD ROLE:

1.   To encourage NORMAL OPERATIONS. (A small part of his time).
2.   To handle PROBLEM AREAS. (A major part of his time).

This is known as MANAGEMENT BY EXCEPTION

This principle has a Biblical basis and is illustrated by the shepherd who leaves the ninety-nine sheep in the security of the fold and goes in pursuit of the one sheep that has gone astray.

If the manager can keep on solving problems in order to keep them down to a minimum, then they will never mount up to the degree where they will jeopardise the normal operation of the entire enterprise.

4.1   Each Level Deals with its Own Problems

Obviously, it is not the responsibility of the Managing-Director to deal with ALL the problems, because problems should be handled on each level. For example, a problem with the mailing list and postage should be handled by the people in that department. If they are unable to settle the matter satisfactorily, they may request help from a superior.

5.   MANAGING INVOLVES CONFRONTATION OF A PROBLEM BEFORE IT BECOMES A MAJOR ISSUE

One of the less enviable tasks of a manager is the task of **confrontation**; unenviable, but often essential. Many people are neither able nor willing to confront a situation. Failure to confront or to be willing to confront actually disqualifies us from leadership. It is an unavoidable part of the responsibility of leadership.
Postponing confrontation indefinitely will turn the problem into an issue.

5.1   The Act and Attitude of Confrontation

It is amazing to see how many people, including many committed Christians, will do anything to avoid confrontation. Many church boards simply refuse to confront sin in the lives of leaders or people in the congregation, and will endlessly play for time. They hope that things will improve or that the problem will evaporate, but that very seldom ever happens. Actually, refusing to confront is to disobey God, or to say that we know better than God.

When a leader fails to confront a problem or a person that should be confronted, he actually becomes party to the problem that sooner or later will backfire on him. Confronting a person involves personally meeting with that person and speaking face to face with him. It also involves being open, honest and firm with him about the problem that has emerged.

When confronting a situation it is very important to **have the right attitude**. To confront is not to affront - to insult openly. Confrontation in an attitude of humility and love always produces the best results. Avoid being paternalistic. Try and be as understanding as possible, for we certainly all make mistakes. The Bible says, *"Let him who thinks he stands take heed lest he fall."* [1 Corinthians 10;12].

Confrontation must always be on a person to person basis. One of the principles in confrontation could be stated as follows: "Always speak to a person about a problem you have with them, before you speak to someone else about the problem you have with the first person".

5.2   Jesus Taught Us to Confront Problems

Our attitude always should be one of recognising that God knows best and that His way of doing things always is best.

Jesus gave us a clear instructions about confronting a problem in Matthew 18:15 - 20. Note the four very clear steps that Jesus says we must follow.

"Moreover if your brother sins against you,

Step 1:   *GO AND TELL HIM HIS FAULT BETWEEN YOU AND HIM ALONE.*
If he hears you, you have gained your brother.
16 "But if he will not hear you,

Step 2:   *TAKE WITH YOU ONE OR TWO MORE,*
" .. that 'by the mouth of two or three witnesses every word may be established.'
17 "And if he refuses to hear them, .. ".

Step 3:   *TELL IT TO THE CHURCH.*
"But if he refuses even to hear the church,

Step 4:   *LET HIM BE TO YOU LIKE A HEATHEN AND A TAX COLLECTOR.*
18 "Assuredly, I say to you, whatever you bind on earth will be bound in heaven, and whatever you loose on earth will be loosed in heaven.
19 "Again I say to you that if two of you agree on earth concerning anything that they ask, it will be done for them by My Father in heaven.
20 "For where two or three are gathered together in My name, I am there in the midst of them."

5.3   The Apostle Paul Confronted Peter

In Galatians 2:11 we read,

> *"But when Peter was come to Antioch, I WITHSTOOD HIM TO THE FACE, because he was to be blamed".*

The following verses give more details with regard to this specific case.

The issue, as far as we are concerned, is that CONFRONTATION HAS A BIBLICAL BASIS.

III. PRACTICAL GUIDELINES FOR MANAGING OR CONTROLLING

1.   ESTABLISH EFFECTIVE METHODS FOR OBTAINING REGULAR FEEDBACK

A manager can control effectively **only if** he is given the correct information through feedback. Feedback should be given as follows:

1.   It must be **regular!**
      That is, daily, weekly, monthly or quarterly reports, or whatever is required in a particular situation.

2.   It must be **specific.**
      Foggy information clouds the issue and leads to for wrong decisions.

3.   It must be **accurate.**
      If a financial report is incorrect, it can soon cause major financial problems.

4.   It must be **succinct and concise.**
      Short, to the point reports are far more effective; nobody reads long, drawn-out reports.

1.1   How Does One Gather this Information?

Today, with the aid of computers, things are made considerably easier. With the right software program a daily cash balance can be obtained with great ease. To some businesses this is absolutely crucial information. Other businesses can be run successfully on the basis of a weekly or a monthly financial statement.
It is essential that you **assess what information or feedback is necessary** for your

business or church to operate efficiently, and then make arrangements to be provided with this information on a regular basis.

Two important matters that should always be controlled in any business are:

1.   You should be sure to work on the basis of a budget and
2.   Capital expenditure should be budgeted, controlled and monitored carefully.

2.   EFFECTIVE REPORT BACK MUST BE RELATED TO JOB DESCRIPTION

In the local church where I am privileged to serve, when we appoint a pastor to our pastoral team, we clearly define his particular responsibilities. Many of our pastors carry a THREEFOLD RESPONSIBILITY:

1.   Shepherd the flock they oversee.

2.   Identify and raise up leaders whom they can release into the team that works with them,

3.   Handle a specific area of responsibility such as the Media, Follow-up, Children's Church, the Youth, the baptismal candidates, etc.

It therefore would be logical to ask them to report on each of the three responsibilities they carry:

PASTOR'S REPORT

Pastor's Name:		Month:	

1. SHEPHERDING:

a.	Number of members	
b.	Number of counselling appointments:	
c.	Number of visitations:	
d.	Led anyone to the Lord?	
e.	Prayed for any for healing / baptism?	
f.	Any in hospital?	
g.	Any marriages, deaths, births?	
h.	Any applications for membership?	
i.	Any resignations / removals?	
j.	Anyone moving out of town?	
k.	Any contact with other pastors in city ?	
l.	Anything else you'd like to report ?	

2. LEADERSHIP TEAM:

a. How many on your team?	
b. Did you meet with your leaders this month?	
c. Any problems ?	
d. Any added to your "potentials" list ?	
e. Do you have a specific plan of action ?	

3. SPECIFIC RESPONSIBILITY:
What responsibility?

Report:

In summary:
1. Effective feedback methods are essential for effective Management!
2. Effective reportback must be related to job description!

3. CAREFULLY PLAN HOW YOU WISH TO MEASURE YOUR RESULTS

This is a matter of major importance, and deserves very careful attention and must not be left until a satisfactory measuring method has been established.
THIS POINT CANNOT BE EMPHASISED ENOUGH!
It is precisely at this point that many churches, ministries and Christian organisations have missed the boat completely and have settled for mediocrity. Don't allow this to happen to you !

One of the reasons why Christians tend to miss it at this point is because of a basic attitude that says, "We have not been called to be successful but to be faithful," or "I must do only what my hand finds to do and I must leave the results to God."

This crippling attitude often is the father of laziness and lack of motivation. Jesus said that we are to go into all the world to make disciples of all nations, but this careless attitude mentioned above won't even take us into our neighbourhoods. Quite frankly, it is an attempted dodge used to release us from our responsibility to WORK and DO the will of God. Jesus Himself said, *"I must work the works of Him that sent me, while it is day; the night comes when no man can work."* (John 9:4).

3.1 Jesus is Interested in Results!

The Living Bible says: *"And He called his twelve disciples together and sent them out two by two, with power to cast out demons . . . The apostle now returned to Jesus from their tour and told Him all they had done and what they had said to the people they had visited."* Mark 6:7,30. Obviously Jesus was interested in the results of their trip.

3.2 The Holy Spirit is Also Interested in Results!

That is why He recorded for us how many were added to the church on the day of Pentecost. That is why He recorded for us the fact that in a short period of time the church had grown to 5000 people.
Thereafter, in the Acts of the Apostles many references to their growth and to their growth rate are recorded. Check out the words "added", "multiplied" and "increased". e.g.: Acts 2:41; 2:47; 4:4; 5:14; 11:24; 6:1,7; 9:31; and 16:5.
This is clear evidence that the Holy Spirit is interested in results!

Acts 2:41 "Then those who gladly received his word were baptized; and that day *about three thousand souls were **added** to them."*

*Acts 2:47 "praising God and having favor with all the people. And the Lord **added** to the church daily those who were being saved."*

*Acts 4:4 "However, **many** of those who heard the word **believed;** and the number of the men came to be about **five thousand**."*

*Acts 5:14 "And believers were **increasingly added** to the Lord, **multitudes** of both men and women,"*

*Acts 6:1 "Now in those days, when the number of the disciples was **multiplying,** there arose a murmuring against the Hebrews by the Hellenists, because their widows were neglected in the daily distribution.*

*7 And the word of God spread, and **the number of the disciples multiplied greatly** in Jerusalem, and **a great many of the priests were obedient to the faith**."*

*Acts 9:31 "Then the churches throughout all Judea, Galilee, and Samaria had peace and were edified. And walking in the fear of the Lord and in the comfort of the Holy Spirit, they were **multiplied**."*

*Acts 11:24 "For he was a good man, full of the Holy Spirit and of faith. And **a great many people were added** to the Lord."*

*Acts 16:5 "So the churches were strengthened in the faith, and **increased in number daily**."*

These Scripture references are clear evidence of the Holy Spirit's interest in results.

A very important question that needs to be answered is:

3.3   What Do You Want to Measure?

There are two very important things that need to be measured :

*   The PROGRESS of your PLAN, and

*   The DEVELOPMENT of your PEOPLE

3.3.1 The Progress of Your Plan

The constant monitoring of your plan is CONTROLLING, but it is important to determine WHAT you want to monitor or measure. The most commonly used monitoring methods are :

A.   Statistical Reports

This method is used universally. It gives a clear quantitative measurement but not necessarily a qualitative measurement. In accounting it always is best to give both the budgeted and the actual figures by way of comparison. The same is true of any numerical projection.

Statistics help to ascertain to what extent progress has been made in the implementation of a plan.

A word of warning! Statistics can be intimidating, especially to those who are responsible for producing them, but this does not mean that we must do away with statistics.

However, sensitivity in this area is wise.

B.   Written Reports

A written report gives an overview that statistics cannot give. It often exposes the frustrations that a staff member is facing and also reveals the successes that a person has achieved. It can bring interpersonal relationship issues and administrative difficulties into focus that usually can be rectified. It can more easily state WHAT happened and WHY it happened. The advantages of a written report therefore are clear.

There are, however, also disadvantages to written reports:

> * They are time-consuming.
> * Some people have difficulty in reporting effectively.
> * The exercise is futile if the report is not ready and there is no feedback.

Despite these and other disadvantages written reports can be most useful.

C.   Verbal Reports

A face to face or a telephonic verbal report can prove most useful. In a short time a lot can be conveyed AND difficulties can be discussed and handled immediately. Attitudes and emotions often can be picked up more easily in a verbal report. Probing questions that are asked can uncover something that otherwise would have festered for a long time. A verbal report also can produce a feeling of "I'm cared about - he's willing to talk about my problems." This is desirable.

BUT OF COURSE, a written report that is discussed with the reporter can be even more effective. Details of a verbal report may be denied or questioned at a later stage but the written report can be placed on record.

D.   Observation

Spending some time with your staff or helpers in the office or on the job can be very informative. Although it tends to be very subjective, it will provide a lot of information on the morale, team spirit and enthusiasm of your staff. It also will make them feel that you are interested in and concerned about them.

The DANGER of this method could be that they might feel that they are being policed, but of course, that will depend entirely on your approach and attitude.

If you take the following exercise seriously it could well transform your whole way of life and make you far more productive! For your own sake please take it very seriously!

MANAGING WORKSHEET No 1   [MW:1]

1. WHAT KIND OF INFORMATION DO YOU NEED REGULARLY?

1		6	
2		7	
3		8	
4		9	
5		10	

2. FROM WHOM WILL YOU NEED TO GET THIS INFORMATION?

1		6	
2		7	
3		8	
4		9	
5		10	

3. WHAT METHODS CAN YOU EMPLOY TO SECURE THIS INFORMATION?

1	
2	
3	
4	
5	
6	
7	

Asking and answering the above three questions is vitally important to you and your organisation. If you fail to answer these questions and as a result also fail to implement action in this regard, then you might as well give up the idea of being a manager!

THE CRUX OF THE MATTER IS:

* Monitoring and measuring are essential.
* Select the best method for your particular situation.
* Usually you will need to use more than one method.

3.3.2 The DEVELOPMENT of your PEOPLE

This very important area often is completely neglected. It should be given far more attention, especially in Christian circles. One of our goals as Christian leaders is "to present every one fully mature in Christ". We should major on developing our people.

The next logical question to ask is:

HOW CAN WE DEVELOP OUR PEOPLE?

If we take for granted that we are responsible for developing those people who are reporting to us, we can take the following steps to assist them in their development:

1.   Arrange A Personal Interview with Each Person Every Six Months

This interview must not be hurried, it must be free from interruptions, it must not be over structured and should be as relaxed as possible. Ask questions and be a good listener. Do not preach.

* Ask the person for their assessment of their own progress.
* Discuss any improvements or deteriorations.
* Ask for their suggestions in terms of definite steps for improving their weaknesses

AT THE CONCLUSION:

* SUMMARISE the situation: Their development
                                 Their strengths/ weaknesses
                                 Their potential

* SPECIFY your expectations of their improvement and development.

* ASSURE them of your availability and sincere help in any of these areas, and that the interview with them was with a view to their own development.

* THANK them for their support.

2.   Prior to this Interview Ask the Person to Fill in A Personal Progress Form

This form will be the basis of discussion at the interview.
Take a look now at the PROGRESS EVALUATION FORM **[MW:4]** Pages 161 - 164.
This form was drawn up to evaluate the progress of pastors on my pastoral team.
Using this form as a guideline, you would need to draw up a form that is adjusted according to the needs of your organisation.

4.   MUTUALLY SETTLE WHAT ARE REASONABLE STANDARDS OF PERFORMANCE

If a man knows that his superior is happy with ten calls a week, then when he reports twelve calls he has a sense of job satisfaction.

In the secular field establishing such standards is perhaps somewhat easier than in the Christian field. A salesman operates on the basis of the number of calls he makes and the number of orders or on the value of orders he writes up, and this is relatively easy to add up.

Bringing people to spiritual maturity and raising up leaders is not so easy to measure, yet hard work and consistently contacting people certainly produces results even in the spiritual realm. Perhaps it IS a matter of "if we do our part we can expect the Lord to do his part".

Defining OUR PART will assist us in establishing reasonable standards of performance.

4.1   How is this Done?

At this point it is important that there should be interaction between the two parties concerned. Always start with the person reporting to you. Based on their job description ask them to prepare "a first draft" as a "guide for discussion" of activities for which they are responsible.

Ask him to answer the questions:

What are your major responsibilities ?

What standards would you rate as fair standards of performance for your job?
[A pastor may say : 10 visits per week; A salesman may say : 10 calls a day].

Once they have given you their written answer, discuss it with them and then mutually agree on the performance standards to be set. This will assist you in your task of controlling.

5. ESTABLISH A METHOD OF MAKING CORRECTIONS

It is very seldom that people accomplish their goals without ever making any changes in their planning or in their strategy. Circumstances change, staff changes, demands change and therefore we must be prepared to change for the better.

To be immovable, unchangeable or unadjustable can be very dangerous. We constantly should remain open to change and improvement; we must remain flexible.

The apostle Paul was given clear objectives for his life when he met with the Lord on the Damascus road:

"But rise and stand upon thy feet; for I have appeared unto thee FOR THIS PURPOSE, to make thee a minister and a witness both of those things which thou hast seen, and of those things in which I will appear unto thee; Delivering thee from the people, and from the Gentiles, unto whom now I send thee; To open their eyes, and to turn them from darkness to light, and from the power of Satan unto God, and that they may receive forgiveness of sins, and inheritance among them who are sanctified by faith that is in me. Whereupon, O King Agrippa, I WAS NOT DISOBEDIENT unto the heavenly vision." Acts 26:16 - 19.

He never lost sight of these objectives! BUT his plan changed constantly! At times God changed it, and at times circumstances changed it. Remember when certain people vowed to kill Paul and some of his friends helped him to escape? (Acts 23:12 and the following verses). This was an unexpected change of plan.

5.1   How Does One Go About Making Corrections?

When it becomes obvious that a specific plan is not working:

A.   Identify the Problem As Being Distinct From the Symptoms.

A headache could be the result of a stomach disorder. An eye problem could be caused by tension, or by a tumour in the brain. The treatment in each case would be different. To treat the headache without looking for the actual cause will of necessity only be a temporary solution.

We need to identify the cause of the problem, and therefore the actual problem itself, in order to find an answer.

How does one distinguish between the symptom and the problem?
It is best to rate everything as a symptom initially and then, as you consider the factors that could have caused the symptoms, the basic problem will begin to emerge.

B.   Clearly Restate What You Are Trying to Accomplish

For this you need to go back to your objectives and goals and clarify WHAT you have in mind.

For example:
What we have in mind is TO FOLLOW UP ALL WHO RESPOND TO THE ALTAR CALLS IN THE CHURCH SERVICES EFFECTIVELY.

The **SYMPTOM** is that people come to our church and do not get slotted in. They get baptised and we see them for a couple of weeks and then they vanish. Folks who respond to the appeals do not seem to mean business with God. This is the symptom.

IDENTIFYING THE PROBLEM involves getting behind the symptom and realising that the people who respond need friendship and individual attention that will not dry up after ten days.

We therefore need to do something about it.

C. Clearly Determine the Conditions That Must Exist in Any Solution You May Suggest

In other words, any solution we may wish to suggest must include the following:

The people who respond must be

* genuinely befriended;

* walked with for some time and as a result feel wanted and needed;

* accompanied to church or at least be met at church and be given constant personal attention at church

* be shown hospitality in the home of the person befriending them.

THESE ARE SOME OF THE CRITERIA!
Any suggested solutions must meet these criteria.

D. List the Alternative Solutions

This can be done very effectively through BRAINSTORMING, in an atmosphere of total dependence on the Holy Spirit.

E. Select An Alternative Or Alternatives

F. Implement Your Solution

Carefully plan the action steps you will take to implement your new solution. Write it into your planning. Take the necessary steps.

G. Set Dates for Evaluating Your Decision

A PARENTHESIS ON BRAINSTORMING

BRAINSTORMING as Christians, in total dependence on the Holy Spirit, can be a very enlightening and productive exercise.

It can be a very effective way of discovering God's plan for your church, your cell, your home, your business or for many other aspects of your life.

BRAINSTORMING is based on the assumption that, as God gave Solomon wisdom to lead his people into blessing and prosperity, so we too CAN and SHOULD go to Him for His wisdom for ourselves. James 1:5 - 6 assures us that **God's wisdom is available**!

> *James 1:5 "If any of you lacks wisdom, let him ask of God, who gives to all liberally and without reproach, and it will be given to him.*
> *6 But let him ask in faith, with no doubting, for he who doubts is like a wave of the sea driven and tossed by the wind."*

We also have the gift of the **discerning of spirits** to protect us against the enemy and his deception.

BRAINSTORMING, in dependence on the Holy Spirit, provides an ideal situation for the Holy Spirit to birth in us HIS DREAMS AND VISIONS. It also places us, as a group, in a place where we can ask the Holy Spirit to speak to us, and then we can write down what He says to us as a group.

WHAT TO DO AND HOW IT WORKS

1. **Gather a group of selected people who relate to the situation and who can contribute to the brainstorming.**

2. **Ask God for His wisdom and tell Him that you believe that He will impart it to you.**

3. **Explain to those participating how brainstorming works.**

   A. Husbands and wives are to work together as a man-and-wife team.
   B. A specific question to be brainstormed will be asked at the appropriate moment.
   For example:
   [1] "What can we do to improve our follow-up of those who respont to the altar call?"
   [2] What can we do to
   C. When it is asked, discuss it with your partner.

4. **Write down any suggested answers that may occur to you no matter how unimportant you may think they are.**

5. **Follow this up with a "Round Robin" recording of ideas.**

   This involves the following :
   a. The preappointed chairman asks the participants to share their answers and suggestions. This is to be done in an orderly manner, preferably going down the line from person to person.

   THE GOLDEN RULE in brainstorming is:
   "There must be no criticism of any idea shared nor must there be any audible support for any idea shared".
   e.g.: "How ridiculous!" or "Amen ! At last they're getting some sense into their heads."

   b. The chairman will lead by asking the people to share an idea - each person or team sharing only one idea at a time. After each person or team has had the opportunity of sharing one answer or suggestion, the first person will be given an opportunity to share his second suggestion.

   c. These suggestions must be recorded by a scribe on a flip chart or blackboard. As each idea is recorded it is numbered successively and written down in a paraphrased (shortened) form. Do not state "same ideas" unless they have a totally different angle to them.

d. "Piggy-backing" is to be encouraged. In other words, if someone shares an idea that you can add to you, are encouraged to do so.

e. When you run out of ideas and you are offered another turn to speak, all you need to say is "PASS", and the chairman will then pass on to the next person.

f. Be sure to work together as a team. Do not talk out of order. Work quietly together - try not to disturb the folks near you.

g. When there are no more ideas to be recorded the time for evaluation has come.

6. Time for EVALUATION!

a. The chairman reads all the ideas and eliminates any misunderstandings.

b. Vote for items of priority. To do this :

* Pray and thank the Lord for all the ideas He has given.

* Specifically ask Him to show YOU which are the most important ideas.

c. At this point, 5 or 7 small sheets of paper should be given to you. (This number is decided upon by the chairman, depending on how much feedback he wants.)

Draw a small block in the two corners of each page as illustrated:

Item Number
(as per black board)

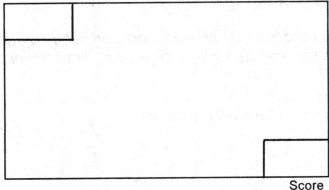

Score

d. Select the SEVEN most important items on the board and write down one item and its relevant number per piece of paper.

e. The chairman must then lead the group in the following SELECTION PROCESS. If you are looking for the SEVEN most important items, do as follows:

(1) Select "most important" and score it "7" and place aside.

(2) Select "least important" and score it "1" and place aside.

From the balance,

(3) Select "most important" and score "6" and put it aside.

(4) Select "least important" and score "2" and put it aside.

From the balance,

(5) Select "most important" and score "5" and put it aside.

(6) Select "least important" and score "3" and put it aside.

(7) The last remaining one is then scored "4".

f. At this point the chairman must COLLECT ALL THE CARDS.

g. He privately must do three things:

(1) Stack the cards according to their item number.

(2) Add up the total scores for each item.

(3) Select the seven items with the highest scores and announce them in terms of priority rating.

If the people heard from God, this will give them a clear idea of what God is saying to the group.

Remember that Proverbs 3:5 and 6 says,

"Trust in the Lord with all thy heart, and lean not unto thy own understanding. In all thy ways acknowledge Him and He shall direct thy paths".

This ends the section on BRAINSTORMING!

6. FACILITATE YOUR CONTROLLING

There are several aids we can use to help us in our controlling. If we will take a little time to think about them and then implement them, they will be of great help to us.

2.1 The Correct Use of Our Diaries

Diaries are not only for recording appointments! We can use them to remind us of tasks that we need to do as well as of tasks we have delegated. All delegated tasks as well as the date on which you should receive feedback should be diarised. It is also very useful to diarise a week before that date and get your secretary to remind the man of the fact that he is due to report back to you within a week.

When involved in our own planning it is most important that we should see to it that all our projections are recorded in terms of their dates and that a date for a week before or a month before also be recorded in order to jog our memories.

We should also diarise all controlling activities regularly so that we do not neglect to control on a regular basis. For example, once we have decided to interview a person reporting to us on a weekly basis, it is vital that we do it on a regular basis. Here our diaries come to our aid. USE YOUR DIARY!

2.2 Effective Use of Your Secretary

Your secretary can be of tremendous help to you, especially in reminding you in good time about deadlines, controlling responsibilities and staff interviews. She also can assist you in seeing to it that a man reporting to you, who is due to have a "Development Review" with you, is furnished with the form he needs to fill in on time.

BUT REMEMBER! Secretaries can help only if they have been programmed to help, and YOU are the programmer.

2.3 Using Guidelines and Check Lists

All of us need help in the things we do. Guidelines from those who have handled a situation before can make it so much easier for us and can make us so much more efficient in discharging our responsibilities.
Give them guidelines wherever you can. These guidelines can take the form of CHECK LISTS and will prevent you from leaving out major areas of importance.

For example, when asking a man to draw up a job description for a sub-ordinate, he will need definite guidelines. Assist him by giving him a guideline.

Check lists of points to be covered in preparing for a particular event, make for excellence and peace, because you know that all the necessary matters will be covered.

Different members of your team can help you in compiling different check lists. In the

context of a local church some of the following check lists could prove very useful:
> A list of points that need to be covered in preparation for a wedding.
> A list of points that need to be covered in preparing for a youth camp.
> A list of points that need to be attanded to when arranging a christmas party.
> A list of pints that need to be covered when leading a person to Christ.

Be sure to carefully look at MANAGING WORKSHEET No. 2 [MW:2] right now and spend four or five minutes filling it in. You will need to come back to it a little later as you think of more check lists that need to be compiled.

2.4   Regular Meetings with Key People

Communication is the name of the game! Regular meetings with key people open up the channels of communication.

To assist you in keeping these meetings regular, ask your secretary to arrange these meetings for you on the suggested basis.

Not only will the lines of communication be kept open at these meetings, but you have the additional advantage of developing relationships and a growing understanding of each other.

Controlling therefore has a great deal to do with BEING ORGANISED and therefore relates closely to the organising phase of management.

IV. MANAGING AS A LIFESTYLE

Every effective manager should organise his life in such a way so that he constantly be taking up his responsibility to control. He will learn to pick up all the "vibes" that he needs to pick up and he will be able to nudge his way gently into any situation and assist the people. Controlling will become a way of life for him.

Because managing implies CLOSENESS, he will automatically seek opportunities to get alongside his staff and his customers or congregation. Through COMMUNICATION and INVOLVEMENT his control will become a lifestyle.

In actual fact, the trend today is away from large and complex infrastructures and information systems to control the performance of people.

If you have carefully DEFINED MEASURABLE GOALS and OBJECTIVES, controlling is an easy process.

Every attempt should be made to keep controlling VERY SIMPLE.
SHORT, SWEET and SIMPLE !

MANAGING WORKSHEET No. 2   [MW:2]

COMPILING OF CHECK LISTS

	1. CHECK LISTS that need to be drawn up:	2. Person who will compile Check List:	2. Completion date :
1			
2			
3			
4			
5			
6			
7			
8			
9			
10			
11			
12			
13			
14			
15			
16			
17			
18			

PEOPLE I NEED TO MEET WITH REGULARLY

	KEY PEOPLE OR GROUPS I NEED TO MEET WITH REGULARLY:	DATES OF MEETINGS:
1		
2		
3		
4		
5		
6		
7		
8		
9		
10		
11		
12		
13		
14		
15		
16		
17		
18		
19		
20		
21		
22		
23		

PROGRESS EVALUATION FORM

FOR PASTORS

Name:	
Position:	
Years with organization:	
Date:	
Signature:	

SELF ASSESSMENT OF YOUR DEVELOPMENT!

1. SPIRITUAL DEVELOPMENT

Give yourself a rating of 1 to 10	1	2	3	4	5	6	7	8	9	10	Action that needs to be taken
1. I am consistent.											
2. I am teachable and have a non-critical attitude											
3. I regularly prayer and study my Bible.											
4. I show love and concern for others											
5. I feel I am fruitful in my ministry.											
6. I endeavour to constantly walk in the Spirit.											
7. I manifest the FRUIT of the Spirit.											
8. I regularly flow in the GIFTS of the Spirit.											

2. PERSONAL DEVELOPMENT

Give yourself a rating of 1 - 10.	1	2	3	4	5	6	7	8	9	10	Action that needs to be taken
1. I am emotionally stable.											
2. I am alert and physically energetic.											
3. I fit in socially with my people and am consistently good mannered.											
4. My home life in good shape											
5. My wife regularly attends church and other meetings											

3. PLANNING

Give yourself a rating of 1 to 10	1	2	3	4	5	6	7	8	9	10	Action that needs to be taken
1. I plan adequately before acting											
2. I maintains clear objectives											
3. I regularly ask God for direction											
4. I have clearly defined objective											
5. I keep a list of prospective leaders											

4. ORGANISING

Give yourself a rating of 1 to 10	1	2	3	4	5	6	7	8	9	10	Action that needs to be taken

1. I am able to effectively organise
    People
    My ministry activities.											

2. I am well organised financially:
    Personally
    In your ministry											

3. I delegate responsibility and authority effectively.											
4. I have clearly stated job descriptions for my team members											

5. I carefully plan
    each year
    each term
    each week											

5. LEADING / DIRECTING

Give yourself a rating of 1 to 10	1	2	3	4	5	6	7	8	9	10	Action that needs to be taken
1. I am sure of God's calling and accept this God-given responsibility											
2. I am able to motivate others											
3. I am a soul winner.											
4. I am able to build disciples effectively											
5. I communicate effectively when teaching others											
6. I am able to deal with interpersonal problems.											
7. I develop people to assume greater responsibility.											
8. I am decisive in making good decisions.											

6. CONTROLLING / MANAGING

Give yourself a rating of 1 - 10											Action that needs to be taken
1. I submit reports and data requested on time.											
2. I identify problems my team members are facing, and address them.											
3. I clearly understand what are my areas of responsibility.											
4. I have clearly defined the different roles of my team members.											
5. I regularly meet with my Team members.											
6. I often phone many of my team members.											

7. PHILOSOPHY OF MINISTRY

Give yourself a rating of 1 to 10	1	2	3	4	5	6	7	8	9	10	Action that needs to be taken
1. I am committed to the vision of my organisation.											
2. I could easily recite the Mission Statement of my organisation.											
3. I constantly present the Mission Statement to my team.											
4. In my heart I support the objectives of our Mission Statement											
5. I actively pursue the objectives of the Mission Statement.											
6. I demonstrate compatibility with my organisation's philosophy.											
7. I am happy to work within the structure of my organisation.											
8. I would like to speak to my superior about the following:	1. 2. 3.										

GENERAL

THE PERFECT SECRETARY

THE PERFECT SECRETARY is published by THE KELLY PERSONNEL GROUP in the interests of better business practice in South Africa. [Used with permission.]

Author Neville W Mackay, Chief Executive Officer of the Kelly Group, is a recognised authority on office staff recruitment and training.

He is a popular speaker at Secretaries' Receptionists' seminars and has written two guides for Switchboard Operators. One of them, commissioned by the Junior Chamber, South Africa was translated into five languages and transcribed into Braille fir blind Receptionists.

Booklets in the series, YOU AND YOUR JOB, are available free on request at all KELLY GIRL-KELLY TEMP and KELLY PERMS branches throughout the Republic of South Africa.

Does the Perfect Secretary Exist?

She does! She is recognised by her skills and personal attributes, attitude, efficiency, acceptance of responsibility, initiative, loyalty, commitment, grooming, tact and charm - 10 qualifications that add up to the sort of Secretary every business executive needs.

If you have that combination, you have what it takes to get right to the top of a career which can be satisfying and rewarding.

If you have chosen to be a Secretary, it makes sense to aim high and strive to become "The Perfect Secretary". Real career satisfaction and success lie in being excellent in your chosen field.

The role of the Executive Secretary

As thousands of busy executives will testify, the role of an Executive Secretary, if properly fulfilled, is truly that of a Personal Assistant - the boss's "right hand" - and a great asset to any business or professional office.

It is an exciting role, loaded with job satisfaction - and tangible rewards. Top secretaries today command high salaries.

As an executive secretary, you are close to the planning and decision-making of commercial companies and public institutions, and will be associated personally with the dynamic people who lead them.

Every working day can be a stimulating challenge if you demonstrate a willingness to accept full responsibility and stay professional in all you do.

Are you "The Perfect Secretary"? Run through our checklist of 10 vital qualifications to see how you rate in this specialised and competitive field.

1. SKILLS AND PERSONAL ATTRIBUTES

On today's multi-faceted offices, the more skills you have, the better your chances of succeeding in the secretarial field. You need to:

* Be computer literate together with accurate typing skills. A good knowledge of word processing and spreadsheet packages is essential. A willingness to learn new packages, will add an extra dimension to your prospects and earning power.

* Have the ability to communicate effectively in writing, as well as face to face and on the telephone. All essential for the truly professional Secretary.

* Show readiness to work with figures. You don't need a maths degree to cope with the simple calculations you'd be asked to do in the average office. Machines do all the complicated work these days, so don't be afraid to work with numbers.

* Gain the ability to work under pressure and maintain efficiency.

* Demonstrate a willingness to learn and update your skills. This will ensure you a place in any busy executive's office.

2. ATTITUDE

The Perfect Secretary can truly be the "boss's right hand". Many Secretaries can take dictation, type letters and answer the telephone, but these basic duties are only a part of any Executive Secretary's duties.

An Executive Secretary takes a real interest in the job, as well as the company's business. Each new task is seen as an opportunity, and tackled with zest and imagination. A Secretary's role need not consist of only routine tasks - it's what you make of it.

It's been said that a good secretary can make an executive who is 100% efficient, 150% efficient! If you apply yourself energetically and enthusiastically, you will enhance both you and your executive's value to the company. To do so:

* Fully understand your "boss's role in the management team.

* Adopt a cheerful and positive approach to difficult and tedious tasks.

* Run your office reliably and efficiently, thereby helping to reduce stress in the office.

* Take a sincere interest in the company's overall business, its operation and its mission.

3. EFFICIENCY

The duties of a Secretary vary from job to job, but normally include a number of standard tasks such as handling of correspondence, taking dictation and typing. But it may also include attending business meetings and executive functions, possibly some accounting and administrative tasks such as arranging travel and conferences. You will have some first hand contact with some top clients and suppliers, and will sometimes have to handle their complaints.

SOME USEFUL TIPS ON STAYING EFFICIENT

* Keep a daily "To Do" list of tasks in order of priority, bur rearrange the priorities as you go along. As each job listed is completed, cross it off.

* Know your boss's priorities - they must be yours too.

* Break down big, unpleasant tasks into smaller, less menacing ones.

* Be tidy. Keep everything in its place for ease of reference.

* Note executive instructions carefully. If in doubt, ask questions.

* Check your work thoroughly.

* Use your lunch-break to get out of the office and give your mind a rest from work. It pays of in improved concentration later in the day.

* Last thing on Fridays, summarise your next week's tasks and set yourself deadlines.

4. ACCEPTANCE OF RESPONSIBILITY

The Perfect Secretary, as a trusted Personal Assistant, must be ready and able to accept responsibility for action and decisions taken in the absence of the boss.

Even when your boss is in the office, he or she can be relieved of some routine tasks - such as writing letters of acknowledgement,, thanks, or apology. Such letters should be polite, brief, confined to facts and signed with your name and title.

5. INITIATIVE

Initiative and readiness to take on extra tasks are qualities which distinguish the Perfect Secretary from the rest. The Perfect Secretary doesn't wait to be told what to do around the office, but finds ways to be of help. There can never be time to read magazines during working hours. Look for ways to lighten your employer's load.

If your employer regularly performs routine jobs which you can handle, offer to attend to them. You are qualified to handle travel arrangements, set up meetings and gather information. By doing such tasks, you free your boss for the other important duties for which he of she is best qualified.

6. GROOMING

The Perfect Secretary should always be well groomed. Flamboyant clothes, startling make-up and loads of jewellery have no place in a business environment - except, perhaps, that of a seaside fortune-teller. Hair, nails, shoes and other accessories should be clean and well cared for, and overpowering perfume kept for after five.

Clothes need not be expensive - a simple, uncluttered appearance is always acceptable.

7. COMMITMENT

Being committed to your job means identifying yourself completely with its struggle for success. Do not bring problems to work, or conduct private business during your employer's time.

There should be no lengthy absences from your desk while you chatter to colleagues. Keep private telephone calls to a minimum. You should be willing to stay late occasionally to finish urgent work which cannot be left over for the next day. Arrive punctually each morning. Such discipline will not be overlooked when you occasionally have to ask for time off to attend to a personal matter during business hours.

Total commitment is one of the hallmarks of the Perfect Secretary. It springs naturally from really caring about your work, and striving for the highest possible standards.

8. LOYALTY

Loyalty to your boss and the company you serve is of paramount importance. You must either like or respect your boss - preferably both. If you can't, you should almost certainly change your job, for you will never be able to serve him or her effectively. Mutual respect is the foundation of all Boss-Secretary relationships.

Never, ever, discuss confidential company business inside or outside your office, or voice criticism of your employers.

9. TACT

The ability to handle people tactfully is one of the most important attributes of the Perfect Secretary. You may sometimes have to shield your boss from unnecessary interruptions or demands on his or her time, but you must do it tactfully. Keep your boss informed on matters of importance, when you have diverted callers.

10. CHARM

Remember that the executive you work for, however exalted and awe inspiring, is a human being too. He or she will respond positively to a warm and charming Secretary, but not to a tight-lipped dragon running the office with military precision and icy disdain.

YOUR PLACE IN THE TEAM

When you've finally arrived in the prestigious post you've dreamed about and worked towards for years, don't let it go to your head! Start off on the right foot by examining the management structure of the company and see and understand where you fit in. Keep a sense of proportion.

Being Executive Secretary to the Managing Director or the Personal Assistant to the Chairman is important, but remember that you are a member of a larger team.

A dash of modesty, added to your efficiency, reliability and effectiveness in the company will make you invaluable to your employers and appreciated by everyone you encounter in the course of your work. In short you will be "The Perfect Secretary".